1997

Fraud Auditing and Forensic Accounting

Second Edition

Fraud Auditing and Forensic Accounting

New Tools and Techniques

Second Edition

G. Jack Bologna, B.B.A., J.D., CFE
Associate Professor of Management
Siena Heights College
Adrian, Michigan

Robert J. Lindquist, B. COMM., C.A., CFE
Chairman
Lindquist Avey Macdonald Baskerville Inc.
Toronto, Ontario,
Washington, D.C.

JOHN WILEY & SONS, INC.
New York • Chichester • Brisbane • Toronto • Singapore

This publication is designed to provide accurate and
authoritative information in regard to the subject
matter covered. It is sold with the understanding that
the publisher is not engaged in rendering legal, accounting,
or other professional services. If legal advice or other
expert assistance is required, the services of a competent
professional person should be sought.

Library of Congress Cataloging-in-Publication Data:
Bologna, Jack.
    Fraud auditing and forensic accounting : new tools and techniques
/ G. Jack Bologna, Robert J. Lindquist. — 2nd ed.
        p.   cm.
    Includes bibliographical references (p.   –   ) and index.
    ISBN 0-471-10646-1 (Cloth)
    1. White collar crime investigation—United States. 2. Forensic
accounting—United States. 3. Fraud investigation—United States.
I. Lindquist, Robert J. II. Title.
HV8079.W47B65   1995
364. 1′63—dc20   95-5510

Preface

One does not write a book for ego gratification or monetary reward. Indeed, most books provide authors with little fame or fortune, and a book for a limited audience of technical specialists provides an even more modest return on effort. So why do authors take on such enormous tasks for so little reward?

Most often such books are written from a compulsion to share a few professional insights and anecdotes with professional colleagues who appreciate the writer's lifelong interests. Indeed, that was our primary purpose.

Our goal in writing this book was to contribute to the literature of auditing, investigation, and forensics. Beyond that, we hope our work creates and awareness of the meaning and value of fraud auditing and forensic accounting.

This book deals with deceptions of many kinds but mainly of an accounting nature. Deception undermines our faith in people. It makes *all* of us a little poorer, not merely the victim. So, whereas we may speak of all manner of deceptions in this book, we hope not to destroy faith in people but to reduce the temptations in our society and in organizations that can foster accounting fraud.

Accordingly, this book is intended as a formula neither for financial deception nor for fraud detection, because there is no successful formula for either.

Deception and its detection are qualitative things—not quantitative. They are mainly states of mind.

Deception deals with human character or, more properly, with its lack. Character is a mental quality, a matter of personality and upbringing. Detection deals with a mind-set too; one that suggests that truth, justice, and fairness in human relationships and business transactions are important values that should be preserved and promoted. To that end we commit this book.

In the broadest terms possible, then, this book deals with the growing international problems of white-collar crime from the perspective of how forensic accountants can investigate and document such crimes, how internal and external auditors can detect them, how police and security authorities can investigate them, and how good management practices can prevent and detect them.

White-collar crime does not create the public fear or concern that street crime does. Yet a recent Joint Economic Committee of the U.S. Congress report states that street crimes produce yearly losses of about $4 billion, whereas white-collar crimes may cost U.S. citizens over $80 billion annually. In terms of dollar loss alone, we might question society's permissive attitude toward white-collar crime.

Our dichotomous perspectives on street crime and white-collar crime are based mainly on media coverage. The media report mostly street crime, and unless a political figure, a social lion, or an economic giant is involved, tend to overlook white-collar crime.

If our role models (economic, political, and social leaders) are corrupt, greedy, or inept, can we realistically expect their subordinates to behave much better? Imitating superiors is one way we all learn. If our superiors value honesty and behave honestly, we tend to mimic that behavior. If they behave dishonestly, that creates a need for fraud auditors and forensic accountants.

SIGNIFICANT EVENTS IN THE RECENT HISTORY OF FRAUD AUDITING AND FORENSIC ACCOUNTING

- The expression *litigation support* added to the lexicon of forensic accounting
- Founding of the Association of Certified Fraud Examiners, the National Association of Forensic Accountants, and the National Litigation Support Services Association
- Treadway and MacDonald Commission Reports
- Issuance of SAS No. 53, The Auditor's Responsibility to Detect Errors and Irregularities, by the AICPA (American Institute of CPAs)
- Issuance of Statement on Internal Auditing Standards, No. 3, "Deterrence, Detection, Investigation and Reporting of Fraud," by the IIA (Institute of Internal Auditors)
- AICPA issuance of SAS No. 54 on the Auditor's Responsibility to Report Illegal Acts
- Establishment of college-level courses on fraud auditing at Brigham Young University and the University of Nebraska
- Publication of the first auditing text with a full-chapter treatment of fraud auditing
- Adoption of policies on fraud detection by the Institute of Financial Executives and Management Accountants
- U.S. litigation proposed to hold external auditors liable for fraud detection and reporting of criminal acts to audit committees and SEC (public companies)
- Federal sentencing guidelines
- Money laundering legislation

- Redefinition of internal controls
- RICO judicial interpretations

We have seen other things that were far from happy bits of news: frauds of gigantic size, like BCCI, for example, and Volkswagen and Phar-Mor, to say nothing of S&L insolvencies, Wall Street insider trading, defense-contractor price gouging, and so on. Fraud in business may not be endemic, but it is a matter of grave social and economic concern. The Hallcrest Report II estimates that economic crime in the United States cost $114 billion in 1990 or about 2 percent of the GNP. Spending on security costs U.S. businesses and consumers another $52 billion annually. Fraud is, therefore, no simple vice. It demands full-time, professional attention.

Our purpose in writing this is to share our experience and knowledge with other practitioners of the arcane arts of fraud auditing and forensic accounting, now often called *litigation support.* Generally, we limit our discussions to fraud in books of account; that is, fraud in financial statements and business transactions, such as sales, purchases, payments, and receipts. Other serious frauds such as investor and consumer frauds receive incidental attention.

Litigation support, which has come to mean using particular accounting skills to estimate losses, damages, and asset values in civil suits for negligence, contract breaches, and divorce, are covered only peripherally.

The major news stories of fraud in books of account (transaction and statement frauds) may provide some further insight on the nature and scope of that problem. We have, therefore, abstracted the following news items and editorial comments from the *Forensic Accounting Review:*

Inventory Plugging is the favored technique to overstate profits. Recent incidents included Laribee Wire Manufacturing, L.A. Gear, Digital Equipment, Phar-Mor, Comptronix, Leslie Fay Co., Miniscribe Corp., F&C International, and Fingerhut Cop.

"When companies are desperate to stay afloat, inventory fraud is the easiest way to produce instant profits and dress up the balance sheet," says Felix Pomerantz, director of Florida International University's Center for Accounting, Auditing and Tax Studies in Miami, in a front-page story on that subject in the 12/14/92 issue of *Wall Street Journal.*

Pomerantz adds, "If auditors were more skeptical of management claims, they would look at a far greater portion of the inventory and do more surprise audits. . . ."

The *New York Times,* 1/3/93, labeled 1992 as the "year of the scam," quoting Howard M. Schilit, professor of accounting at American University in Washington, D.C. The article recounts the problems that engulfed Comptronix Corp., National Health Laboratories, and Sequoia Systems. Professor Schilit was awarded (tongue in cheek) the Baker Street Irregulars Award by the *Times* because he figured that something was awry at Comptronix; "sales and accounts receivable usually move in tandem, because customers don't pay on the spot if they can avoid it. But Comptronix's receivables were not growing nearly so fast as sales. Was every new customer paying on delivery? Similarly, inventory usually keeps pace with accounts payable, because companies do not usually pay cash at the delivery dock for goods ordered as inventory. But at Comptronix, inventories were soaring while payables were standing still. Lastly, inventories were turning over much more slowly than the company's robust reported sales growth would suggest."

G.J. BOLOGNA
R.J. LINDQUIST

Plymouth, Michigan
Toronto, Ontario
Washington, D.C.
June 1995

Acknowledgments

We owe our most heartfelt thanks to many, many people who supplied us with information, inspiration, and motivation to complete this book. Chief among them are our wives, Jean Bologna and Angela Lindquist; Barbara Davis of Computer Protection Systems, Inc., who toiled through the whole editorial process without once showing signs of exhaustion or frustration; the Toronto staff of Lindquist, Avey, Macdonald, Baskerville, particularly Brain Crockatt, Peter Steger and Vivian Kanargelidis; to more than 10,000 members of the Association of Certified Fraud Examiners and the Association's founder, Joseph Wells, who has done so much to professionalize our field of study.

We also thank our acquisitions editor at John Wiley & Sons, Sheck Cho, for encouraging us to update our first edition and for waiting patiently for the second edition's completion.

A special note of thanks is owed to Butterworth-Heinemann Publishers, who allow us to reprint material that saw the light of day in coauthor Bologna's 1993 book *Handbook on Corporate Fraud.*

Finally, we thank the many purchasers of the first edition of this book who offered us feedback on new areas of coverage and anecdotes from their own experiences with fraud auditing and forensic accounting.

Contents

Introduction   1

1. Fraud Definitions and Taxonomy   3

Consumer and Investor Frauds   3

Criminal, Civil, and Contractual Fraud   3

Fraud, Theft, and Embezzlement   3

Fraud For and Against the Company   4

Internal and External Fraud   4

Management and Non-Management Fraud   5

Fraud Auditing, Forensic Accounting, and Financial Auditing   5

Fraud Auditors, Forensic Accountants, and Financial Auditors   5

Transaction and Statement Fraud   6

Motivation and Opportunities Fraud   7

Payment and Receipt System Fraud   7

Fraud Prevention and Detection   7

Skimming, Lapping, and Kiting   8

Bribery, Related-Party Transactions, and Conflict of Interest   8

High-Level and Low-Level Thieves   8

What Is Fraud?   9

Why Is Fraud Committed?   10

Who Commits Fraud?   11

Who Is Most Often Victimized By Fraud?   13

Why Do Employees Lie, Cheat, and Steal on the Job?   13

What Are the Varieties of Fraud?   15

What Do We Know about White-Collar Crime?   21

How Serious Is the Fraud (White-Collar Crime) Problem?   21

2. **Forensic Accounting and Fraud Auditing**
   Fundamentals   **26**
   Who Needs Fraud Auditing?   27
   What Should A Fraud Auditor Know and Be Able to Do?   28
   Thirteen Principles of Fraud Auditing   31
   Financial Auditing and Fraud Auditing   32
   Thinking as a Fraud Auditor   36
   The Fraud Auditor's General Mind-set   39
   What Is Forensic and Investigative Accounting?   42
   Who Needs Forensic Accounting?   43
   What Should a Forensic Accountant Be Able to Do?   44
   Some Reflections on Forensic Accounting   46
   Training Fraud Auditors   49
   Fraud Auditing Software Tools   53
   Using Computers As Investigative Aids   59
   Investigative Data Base Resources Bibliography   62

3. **Auditor Liability for Undetected Fraud**   **64**
   Are Auditors Liable for Fraud Detection?   64
   Fraud Detection and Disclosure: Are New Teeth Needed?   71
   What about Auditors' Expectations? (by Ron E. Ellis
      and David C. Selley)   72
   What Liability Crisis? (by Mindy Paskell-Mede)   88

4. **Forensic and Investigative Accounting:**
   A Case Approach   **92**
   Fraud Within the Purchases, Payables, and Payments System   93
   Fraud Within the Sales, Receivables, and Receipts System   95
   Management Fraud Within the Purchases, Payables, and
      Payments System   97
   Employee Fraud Within the Purchases, Payables, and
      Payments System   99
   Vendor Fraud Within the Purchases, Payables, and
      Payments System   104
   Management Fraud Within the Sales Receivable
      Receipts System   106

Employee Fraud Within the Sales, Receivables, and
　　Receipts System　　　　　　　　　　　　　　　　　　109

Customer Fraud Within the Sales, Receivables, and
　　Receipts System　　　　　　　　　　　　　　　　　　111

Investigative Accounting in Murder, Arson, and
　　Commercial Bribery Cases　　　　　　　　　　　　　　114

5. Prevention and Detection of Fraud　　　　　　　　　**129**

Invitations to Corporate Fraud, Theft, and Embezzlement　　129

Landmark Cases in Corporate Fraud　　　　　　　　　　130

How Can Management and Corporate Fraud Be Detected?　　133

Telltale Signs of Management and Corporate Fraud　　　　134

Embezzlement: Would You Know One If You Saw One?　　137

Is Corporate Fraud Cyclical?　　　　　　　　　　　　　138

Can Management Controls Become Too Much of a
　　Good Thing?　　　　　　　　　　　　　　　　　　　138

The Classic Approaches to the Reduction of Employee
　　Theft, Fraud, and Embezzlement　　　　　　　　　　140

Preventing Fraud in Particular Account Categories　　　　141

Cases　　　　　　　　　　　　　　　　　　　　　　142

6. Fraud Risk Assessment　　　　　　　　　　　　　　**146**

High-Fraud and Low-Fraud Environments　　　　　　　　148

Risk-Management Checklist　　　　　　　　　　　　　　151

Embezzlement Risk Assessment for the Banking Industry　　151

Risk Financing　　　　　　　　　　　　　　　　　　　151

Evolution of an Accounting System Fraud　　　　　　　　157

7. Accounting Systems and Cycles　　　　　　　　　　**159**

Revenue Cycle　　　　　　　　　　　　　　　　　　　159

Payments Cycle　　　　　　　　　　　　　　　　　　160

Bank Reconciliation　　　　　　　　　　　　　　　　　161

General Ledger　　　　　　　　　　　　　　　　　　　161

Other Corporate Records　　　　　　　　　　　　　　　162

Computerized Accounting Systems　　　　　　　　　　　164

Personal Computers　　　　　　　　　　　　　　　　　167

Financial Statement Reporting　　　　　　　　　　　　　169

8. Computer-Related Fraud   **171**

History and Evolution of Computer-Related Crimes   172

The Most Common Computer-Related Crimes   176

The Nature of Computer-Related Crime   177

Hackers and Phone Phreaks   178

The Value of Stored Data   185

Computer Communications   185

Characteristics of the Computer Environment   186

Computer Systems Threats   188

9. The Auditor As An Expert Witness   **190**

Qualification and Admissibility of Accounting Schedules   192

Profile of the Expert Witness   196

The Expert's Role in the Litigation Team   197

Pretestimony Activities   198

On the Stand: Demeanor and Appearance   199

Direct Examination   200

Cross-Examination   200

Survival Techniques   205

10. General Criteria and Standards for Evaluating an Expert's Qualifications   **207**

Credentials   207

Sources for Locating Expert Witnesses   216

Distinguishing the Actual Area of Competence   216

11. Gathering Evidence   **219**

Rules of Evidence   219

Hearsay Exceptions   221

Other Rules of Evidence   223

Admissions and Confessions   225

12. Case Studies   **228**

Dave Flag Case   228

Maxi Lumber Case   229

Roy's Retail Case   229

Plastics, Ltd. Case   230

U.S. Jewelry Consortium   230

Money, Money, Money Case   230

Trading Mania   233

Sharp Rentals Case   234

Double-Paid Vacations Case   235

The Money Laundering Lawyer Case   237

Living High with Your Partner's Money   238

The 28-Hour-Day Case   240

Secret Commissions Case   241

The Rainbow Syndrome Case   242

Index   **245**

Introduction

The first edition of this book was published in 1987. At that time fraud auditing and forensic accounting were terms few accountants understood. Today both Canadian and American auditing authorities have had their say regarding auditor liability for nondetection of fraud in books of account. We now have the International Association of Certified Fraud Examiners, which numbers over ten thousand members and is still growing. Hundreds of practicing public accounting firms specialize in fraud auditing and forensic accounting. Colleges are beginning to offer courses and training on these subjects. The Institute of Internal Auditors offers a regular feature on fraud in each issue of its monthly magazine and sponsors several training sessions a year on fraud auditing for internal auditors. The National Association of Management Accountants and the Financial Executive Institute also sponsor such training sessions for their members, and the International Association of Certified Fraud Examiners conducts a rich variety of fraud training programs throughout the year, which are warmly received.

Why a book on fraud auditing and forensic accounting right now, written by the two of us, a Canadian public accountant who specializes in forensic accounting and an American management generalist who specializes in skills training for managers and in organizational development? Does the world really need another book on human greed and deception? Haven't these topics been exhausted by now?

The foregoing questions were posed to us by friends, colleagues, and publishers when we proposed to do this book. You may be asking those questions yourself. Let us attempt to clarify our intentions by explaining why the book was written and for whom, what benefits readers might derive from it, why the book is organized as it is, and what we hope to accomplish by this combined effort.

A Canadian public accountant and an American management consultant may seem an unlikely pair to join in any endeavor, much less the coauthoring of a book on accounting-type frauds. Yet, that may have been our original attraction. We tend to be more unalike than alike—in style, approach, and orientation. But we share a common interest in the use of accounting, auditing, and investigative skills to ferret out financial frauds and solve financial crimes. Indeed, our common interest is almost a passion. We both thoroughly enjoy the challenge of preventing, detecting, investigating, and documenting fraudulent transactions. So lesson one of this book is the notion that when experts agree on anything, it is probably because they share a common bias.

But there are a number of other good reasons why we joined in this writing endeavor. Teaming a Canadian authority on fraud and forensic accounting with an American authority on organizational behavior has decided advantages for readers. Our perspectives, experiences, and skills are broader and deeper. Our knowledge bases are diverse, yet stem from the same original source—the discipline of accounting—a chance for each author to address the different, yet in many ways similar, subjects of fraud auditing and forensic accounting. So even in diversity there is unity of purpose. The benefits to the reader include practical and tested techniques, sage advice, and broad perspectives.

Chapter 1

Fraud Definitions and Taxonomy

Most technical books have a glossary at the end. This one provides a taxonomy at the beginning to lay a simple but expanded foundation for what follows in the text. Another benefit of the taxonomy is that it provides a periodic quick review and thus reinforces the lessons learned at the first reading. In essence, the taxonomy summarizes the major principles of fraud auditing and forensic accounting.

CONSUMER AND INVESTOR FRAUDS

Fraud, in a nutshell, is intentional deception, commonly described as lying, cheating, and stealing. Fraud can be perpetrated against customers, creditors, investors, suppliers, bankers, insurers, or government authorities, e.g., tax fraud, stock fraud, short weights and counts. For our purposes, we will limit coverage to frauds in financial statements and commercial transactions. Consumer fraud has a literature of its own. Our aim is, therefore, to assist accountants and investigators in their effort to detect and document fraud in books of account.

CRIMINAL, CIVIL, AND CONTRACTUAL FRAUD

A specific act of fraud may be a criminal offense, a civil wrong, and grounds for the rescission of a contract. *Criminal fraud* requires proof of an intentional deception. *Civil fraud* requires that the victim suffer damages. Fraud in the inducement of a contract may vitiate consent and render a contract voidable.

FRAUD, THEFT, AND EMBEZZLEMENT

Fraud, theft, and embezzlement are terms that are often used interchangeably. Although they have some common elements, they are not identical in the criminal law sense. For example, in English common law, theft is referred to as *larceny*—the taking and carrying away of the property of another with the intention of permanently depriving the owners of its possession. In larceny, the perpetrator comes into possession of the stolen item illegally. In *embezzlement,* the perpetrator comes into initial possession lawfully, but then converts it to his or her own use. Embezzlers have a fiduciary duty to care for and to protect the property. In converting it to their own use, they breach that fiduciary duty.

FRAUD FOR AND AGAINST THE COMPANY

This text focuses mainly on fraud in an organizational setting. This is sometimes called *corporate* or *management fraud.* In that context, we can distinguish between organizational frauds that are intended to benefit the organizational entity and those that are intended to harm the entity. For example, price fixing, corporate tax evasion, violations of environmental laws, false advertising, and short counts and weights are generally intended to aid the organization's financial performance. Manipulating accounting records to overstate profits is another illustration of a fraud intended to benefit the company but which may benefit management through bonuses based on profitability. Frauds *against* the company, on the other hand, are intended to benefit only the perpetrator, as in the case of theft of corporate assets or embezzlement.

There are several other financial crimes that do not fit conveniently into our schema here but also are noteworthy, for example, arson for profit, planned bankruptcy, and fraudulent insurance claims.

INTERNAL AND EXTERNAL FRAUD

Frauds referred to as corporate or management frauds can be categorized as *internal frauds* to distinguish them from *external fraud* (a category that includes frauds committed by vendors, suppliers, and contractors, who might overbill, double bill, or substitute inferior goods). Customers may also play that game by feigning damage or destruction of goods in order to gain credits and allowances.

Corruption in the corporate sense may be practiced by outsiders against insiders, like purchasing agents, for example. Corruption can also be committed by insiders against buyers from customer firms. Commercial bribery often is accompanied by manipulation of accounting records to cover up its payment and protect the recipients from the tax burden.

MANAGEMENT AND NON-MANAGEMENT FRAUD

Corporate or organizational fraud is not restricted to high-level executives. Organizational fraud touches senior, middle, and first-line management, as well as non-management employees. There may be some notable distinctions between the means used, and the motivations and opportunities the work environment provides, but fraud is found at all levels of an organization—if you bother to look for it. Even if internal controls are adequate by professional standards, we should not forget that top managers can override controls with impunity, and often do so.

FRAUD AUDITING, FORENSIC ACCOUNTING, AND FINANCIAL AUDITING

In the lexicon of accounting, terms such as *fraud auditing, forensic accounting, investigative accounting, litigation support,* and *valuation analysis* are not clearly defined. By today's usage, the broadest term is *litigation support,* which incorporates the other four terms. But traditional accountants still feel some distinctions apply between fraud auditing and forensic accounting. Fraud auditing, they say, involves a proactive approach and methodology to discern fraud; that is, one audits for evidence of fraud. The purpose is to detect fraud. Forensic accountants, on the other hand, are called in *after* evidence or suspicion of fraud has surfaced through an allegation, complaint, or discovery.

Financial auditing generally is not intended to search for fraud but to attest that financial statements are presented fairly. Movements are afoot to compel financial auditors to design their audits in such a way that fraud can be discerned and criminal acts can be discovered. But at this writing no law has been passed to that effect, nor have professional societies included those obligations as a matter of professional diligence.

FRAUD AUDITORS, FORENSIC ACCOUNTANTS, AND FINANCIAL AUDITORS

Fraud auditors are accountants who, by virtue of their attitudes, attributes, skills, knowledge, and experience, are experts at detecting and documenting frauds in books of account. Their particular attitudes include the following beliefs:

- That fraud is possible even in accounting systems in which controls are tight

- That the visible part of a transaction fraud may involve a small amount of money, but the invisible portion can be substantial
- That red flags of fraud are discernible if one looks long enough and deep enough
- That fraud perpetrators can come from any level of management or society

The personal attributes of fraud auditors include self-confidence, persistence, commitment to honesty and fair play, creativity, curiosity, an instinct for what is out of place or what is out of balance, independence, objectivity, good posture and grooming (for courtroom testimony), clear communication, sensitivity to human behavior, common sense, and an ability to fit pieces of puzzle together without force or contrivance.

The skills fraud auditors require include all of those that are required of financial auditors, plus a knowledge of how to gather evidence of and document fraud losses for criminal, civil, contractual, and insurance purposes; how to interview third-party witnesses; and how to testify as an expert witness.

Fraud auditors must know what a fraud is from a legal and audit perspective, an environmental perspective, a perpetrator's perspective, and a cultural perspective. They also need both general and specific kinds of experience. They should have a fair amount of experience in general auditing and fraud auditing, but should have industry-specific experience as well: banking industry fraud; insurance industry fraud; construction industry fraud; manufacturing, distribution, and retailing frauds.

Forensic accountants may appear on the crime scene a little later than fraud auditors, but their major contribution is in translating complex financial transactions and numerical data into terms that ordinary laypersons can understand. Their areas of expertise are not only in accounting and auditing but in criminal investigation, report writing, and testifying as expert witnesses. They must be excellent communicators, professional in demeanor, conservative in dress, and otherwise well groomed.

TRANSACTION AND STATEMENT FRAUD

Fraud in books of account comes in two major categories: transaction and statement frauds. *Statement frauds* involve the intentional misstatement of certain financial values to enhance the appearance of profitability and deceive shareholders or creditors. *Transaction frauds* usually are intended to facilitate the theft or conversion of organizational assets to one's personal use. Senior managers commit statement frauds hoping to gain some personal benefit (promotion, raise, bonus) from their fraud. Low-level personnel generally commit transaction fraud to cover up or facilitate a theft or embezzlement.

The most common forms of statement fraud are overstated revenue and inventory. The most common forms of transaction fraud are fictitious payables and the conversion of corporate assets to personal use.

MOTIVATION AND OPPORTUNITIES FRAUD

On-the-job fraud, theft, and embezzlement are products of motivation and opportunity. The motivation may be economic need or greed, egocentricity, ideological conflicts, and psychosis. Most on-the-job frauds are committed for economic reasons, and are often attributable to alcoholism, drug abuse, gambling, and high living. Loose or lax controls and a work environment that does not value honesty provide the opportunity.

Motivations and opportunities are interactive: the greater the economic need, the less weakness in internal controls is needed to accomplish the fraud. The greater the weakness in controls, the less motivational need.

PAYMENT AND RECEIPT SYSTEM FRAUD

Accounting systems in the computer era are subclassified into payment and receipt systems. *Payment systems* include such accounts as payroll, purchases, and payables. *Receipt systems* include sales and receivables. Both systems also impact on the inventory and cash accounts.

The favorite scam low-level insiders practice is the payables scam, in which phony employees and vendors are added to master files and then funds are disbursed to them for goods and services that were never delivered.

Receivable scams are possible, too, by issuing credits for returns that were never received or for alleged damage to goods.

FRAUD PREVENTION AND DETECTION

Usually, it is less expensive to prevent fraud than to detect it. Therefore, fraud prevention should take precedence over detection. Internal controls alone do not prevent fraud in books of account; they merely facilitate its detection. Fraud prevention measures include hiring honest people, paying them competitively, treating them fairly, and providing a safe and secure workplace, real-time feedback on their performance (and positive reinforcement when their performance meets standards), adequate tools and training to do their jobs right, role-modeling honesty, and codes of ethics.

Fraud prevention means creating a work environment that values honesty. Senior managers who role-model truth and fairness in their daily interactions with their peers and subordinates can create such an environment. Prevention also means regularly monitored and enforced internal controls. Therefore, prevention strategies include tight controls, ethical codes, fair treatment, awareness training, applicant screening, and honest role models.

Detection strategies include monitoring variance reporting systems, internal auditing, compliance auditing, and intelligence gathering.

SKIMMING, LAPPING, AND KITING

Skimming is often called "front-end fraud." Funds are stolen before a book entry is made. It is a common practice in cash businesses such as bars, restaurants, vending machines, home modernization contracting, gas stations, and retail stores.

Lapping is a form of robbing Peter to pay Paul. One takes in customer A's money, steals it, and pays it back the next day with customer B's money. The problem is that there often is a balloon effect from lapping. It is so easy to steal that the perpetrator takes a little more every time, and the balance grows larger and larger until the balloon bursts. There is not enough cash flow to sustain the scam any longer.

Kiting involves using checks from different banks in different federal reserve districts as props to create a float (free money). Funds are drawn on one bank, deposited in another, drawn down again to a third bank, and on and on. *Check kiting* creates the balloon effect too. When it bursts, millions of dollars have been stolen, wasted, or shipped to Switzerland.

BRIBERY, RELATED-PARTY TRANSACTIONS, AND CONFLICTS OF INTEREST

Technically, bribery is not a form of fraud but a form of corruption. Since it is a breach of trust and loyalty, it often is confused with embezzlement, which is a breach of fiduciary duty. But bribery and embezzlement are close kin, as are related-party transactions and conflicts of interest. Each raises a question of loyalty, honesty, and fair dealing.

HIGH-LEVEL AND LOW-LEVEL THIEVES

All thieves steal as a matter of greed or need and as a matter of ease of opportunity. At high levels of organizational life, it is easy to steal because controls can be bypassed or overridden. The sums high-level managers steal, therefore, tend to be greater than the sums low-level personnel steal. The number of incidents of theft, however, are greater at low levels because of the sheer number of employees.

WHAT IS FRAUD?

One person can injure another either by force or through fraud. The use of force to cause bodily injury is frowned on by most organized societies; using fraud to cause financial injury to another does not carry the same degree of stigma.

Fraud is a word that has many definitions. The more notable ones are as follows:

Fraud as a Crime: The Michigan Criminal Law states:

> Fraud is a generic term, and embraces all the multifarious means which human ingenuity can devise, which are resorted to by one individual, to get an advantage over another by false representations. No definite and invariable rule can be laid down as a general proposition in defining fraud, as it includes surprise, trick, cunning and unfair ways by which another is cheated. The only boundaries defining it are those which limit human knavery.[1]

Fraud as a Tort: The United States Supreme Court in 1887 provided a definition of fraud in the civil sense as:

> *First* That the defendant has made a representation in regard to a material fact;
>
> *Second* That such representation is *false;*
>
> *Third* That such representation was not actually believed by the defendant, on reasonable grounds, to be true;
>
> *Fourth* That it was made with intent that it should be acted on;
>
> *Fifth* That it was acted on by complainant to his damage; and
>
> *Sixth* That in so acting on it the complainant was ignorant of its falsity, and reasonably believed it to be true. The first of the foregoing requisites *excludes such statements as consist merely in an expression of opinion of judgment, honestly entertained; and again excepting in peculiar cases, it excludes statements by the owner and vendor of property in respect of its value.* [Emphasis added.][2]

Corporate Fraud: Corporate fraud is any fraud perpetrated by, for, or against a business corporation.

Management Fraud: Management fraud is the intentional misrepresentation of corporate or unit performance levels perpetrated by employees serving in management roles who seek to benefit from such frauds in terms of promotions, bonuses or other economic incentives, and status symbols.

The Layperson's Definition of Fraud: Fraud, as it is commonly understood today, means dishonesty in the form of an intentional deception or a willful misrepresentation of a material fact. Lying, the willful telling of an untruth, and cheating, the gaining of an unfair or unjust advantage over another, could be used to further define the word *fraud* because these two words denote intention or willingness to deceive.

In short, we might say that fraud, intentional deception, lying, and cheating are the opposites of truth, justice, fairness, and equity. Fraud consists of coercing people to act against their own best interests.

Although deception can be intended to coerce people to act against their own self-interest, deception can also be used for one's own defense or survival. Despite that rationale *for* deception, deception by current standards of behavior is considered mean and culpable. It is considered wrong and evil and can be excused only, if at all, if used for survival. But deception can be intended for a benevolent purpose, too. For example, a doctor might spare a patient from learning that a diagnostic test shows an advanced state of terminal disease. Benevolent deceivers in our society are not looked upon as harshly as are those whose intentions and motives are impure. Those who act out of greed, jealousy, spite, and revenge are not so quickly excused or forgiven.

WHY IS FRAUD COMMITTED?

Fraud or intentional deception is a strategy to achieve a personal or organizational goal or to satisfy a human need. However, a goal or need can be satisfied by honest means as well as by dishonest means. So what precipitates, inclines, or motivates one to select dishonest rather than honest means to satisfy goals and needs?

Generally speaking, competitive survival can be a motive for both honest and dishonest behavior. A threat to survival may cause one to choose either dishonest or honest means. When competition is keen and predatory, dishonesty can be quickly rationalized. Deceit, therefore, can become a weapon in any contest for survival. Stated differently, the struggle to survive (economically, socially, or politically) often generates deceitful behavior.

The same is true of fraud in business, which is perhaps less frequent but far more sophisticated today than in the past. Dollar loss from fraud in business has grown exponentially. Equity Funding (see Chapter 4, *United States v.*

Goldblum, Levin, Lewis et al.) alone involved overstated revenues of $200 million. The overstatement was covered up by several hundred coconspirators who worked feverishly to generate thousands of phony insurance policies by way of company computers. Why did Equity's management persist in such deceitful practices? For survival. Unknown to stockholders and policyholders, despite its spectacular annual increase in volume, Equity Funding was operating at a loss. Telling the truth would have hastened its demise.

Beyond the realm of competitive and economic survival, what other motives precipitate fraud? Social and political survival provide incentives, too, in the form of egocentric and ideological motives. Sometimes people commit fraud (deception) to aggrandize their egos, put on airs, or assume false status. Sometimes they deceive to survive politically. They lie about their personal views or pretend to believe when they do not. Or they simply cheat or lie to their political opponents, or intentionally misstate their opponents' positions on issues. They commit dirty tricks against them.

Motives to commit fraud in business usually are rationalized by the old saw that all is fair in love and war—and in business, which is amoral, anyway. There is one further category of motivation, however. We call it psychotic, because it cannot be explained in terms of rational behavior. In this category are the pathological liar, the professional confidence man, and the kleptomaniac.

In addition to the motives identified above, the internal environment of an organization can provide a climate conducive to committing fraud; the opportunities to commit fraud are rampant in the presence of loose or lax management and administrative and internal accounting controls. When motives are coupled with such opportunities, the potential for fraud is increased.

WHO COMMITS FRAUD?

In view of the foregoing section one might conclude that fraud is caused mainly by factors external to the individual: economic, competitive, social, and political factors, and poor controls. But how about the individual? Are some people more prone to commit fraud than others? And if so, is that a more serious cause of fraud than the external and internal environmental factors we have talked about? Data from criminology and sociology seems to suggest so.

Let us begin by making a few generalizations about people:

- Some people are honest all of the time.
- Some people (fewer than the above) are dishonest all of the time.
- Most people are honest some of the time.
- Some people are honest most of the time.

Beyond those generalizations about people, what can we say about fraud perpetrators? Gwynn Nettler in *Lying, Cheating and Stealing*[3] offers these insights on cheaters and deceivers:

- People who have experienced failure are more likely to cheat.
- People who are disliked and who dislike themselves tend to be more deceitful.
- People who are impulsive, distractable, and unable to postpone gratification are more likely to engage in deceitful crimes.
- People who have a conscience (fear, apprehension, and punishment) are more resistant to the temptation to deceive.
- Intelligent people tend to be more honest than ignorant people.
- Middle- and upper-class people tend to be more honest than lower-class people.
- The easier it is to cheat and steal, the more people will do so.
- Individuals have different needs and therefore different levels at which they will be moved to lie, cheat, or steal.
- Lying, cheating, and stealing increase when people have great pressure to achieve important objectives.
- The struggle to survive generates deceit.

People lie, cheat, and steal on the job in a variety of personal and organizational situations. The following are but a few:

1. **Personal variables**
   Aptitudes/abilities
   Attitudes/preferences
   Personal needs/wants
   Values/beliefs
2. **Organizational variables**
   Nature/scope of the job (meaningful work)
   Tools/training provided
   Reward/recognition system
   Quality of management and supervision
   Clarity of role responsibilities
   Clarity of job-related goals
   Interpersonal trust
   Motivational and ethical climate (ethics and values of superiors and co-workers)

3. **External variables**

Degree of competition in the industry

General economic conditions

Societal values (ethics of competitors and of social and political role models)

WHO IS MOST OFTEN VICTIMIZED BY FRAUD?

One might think that the most trusting people are also the most gullible and therefore most often the victims of fraud. Using that rationale, we could postulate that organizations with the highest levels of control would be least susceptible to fraud. But organizations that go overboard on controls do not necessarily experience less fraud; and they have the added burden of higher costs.

Controls to protect against fraud by either organization insiders or outside vendors, suppliers, and contractors must be adequate; that is, they must accomplish the goal of control—cost-feasible protection of assets against loss, damage, or destruction. Cost-feasible protection means minimal expenditures for maximum protection. Creating an organizational police state would be control overkill. A balanced perspective on controls and security measures is the ideal, and that may require involving employees in creating control policies, plans, and procedures. A balanced perspective weighs the costs and benefits of proposed new controls and security measures. It means that a measure of trust must exist among employees at all levels. Trust breeds loyalty and honesty; distrust can breed disloyalty and perhaps even dishonesty.

Fraud is therefore most prevalent in organizations that have (1) no controls, (2) no trust, (3) no ethical standards, (4) no profits, and (5) no future.

WHY DO EMPLOYEES LIE, CHEAT, AND STEAL ON THE JOB?

The following 25 reasons for employee crimes are those most often advanced by authorities in white-collar crime (criminologists, psychologists, sociologists, risk managers, auditors, police, and security professionals):

1. The employee believes he or she can get away with it.
2. The employee thinks he or she desperately needs or desires the money or articles stolen.
3. The employee feels frustrated or dissatisfied about some aspect of the job.
4. The employee feels frustrated or dissatisfied about some aspect of his or her personal life that is not job related.

5. The employee feels abused by the employer and wants to get even.

6. The employee fails to consider the consequences of being caught.

7. The employee thinks: "Everybody else steals, so why not me?"

8. The employee thinks: "They're so big, stealing a little bit won't hurt them."

9. The employee doesn't know how to manage his or her own money, so is always broke and ready to steal.

10. The employee feels that beating the organization is a challenge and not a matter of economic gain alone.

11. The employee was economically, socially, or culturally deprived during childhood.

12. The employee is compensating for a void felt in his or her personal life and needs love, affection, and friendship.

13. The employee has no self-control and steals out of compulsion.

14. The employee believes a friend at work has been subjected to humiliation or abuse or has been treated unfairly.

15. The employee is just plain lazy and won't work hard to earn enough to buy what he or she wants or needs.

16. The organization's internal controls are so lax that everyone is tempted to steal.

17. No one has ever been prosecuted for stealing from the organization.

18. Most employee thieves are caught by accident rather than by audit or design. Therefore, fear of being caught is not a deterrent to theft.

19. Employees aren't encouraged to discuss personal or financial problems at work or to seek management's advice and counsel on such matters.

20. Employee theft is a situational phenomenon. Each theft has its own preceding conditions, and each thief has his or her own motives.

21. Employees steal for any reason the human mind and imagination can conjure up.

22. Employees never go to jail or get harsh prison sentences for stealing, defrauding, or embezzling from their employers.

23. Human beings are weak and prone to sin.

24. Employees today are morally, ethically, and spiritually bankrupt.

25. Employees tend to imitate their bosses. If their bosses steal or cheat, then they are likely to do it also.

Laws to be respected and thus complied with must be rational, fair in application, and enforced quickly and efficiently. Company policies that relate to employee honesty, like criminal laws in general, must be rational, fair, and intended to serve the company's best economic interests. The test of rationality for any company security policy is whether its terms are understandable, whether its punishments or prohibitions are applicable to a real and serious matter, and whether its enforcement is possible in an efficient and legally effective way.

But what specific employee acts are serious enough to be prohibited and/or punished? Any act that could or does result in substantial loss, damage, or destruction of company assets should be prohibited.

The greatest deterrent to criminal behavior is sure and evenhanded justice; that is, swift detection and apprehension, a speedy and impartial trial, and punishment that fits the crime: loss of civil rights, privileges, property, personal freedom, or social approval. Having said all that, why is it that despite the dire consequences of criminal behavior we still see so much of it? Apparently because the rewards gained often exceed the risk of apprehension and punishment; or, stated another way, because the pains inflicted as punishment are not as severe as the pleasures of criminal behavior. The latter seems to be particularly true in cases of economic or white-collar crimes.

Are white-collar criminals more rational than their blue-collar counterparts? If so, they probably weigh the potential costs (arrest, incarceration, embarrassment, loss of income) against the economic benefit—the monetary gain from their crime. If the benefit outweighs the cost, they opt to commit the crime—not just any crime, but crimes against employers, stockholders, creditors, bankers, customers, insurance carriers, and government regulators.

WHAT ARE THE VARIETIES OF FRAUD?

As stated earlier, fraud is intentional deception. Its forms are generally referred to as lying and cheating. But theft by guile (larceny by trick, false pretenses, false tokens) and embezzlement are sometimes included as fraudulent acts. The element of deception is the common ground they all share.

But fraud and deception are abstract terms. They go by many other names as well. For example, in alphabetical order:

Accounts Payable Fabrication	Business Opportunity Fraud
Accounts Receivable Lapping	Bust Out
Arson for Profit	Cash Lapping
Bank Fraud	Check Forgery
Bankruptcy Fraud	Check Kiting
Benefit Claims Fraud	Check Raising
Bid Rigging	Collateral Forgery
Breach of Trust	Commercial Bribery
Breach of Fiduciary Duty	Computer Fraud

Concealment
Consumer Fraud
Conversion
Corporate Fraud
Corruption
Counterfeiting
Credit Card Fraud
Defalcation
Distortion of Fact
Double Dealing
Duplicity
EFTS Fraud
Embezzlement
Expense Account Fraud
False Advertising
False and Misleading Statements
False Claim
False Collateral
False Count
False Data
False Document
False Entry
False Identity
False Information
False Ownership
False Pretenses
False Report
False Representation
False Suggestion
False Valuation
False Weights and Measures
Fictitious Person
Fictitious Vendors, Customers, and
   Employees
Financial Fraud
Financial Misrepresentation
Forged Documents/Signatures
Forgery
Franchising Fraud
Fraud in Execution
Fraud in Inducement
Fraudulent Concealment

Fraudulent Financial Statement
Fraudulent Representation
Industrial Espionage
Infringement of Patents, Copyrights,
   and Trademarks
Input Scam
Insider Trading
Insurance Fraud
Inventory Overstatement
Inventory Reclassification Fraud
Investor Fraud
Kickbacks
Land Fraud
Lapping
Larceny by Trick
Loan Fraud
Lying
Mail Fraud
Management Fraud
Material Misstatement
Material Omission
Misapplication
Misappropriation
Misfeasance
Misrepresentation
Oil and Gas Scams
Output Scams
Overbilling
Overstatement of Revenue
Padding Expenses
Padding Government Contracts
Payables Fraud
Payroll Fraud
Performance Fraud
Price Fixing
Pricing and Extension Fraud
Procurement Fraud
Quality Substitution
Restraint of Trade
Sales Overstatements
Securities Fraud
Software Piracy

Stock Fraud

Subterfuge

Swindling

Tax Fraud

Tax Shelter Scam

Technology Theft

Theft of Computer Time

Theft of Proprietary Information

Throughput Scam

Trade Secret Theft

Undue Influence

Understatement of Costs

Understatement of Liabilities

Unjust Enrichment

Vendor Short Shipment

Watered Stock

Wire Fraud

Wire Transfer Fraud

Another way to view the pervasiveness and complexity of fraud might be to design a fraud typology, as in Exhibits 1.1, 1.2, 1.3, and 1.4. An array of fraud characteristics may provide such insight. These lists of fraud perpetrators, victims, and fraud types are far from exhaustive. They intend merely to convince the reader that a person's ingenuity, when bent on exploiting another person, possibly is unlimited. As P. T. Barnum is alleged to have said, "There's a sucker born every minute." (He is also alleged to have said, "Trust everyone, but cut the deck.")

Finally, fraud can be viewed from yet another perspective. When we think of fraud in a corporate or management context, we can perhaps develop a more meaningful and relevant taxonomy as a framework for fraud auditing.

Corporate frauds can be classified into two broad categories: (1) frauds directed against the company, and (2) frauds that benefit the company. In the former the company is the victim; in the latter, the company, through the fraudulent actions of its officers, is the intended beneficiary.

Frauds for the company are committed mainly by senior managers who wish to enhance the financial position or condition of the company by such ploys as overstating income, sales, or assets, or by understating expenses and liabilities. In essence, an intentional misstatement of a financial fact is made, and that can constitute a civil or criminal fraud. But income, for example, may also be intentionally understated to evade taxes, and expenses can be overstated for a similar reason. Frauds for the company by top managers are usually to deceive shareholders, creditors, and regulatory authorities. Similar frauds by lower-level profit-center managers may be to deceive their superiors in the organization, to make them believe the unit is more profitable or productive than it is, and thereby perhaps to earn a higher bonus award or a promotion. In the latter event, despite the fact that the subordinate's overstatement of income, sales, or productivity ostensibly helps the company look better, it is really a fraud *against* the company.

In frauds *for* the organization, management may be involved in a conspiracy to deceive. Only one person may be involved in a fraud against the

Exhibit 1.1   Fraud by Corporate Owners and Managers

Victim	Fraud Type
Customers	False advertising
Customers	False weights
Customers	False measures
Customers	False representations
Customers	False labeling/branding
Customers	Price fixing
Customers	Quality substitution
Customers	Cheap imitations
Customers	Defective products
Stockholders	False financial statements
Stockholders	False financial forecasts
Stockholders	False representations
Creditors	False financial statements
Creditors	False financial forecasts
Creditors	False representations
Competitors	Predatory pricing
Competitors	Selling below cost
Competitors	Information piracy
Competitors	Infringement of patents/copyrights
Competitors	Commercial slander
Competitors	Libel
Competitors	Theft of trade secrets
Competitors	Corruption of employees
Competitors	Corruption of employees
Bankers	Check kiting
Bankers	False applications for credit
Bankers	False financial statements
Company/Employer	Expense account padding
Company/Employer	Performance fakery
Company/Employer	Overstating revenue
Company/Employer	Overstating assets
Company/Employer	Overstating profits
Company/Employer	Understating expenses
Company/Employer	Understating liabilities
Company/Employer	Theft of assets
Company/Employer	Embezzlement
Company/Employer	Conversion of assets
Company/Employer	Commercial bribery
Company/Employer	Insider trading
Company/Employer	Related party transactions
Company/Employer	Alteration/destruction of records

Source: Adapted from Jack Bologna, *Forensic Accounting Review,* 1984.

Exhibit 1.1 *(Continued)*

Victim	Fraud Type
Insurance Carriers	Fraudulent loss claims
Insurance Carriers	Arson for profit
Insurance Carriers	False applications for insurance
Government Agencies	False reports/returns
Government Agencies	False claims
Government Agencies	Contract padding
Government Agencies	Willful failure to file reports/returns

Exhibit 1.2 Fraud by Corporate Vendors, Suppliers, and Contractors

Victim	Fraud Type
Customers	Short shipment
Customers	Overbilling
Customers	Double billing
Customers	Substitution of inferior goods
Customers	Corruption of employees

Source: Adapted from Jack Bologna, *Forensic Accounting Review,* 1984.

Exhibit 1.3 Fraud by Corporate Customers

Victim	Fraud Type
Vendors	Tag switching
Vendors	Shoplifting
Vendors	Fraudulent checks
Vendors	Fraudulent claims for refunds
Vendors	Fraudulent credit cards
Vendors	Fraudulent credit applications

Source: Adapted from Jack Bologna, *Forensic Accounting Review,* 1984.

Exhibit 1.4 Fraud by Corporate Employees

Victim	Fraud Type
Employers	False employment applications
Employers	False benefit claims
Employers	False expense claims
Employers	Theft and pilferage
Employers	Performance fakery
Employers	Embezzlement
Employers	Corruption

Source: Adapted from Jack Bologna, *Forensic Accounting Review,* 1984.

organization such as an accounts payable clerk who fabricates invoices from a nonexistent vendor, has checks issued to that vendor, and converts the checks to his or her own use.

Frauds against the company may also include vendors, suppliers, contractors, and competitors bribing employees. Cases of employee bribery are difficult to discern or discover by audit, because the corporation's accounting records generally are not manipulated, altered, or destroyed. Bribe payments are made under the table or, as lawyers say, sub rosa. The first hint of bribery may come from an irate vendor whose product is consistently rejected despite its quality, price, and performance. Bribery may also become apparent if the employee begins to live beyond his or her means, far in excess of salary and family resources.

A rough guide to classification might therefore appear as follows:

1. **Insider fraud against the company**

    Cash diversions, conversions, and thefts, (front end frauds)

    Check raising and signature or endorsement forgeries

    Receivables manipulations such as lapping and fake credit memos

    Payables manipulations such as raising or fabricating vendor invoices, benefit claims, and expense vouchers, and allowing vendors, suppliers, and contractors to overcharge

    Payroll manipulations such as adding nonexistent employees or altering time cards

    Inventory manipulations and diversions such as specious reclassifications of inventories to obsolete, damaged, or sample status, to create a cache from which thefts can be made more easily

    Favors and payments to employees by vendors, suppliers, and contractors

2. **Outsider fraud against the company**

   Vendor, supplier, and contractor frauds, such as short shipping goods, substituting goods of inferior quality, overbilling, double billing, billing but not delivering or delivering elsewhere

   Vendor, supplier, and contractor corruption of employees

   Customer corruption of employees

3. **Frauds for the company**

   Smoothing profits (cooking the books) through practices such as inflating sales, profits, and assets; understating expenses, losses, and liabilities; not recording or delaying recording of sales returns; early booking of sales; and inflating ending inventory

   Check kiting

   Price fixing

   Cheating customers by using devices such as short weights, counts, and measures; substituting cheaper materials; and false advertising

   Violating governmental regulations—for example, EEO, OSHA, environmental securities, or tax violations standards

   Corrupting customer personnel

   Political corruption

   Padding costs on government contracts

WHAT DO WE KNOW ABOUT WHITE-COLLAR CRIME?

White-collar crime is a topic much in vogue today. Seminars, symposia, and conferences on that subject abound, sponsored by government agencies, universities, trade groups and professional organizations, chambers of commerce, and business, fraternal, and religious organizations. Most are well attended, particularly because the cost of such crimes to individual businesses and to society is substantial. Reducing such crimes would add greatly to corporate coffers. To appreciate the scope and nature of the white-collar crime problem, let us review some of the literature on that subject.

The classic works on white-collar crime are *White Collar Crime,* by Edwin H. Sutherland; *Other People's Money,* by Donald R. Cressey; *The Thief in the White Collar,* by Norman Jaspan; and *Crime, Law, and Society,* by Frank E. Hartung. These authorities essentially tell us that:

> White-collar crime has its genesis in the same general process as other criminal behavior; namely, differential association. The hypothesis of differential association is that criminal behavior is learned in association with those who define such behavior favorably and in isolation from those who define it unfavorably, and that a person in an appropriate situation engages in such

criminal behavior if, and only if, the weight of the favorable definitions exceeds the weight of the unfavorable definitions.[4]

In other words, birds of a feather flock together, or at least reinforce one another's rationalized views and values.

Trusted persons become trust violators when they conceive of themselves as having a financial problem which is nonshareable, are aware that this problem can be secretly resolved by violation of the position of financial trust, and are able to apply their own conduct in that situation, verbalizations which enable them to adjust their conceptions of themselves as users of the entrusted funds or property.[5]

In other words, "I'm not stealing; I'm just borrowing or getting even."

Jaspan's work *The Thief in the White Collar* is based on his many years of consulting experience on security-related matters, and contains a number of notable and often quoted generalizations. In a nutshell, Jaspan exhorts employers to (1) pay their employees fairly, (2) treat their employees decently, and (3) listen to their employees' problems if they want to avoid employee fraud, theft, and embezzlement. But to temper that bit of humanism with a little reality, he also suggests that employers ought never to place full trust in either their employees or the security personnel they hire to check on employees.

Jaspan's humanitarian generalizations are challenged by Frank Hartung, who fears that Jaspan's book ". . . may serve an end never intended by its author. . . . Sympathetic interpretation of the embezzler . . . may help to perpetuate the vocabulary of motives employed by such people since time out of mind. Their conception of *cause* constitutes, in my judgment, a *vocabulary of motives for the committing of embezzlement!*" [emphasis added][6]

Some examples of these motives described in Jaspan's work are:

- Everyone has a little larceny in his heart.
- Everyone has his own racket.
- Most people will try to cheat on their income tax if they think they can get away with it.
- Circumstances beyond their control forced embezzlers to commit their dishonest acts.
- Mitigating circumstances were involved in the theft, such as protecting a friend, relative, or loved one who is an accomplice in the crime.

Hartung then argues:

It will be noticed that the criminal violator of financial trust and the career delinquent have one thing in common: Their criminality is learned in the process of symbolic communication, dependent upon cultural sources of patterns of thought and action, and for systems of values and vocabularies of motives.

But the career of the trust violator is quite different. First, as we said before, he is most likely not to have a previous record, even though typically he is middle-aged when detected. Second, his education, occupation, residence, friends, and leisure-time activities usually set him in a social class higher than that of the delinquent. Third, even though his crime is deliberate and he attempts to avoid detection, he fails to plan for the securing of immunity if caught. Fourth, even though he may be three or four times as old as the career delinquent, his arrest constitutes a serious crisis for him that he cannot take in his stride. His arrest and conviction and the attendant publicity are a disgrace to him.[7]

A white-collar crime, as currently perceived, is a crime a person employed by a governmental or private-sector organization in a position of trust commits. A position of trust in this context means a position that carries authority over people and/or property belonging to another, usually property owned by an employer organization or property over which the organization has legal custody and control as an agent, bailee, or trustee. The authority vested in the position of trust carries with it certain duties, obligations, and responsibilities such as the honest, diligent, and prudent care, protection, and preservation of the property by the person in whose custody it has been entrusted. In essence, white-collar crimes involve a criminal breach of that trust, a breaking or violation of those duties, obligations, and responsibilities either by acts of commission or by omission, by overt or covert action, as in a willful fraud, theft, or embezzlement of the entrusted property, by inaction, as in oversight and neglect of duty, by negligent performance of duty, as in imprudent action and failure of judgment, or by exceeding one's legal authority.

People in positions of trust never have carte blanche to do as they deem fitting with the property entrusted to them. Laws have been enacted to limit and regulate the nature and scope of their authority. When that authority has not been exercised prudently, violators may be held liable, civilly. When that authority is exceeded or corrupted, the violator may be guilty of a crime.

So the concept of white-collar crime has broadened over the years to include not only criminal breaches of trust by people in authority roles, but breaches in business ethics as well. "Let the buyer beware" no longer carries the legal weight it once did. The seller now has obligations, too, relating to fair dealing, candor, and truthfulness.

HOW SERIOUS IS THE FRAUD (WHITE-COLLAR CRIME) PROBLEM?

In view of the scarcity of hard data on white-collar crime, we undertook a limited survey of our own. Although it is premature to make anything more than generalizations, the survey respondents—40 members of the Toledo Personnel Management Association—rank-ordered the following 25 crimes in terms of seriousness and frequency of occurrence: (Note that two types of crime tied for first and thirteenth places.)

1. Bribing political leaders.
   Padding the bill on government contracts.
2. Employee theft, fraud, and embezzlement.
3. Pilfering small tools and supplies.
4. Computer-related crimes.
5. Bribing union leaders.
6. Expense-account padding.
7. Corporate income tax evasion.
8. Stock frauds and manipulations.
9. Falsifying time-and-attendance reports.
10. False advertising.
11. Selling mechanically defective products.
12. Providing unsafe and unhealthy working conditions.
13. Bribing purchasing agents.
    Making illegal campaign contributions.
14. Selling contaminated or adulterated drugs.
15. Falsifying productivity reports.
16. Falsified company financial statements.
17. Mail fraud.
18. Bribing foreign officials.
19. Selling contaminated or adulterated foodstuffs.
20. Sabotaging company property.
21. Price fixing.
22. Falsifying profitability reports.
23. Selling useless drugs.

In terms of the white-collar crimes that will occur more frequently in the future, the rank ordering was as follows: (Note that two types of crime tied for sixth, seventh, and eighth places.)

1. Computer-related crimes.
2. Bribing political leaders.
3. Expense-account padding.

4. Bribing union leaders.

5. Employee theft, fraud, and embezzlement.

6. Falsifying productivity reports.

Padding the bill on government contracts.

7. Corporate income tax evasion.

Bribing foreign officials.

8. Stock frauds and manipulations.

Polluting the environment.

How pervasive is business fraud? How likely is it to be discovered either by audit design or by accident? The probability of fraud in any audit is not very large. If we were to speculate, we would say the probability of discovering fraud by design is about 20 percent. But we cannot support our thesis with anything stronger than impressions. A few years ago *Fortune Magazine* notated a study it did at the top 1000 industrial corporations and indicated that over a period of about 10 years 11 percent of those firms were charged with some form of accounting irregularity or corruption—commercial and political bribery, antitrust violations, tax violations, and securities violations. These were mainly in the category of frauds for the company. If we add frauds committed against those companies by their own employees, vendors, and customers, the percentage of those Fortune 1000 companies that may have experienced frauds would be higher, perhaps even double the 11 percent.

REFERENCES

1. *Michigan Criminal Law,* Chapter 86, Sec. 1529.
2. *Southern Development Co. v. Silva,* 125 U.S. 247, 8 S.C. Rep. 881, 31 L. Ed, (1887).
3. Gwynn Nettler, *Lying, Cheating and Stealing,* Cincinnati: Anderson Publishing Co., 1982.
4. Edwin H. Sutherland, *White-Collar Crime,* New York: Dryden Press, 1949, p. 234.
5. Donald L. Cressey, *Other People's Money,* New York: The Free Press, 1949, p. 30.
6. Norman Jaspan and Hillel Black, *The Thief in the White Collar,* Philadelphia: J. B. Lippincott, 1960, p. 37.
7. Frank E. Hartung, *Crime, Law, and Society,* Detroit: Wayne State University Press, 1965, pp. 125–136.

Chapter 2

Forensic Accounting and Fraud Auditing Fundamentals

Fraud auditing is creating an environment that encourages the detection and prevention of frauds in commercial transactions. The main thrust of this book is to provide auditors and investigators with further knowledge and insight into fraud as an economic, social, and organizational phenomenon.

Investigating fraud in books of account and commercial transactions requires the combined skills of a well-trained auditor and a criminal investigator. However, finding these skills combined in one person is rare, so part of our mission is to better acquaint auditors with criminal-investigative rules, principles, techniques, and methods and to provide criminal investigators with some knowledge of accounting and auditing rules, principles, techniques, and methods.

Fraud auditing cannot be reduced to a simple checklist. It is an awareness in the broadest sense of many components such as the human element, organizational behavior, knowledge of fraud, evidence and standards of proof, an awareness of the potentiality for fraud, and an appreciation of the so-called red flags. Some of the functions of a fraud auditor follow.

- The fraud auditor should set the standard. This means that the fraud auditor within a company should have in place, and communicated to all employees, an effective corporate code of conduct that should also include conflict-of-interest policy guidelines signed by employees to provide a clear understanding of the intent of management and the level of expectations. There should also be in agreements, especially with vendors, a clause that allows the company to inspect the vendors' records in the normal course of business.

- The fraud auditor must know the realm of fraud possibilities. Fraud auditors should know the types of fraudulent behavior experienced in the past and be able to relate this knowledge to the various segments of any accounting system and/or business operation. For example, knowledge of lapping in the revenue receivable receipt system.

- Fraud auditors should know the most direct route for any investigation to follow to determine if substance exists to support a concern, rumor, or allegation. Fraud auditors should know enough to examine a deposit to determine if receipts from Peter are being applied to reduce the receivable balance of Paul—a quick test to indicate whether lapping is occurring.
- Fraud auditors should look at motive and consider the environment in which the employee operates to determine if there is any possible justification. If a manager has placed more responsibility on an employee, it allows the manager to take less interest in the company's financial well being. Two things occur in this situation: The employee contributes more to the job than the job description requires, and second, the employee sees a poor behavioral model set by the manager. Together, these create within the employee's mind a position of compromise that may form a motivation to steal.
- Fraud auditors have many investigative concerns; one basic concern is opportunity. Can it be shown that the person in question is the only one with the opportunity to steal? Perhaps there are problems in the collection of receipts before that individual receives these monies.
- Another concern of the fraud auditor is to establish benefit and identify assets for possible recovery. Is there clear evidence that the employee suspected is receiving a benefit? Is there a pattern of circumstantial evidence that consistently points in one direction? Is the employee living beyond his or her means? Are there any assets?
- Fraud auditors assess investigative findings. At various stages of an investigation, they must stand back and assess findings measured by the standards of proof, in order to determine if there is substance to an allegation, if a pattern of conduct exists that could suggest intent, or if there is merely a problem in errors and omissions in the accounting system. It may be appropriate for the fraud auditor to merely confront the employee to ask why Peter's money is paying Paul's account. Before doing that, the auditor might need to examine several transactions over an extended period to determine if a pattern of conduct exists and if there has been deceitful reporting to management. The assessment process is one of understanding what one presently has; understanding what may be needed, determining if there is a pattern of conduct consistent with wrongdoing; and, finally, determining if deceitful behavior exists in the employee's reporting to management.

WHO NEEDS FRAUD AUDITING?

Fraud auditing is a relatively new discipline. Whereas financial and operational auditing have long histories of acceptance, fraud auditing has come into its own only during the twentieth century, mainly with the advent of federal, criminal, and regulatory statutes involving business: the Sherman Antitrust Act (1890), the Internal Revenue Act (1913), and the 1934 Securities and Exchange Commission Act (SEC), to name a few. Wartime regulation of pricing and profits such as the Office of Price Administration (OPA) law and the excess-profits-tax law added further impetus to earlier laws related to mail fraud, fraud by wire, the Federal Trade Commission, the Robinson-Patman and Clayton Acts, and the Wage and Hour law. More recent federal laws that have contributed to the growth of fraud auditing include the Labor-Management Reporting and Disclosure Act, the Welfare-Pension Fund Act, Employee Retirement Income Security Act (ERISA), and the Foreign Corrupt Practices Act. These laws, together with the increase in fraud in public companies, waste and abuse in government contracting, and the current public concern over white-collar crime, create a greater need for further development of this new discipline.

The need for fraud-auditing talents is not related solely to compliance with new governmental regulations. Fraud-auditing skills in the private sector are also useful in most cases of financial crime such as embezzlement, misrepresentations of financial facts, arson for profit, bankruptcy fraud, investment frauds of all manner and description, bank fraud, kickbacks and commercial bribery, computer frauds, electronic funds transfer (EFT) systems frauds, and credit card frauds, and scams and shams by vendors, suppliers, contractors, and customers.

Relatively few public accountants and internal auditors are specifically trained and experienced in this discipline. In the United States the largest body of trained and experienced fraud auditors comes from government audit and investigative agencies like the IRS, FBI, GAO, and the SEC. Police authorities on the state and local levels have few audit resources at their disposal; as a consequence, their ability to investigate certain white-collar crimes is limited. There is a need for fraud auditing in both public and private sectors of the economy.

WHAT SHOULD A FRAUD AUDITOR KNOW AND BE ABLE TO DO?

An effective fraud auditor should know, with some degree of depth, what fraud is from the following perspectives:

- Human and individual
- Organizational, cultural, and motivational
- Economic/competitive
- Social

- Regulatory, legal, and evidential (how to discern, detect, and document such frauds)
- Accounting, audit, and internal control (when, where, and how fraud is most likely to occur in books of account and in financial statements)

An effective fraud auditor should be able to do the following competently:

- Conduct a review of internal controls.
- Assess the strengths and weaknesses of those controls.
- Design scenarios of potential fraud losses based on identified weaknesses in internal controls.
- Identify questionable and exceptional situations in account balances.
- Identify questionable and exceptional transactions (too high, too low, too often, too rare, too much, too little, odd times, odd places, odd people).
- Distinguish between simple human errors and omissions in entries and fraudulent entries (intentional error, such as recurring small errors versus unintentional random error and ignorance).
- Follow the flow of documents that support transactions.
- Follow the flow of funds into and out of an organization's account.
- Search for underlying support documents for questionable transactions.
- Review such documents for peculiarities such as raised amounts; forgery; counterfeiting; fake billings; invoicing of claims; destruction of data; improper account classification; irregularities in serial sequences, quantity, pricing, extensions, and footings; and substitution of copies for original documents.
- Gather and preserve evidence to corroborate asset losses, fraudulent transactions, and financial statements.
- Document and report a fraud loss for criminal, civil, or insurance claims.
- Be aware of management, administrative, and organizational policies, procedures, and practices.
- Test the organization's motivational and ethical climate.

The skills of a criminal investigator are in some respects similar to those of an auditor. An auditor and a detective both seek the truth: the auditor with respect to the proper accounting of business transactions and the detective/investigator with respect to the proper (legal) behavior of citizens. Both should have inquisitive minds and challenge things that appear out of order and out of sequence, such as odd times, odd places, and odd people—in a word, things that are the *opposite* of what one would logically expect.

Laypersons call this gift investigative intuition. Investigators call it professional judgment—judgment derived from knowledge, education, training, acquired skills, and experience. No one is born with it. It is acquired mainly by trial and error. It is not a formula, and it cannot actually be taught. But it can be learned.

The hunch of an amateur may not be worth much, based as it is on naiveté. The hunch of a trained investigator is worth much more, because it is based on experience, knowledge, and training. When auditors say they have discovered a fraud in accounting records by accident, it may be no accident; their trained eyes and ears can discern the truth.

Police detectives also attribute some of their investigative insights to accident, chance, or good luck. But, there again, their breakthroughs are not simply random events, but are brought about by their concentration and focus on the issue at hand. It is not black magic or fortuitous circumstances.

So we would like to counter the feigned humility of some investigators and auditors by proposing that "accidental" discoveries of crimes by investigators and frauds by auditors usually are attributable not to pure chance but to know-how. Unfortunately not all investigators or auditors have this skill. The investigative mentality comes with age, training, self-discipline, experience, and a mind-set that understands that crime and fraud are possible in any environment, at any time, by anyone, if the circumstances are ripe.

What are these circumstances? Ripe circumstances are (1) conditions in the environment, such as social values, prevailing moral and ethical standards, and economic, competitive, political, and social conditions; and (2) motives in the mental dispositions of individuals who are most likely to commit a crime.

Although the motive for a crime is not a necessary element of proof in sustaining a conviction (whereas criminal *intent* is), motivation is important to the investigator and the auditor because it tends to identify the more likely suspects when the actual culprit is unknown. The motive also helps to construct a theory of the case; that is, the who, what, when, where, how, and why of the crime. So motivation should not be discounted. It can narrow the search for the culprit and substantially aid in reconstructing the crime.

As a general rule, motives can be separated into four major categories: (1) psychotic, (2) economic, (3) egocentric, and (4) ideological.

Psychotic motivation can impair a successful criminal prosecution when an insanity plea is made. Of the other three motivations, economic motivation is the most common. The individual wants or needs money or wealth. Egocentric motivation means the individual wants more prestige, more recognition, higher social or political status, or even a job promotion. Ideological motivation means that the individuals feel that their cause or values are morally superior to those of the victim, or they feel exploited, abused, or discriminated against by the victim.

Motives should be viewed from another perspective as well; a series of emotions may also serve as motives—motives such as jealousy, spite, revenge, anger, greed, bigotry, hatred, pride, covetousness, gluttony, and sloth; or fears of ridicule, rejection, poverty, sickness, pain, death, failure, loss, and even uncertainty.

It is clear that a competent investigator must know people and their motivations—their needs, wants, demands, and desires; their values, beliefs, and attitudes; and their individual peculiarities.

Auditors, if they hope to become fraud auditors, must be similarly inclined toward the study of people. They must also know how to identify and locate culprits and witnesses and how to interview them, as well as how to gather, classify, and preserve information and evidence and to assess their value, weight, and significance.

THIRTEEN PRINCIPLES OF FRAUD AUDITING

1. Fraud auditing is unlike financial auditing. It is more a mind-set than a methodology.

2. Fraud auditors are unlike financial auditors. Fraud auditors focus on exceptions, oddities, accounting irregularities, and patterns of conduct, not on errors and omissions.

3. Fraud auditing is learned primarily from experience, not from audit textbooks or last year's work papers. Learning to be a fraud auditor means learning to think like a thief—"Where are the weakest links in this chain of internal controls?"

4. From an audit perspective, fraud is intentionally misrepresenting financial facts of a material nature. From a fraud-audit perspective, fraud is an intentional misrepresentation of financial facts.

5. Frauds are committed for economic, egocentric, ideological, and psychotic reasons. Of the four, the economic motive is the most common.

6. Fraud tends to encompass a theory structured around motive, opportunity, and benefit.

7. Fraud in a computerized accounting environment can be committed at any state of processing—input, throughput, or output. Input frauds (entering false and fraudulent data) are the most common.

8. The most common fraudulent schemes by lower-level employees involve disbursements (payables, payroll, and benefit and expense claims).

9. The most common fraudulent schemes by higher-level managers involve "profit smoothing" (deferring expenses, booking sales too early, overstating inventory).

10. Accounting-type frauds are caused more often by absence of controls than by loose controls.

11. Fraud incidents are not growing exponentially, but fraud losses are.

12. Accounting frauds are discovered more often by accident than by financial audit purposes or design. Over 90 percent of financial frauds are discovered by accident.

13. Fraud prevention is a matter of adequate controls and a work environment that places a high value on personal honesty and fair dealing.

FINANCIAL AUDITING AND FRAUD AUDITING

Financial auditing is intended to uncover material deviations and variances from standards of acceptable accounting and auditing practice. But when pretense is used to disguise a transaction or to cover it up, the financial auditor is not likely to become suspicious. Furthermore, the assumption of management integrity can create a false sense of security in the financial auditor concerning the legitimacy of financial transactions. Looking *behind* and *beyond* the transaction forces the fraud auditor to ignore assumptions and to focus on substance instead. The questions the fraud auditor has uppermost in mind are not how the accounting system and internal controls stack up against AICPA and CICA standards but:

- Where are the weakest links in this system's chain of controls?
- What deviations from conventional good accounting practices are possible in this system?
- How are off-line transactions handled, and who can authorize such transactions?
- What would be the simplest way to compromise this system?
- What control features in this system can be bypassed by higher authorities?
- What is the nature of the work environment?

Auditing for fraud is therefore more of an intuitive process than a formal, analytic methodology. It is more of an art than a science. As a consequence, it is difficult to teach. Skill depends on the right mind-set (thinking like a thief, probing for weaknesses) and practice. But it is not *technique* one should master; it is *mental disposition:* doggedness and persistence. No lead, no shred of evidence is too small to be relevant. One seeks relevant information, organizes it in some meaningful way, and then sees the pattern it creates.

The patterns to look for are the exceptions and oddities, the things that do not fit in an organized scheme because they seem too large, too small, too frequent, too rare, too high, too low, too ordinary, too extraordinary, too many, or too few, or feature odd times, odd places, odd hours, odd people, and odd combinations. In a word, one looks for the unusual rather than the usual. Then one goes behind and beyond those transactions to reconstruct what may have led to them and what has followed from them. A more complete assessment of fraud is possible if the data that precedes or follows a questionable transaction are available.

From an accounting and audit standpoint, fraud is an intentional misrepresentation of a material fact in the books of account and ultimately the financial statements. The misrepresentation may be directed against such organizational outsiders as shareholders or creditors, or against the organization itself by covering up or disguising embezzlement, incompetence, misapplication of funds, and theft, or improper use of organizational assets by officers, employees, and agents.

Fraud may also be directed against an organization by outsiders (vendors, suppliers, contractors, consultants, and customers) through overbilling, double billing, substituting inferior materials, or misrepresenting the quality and value of goods purchased or the credit standing of customers. Such outsiders may also be guilty of corrupting insiders (commercial bribery).

Fraud, theft, embezzlement, and commercial bribery are the paramount concerns of fraud auditors. Fraud auditing is the discipline used to discourage, discern, and document such incidents. These incidents may occur for years before they are discovered. Auditing for fraud means identifying intentional irregularities in accounting practices, procedures, and controls.

Financial auditing, as distinguished from fraud auditing, concentrates on the present—on the adequacy of internal controls, on the reliability, validity, and mathematical accuracy of today's entries. But such a narrow focus does not provide a historical perspective. Reasonableness tests, when not related to past relationships and trends, do not provide enough insight. For that reason, we say fraud auditing looks beyond, behind, and before current transactions. It occupies itself as much with the past as the present.

Frauds of this kind occur most often when the following conditions exist:

- Internal controls are absent, weak, or loosely enforced.
- Employees are hired without due consideration for their honesty and integrity.
- Employees are poorly managed, exploited, abused, or placed under great stress to accomplish financial goals and objectives.
- Management models are themselves corrupt, inefficient, or incompetent.
- A trusted employee has an unresolvable personal problem, usually of a financial nature, brought on by family medical needs, or alcoholism, drug abuse, excessive gambling, or expensive tastes.

- The industry of which the company is a part has a history or tradition of corruption.
- The company has fallen on bad times—it is losing money or market share, or its products or services are becoming passé.

Physical custody of property, access to accounting records, and the knowledge and authority to override controls are the main ingredients of fraud in books of account and in financial statements.

People who have access to corporate assets and knowledge of the internal and accounting controls, or who hold management roles in which they can override such controls, are in the best position to commit financial frauds against their companies. The threat of fraud is greatest at the senior management level because access to assets and authority to bypass controls is greatest at that level. But financial fraud is also possible among personnel with accounting, finance, data processing, and property-handling responsibilities. They too may have access to accounting records and can use that knowledge and authority to compromise controls and to access corporate assets.

There is no simple formula for conducting a fraud audit, nor are there any generally accepted checklists or patterned interviews. Fraud is a human phenomenon; humans vary a great deal, as do frauds, in terms of the techniques used.

Most frauds, embezzlements, and thefts of corporate assets are not discovered in the course of routine financial audits. Their existence usually comes to light through (1) an allegation, complaint, or a rumor of fraud brought by a third party (a disgruntled supplier or a fellow employee), (2) an investigator's intuition or general suspicion that something is awry, (3) an exception from an expectation of a person senior to the suspect (an unacceptable condition, profits, sales, costs, assets, or liabilities are too low or too high), or (4) the sudden discovery that something is missing—cash, property, reports, files, documents, or data. Rarely does an auditor know at the outset that a fraud, theft, or embezzlement was committed. One may have some rather sketchy information at best, and then applies the investigative mentality: How to determine whether a fraud, theft, or embezzlement has in fact occurred. The objective is to determine whether a crime exists. A crime exists when the following exist: a proven loss of something of value to a victim; a perpetrator who caused that loss; and a law that makes that loss a crime. The immediate facts to determine are whether there is (1) a criminal law, (2) an apparent breach of that law, (3) a perpetrator, and (4) a victim. These are some of the steps in the fraud auditor's takes:

1. Acquire all available corporate documents relating to the allegation.
2. Meet with the individual making the allegation to determine if the allegation makes sense, and assess the degree of emotion expressed.

3. Assess the allegation against the available documentation to determine the next appropriate move.
4. Determine, if necessary, whether further documentation is available from the company. If so, where? Should other people within the company be interviewed?
5. Assess the corporate environment relative to the person in question.
6. Ask whether a theory of fraud can be developed at this stage. That is, is there motive and opportunity that could possibly benefit the person?
7. The fraud auditor asks himself or herself whether the available evidence makes sense. Does it meet the test of business reality?
8. Should third parties outside the company be interviewed? Does the auditor have a right to meet with these people and examine their documents?
9. Are the proper people within the company informed of the current situation and its direction?
10. How far back in time should one go?
11. Was the problem there before the person suspected assumed a new position?
12. Was the problem present at the person's previous position?
13. What public documents are available?

Accounting-type frauds usually are accompanied by the modification, alteration, destruction, or counterfeiting of accounting information. But accounting information can be either intentionally or accidentally modified, altered, and destroyed, as by human error or omission. The first objective for the fraud auditor, then, is to determine whether a discrepancy in accounting records is attributable to human error. If so, there may be no actual fraud. If the discrepancy (missing records, destroyed records, modified records, counterfeit records, errors, omissions) cannot be attributed to accidental or human error, a full-scale fraud audit/investigation should follow.

Evidence gathered may consist of the testimony of witnesses, confessions of perpetrators, documents, items (means and instruments, or fruits of the crime), and perhaps the testimony of experts. One of those experts may have to be a forensic accountant or fraud auditor, someone who can explain in layperson's terms the financial information available, modified or destroyed records, data, documents, and files.

In the course of routine financial audits, auditors are most likely to uncover cases of active or ongoing embezzlement, *if* they have some degree of fraud awareness. Otherwise, the probability of discovering embezzlement is about 10 percent, if you can believe auditors' impressions. (Auditors claim 90 percent of the frauds they uncover are found by accident.)

THINKING AS A FRAUD AUDITOR

Fraud auditors and detectives tend to be "thinker" types. They are thinkers in the sense that they deal with situations requiring objectivity on their part. Personal feelings and personal biases are inappropriate for making sound decisions and drawing logical conclusions and inferences.

Fraud auditors and detectives tend also to be intuitive in the sense that they enjoy solving new and different problems with a minimum amount of information. Continuous financial auditing would not be the fraud auditor's usual cup of tea.

In circumstances in which evidence is sparse or destroyed, and sometimes nonexistent, fraud auditors can theorize about the facts and play on hunches. They are sensitive to nonverbal cues, are spontaneous in solving problems, and can refine and rework a problem with a variety of approaches until it is solved. They rely more on ingenuity in their work than on a canned audit program.

We owe decisional classifications (sensers, intuitors, thinkers, and feelers) to Carl Jung, who proposed the taxonomy some 60 years ago. Jung also suggested that each of us tends to be dominant in only one of the four functions, but this dominant function is backed up by a paired opposite. The four basic decision combinations are (1) sensation/thinking, (2) intuition/thinking, (3) sensation/feeling, and (4) intuition/feeling.

Updating Jung's theory with recent neurological research, we can also say that some people are left-brain dominant (rational, analytical, sequential, logical, systematic), and some are right-brain dominant (creative, emotional, intuitive, holistic) (see Exhibit 2.1).

There is another distinction between financial auditing and fraud auditing. Financial auditing sees events, transactions, and environments in terms of their overt aspects, whereas fraud auditors tend to look at events, transactions, and environments in terms of their covert aspects (see Exhibit 2.2).

Exhibit 2.1   Left and Right Brain Hemispheres

Left Hemisphere--------------------Right Hemisphere

Sensation/ Thinking	Intuition/ Thinking		Sensation/ Feeling	Intuition/ Feeling
Financial Auditor	Fraud Auditor		Teacher	Artist

Exhibit 2.2 The Iceberg Theory of Fraud

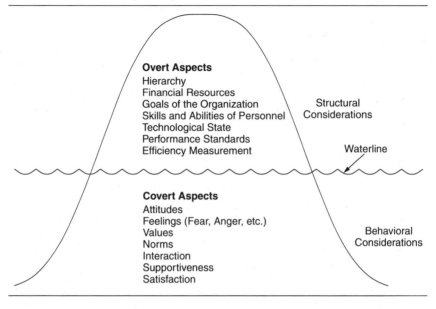

Exhibit 2.2 shows the structural and behavioral considerations of fraud as if they were an iceberg. The structural considerations loom above the surface of the water, visible to anyone who cares to glance in their direction, but the behavioral considerations lurk beneath the surface, posing a danger to the un-suspecting auditor.

Everything we see above the surface is important, but there is a great deal under the surface that also merits close attention. So it seems that financial auditors tend to focus on the structural aspects of control. Are they there, in place, in adequate quantity, and being monitored? Fraud auditors preoccupy themselves with the behavioral aspects of control. Can they be breached? If so, by whom? Under what conditions or circumstances?

Intuition, which we define as professional judgment, is a quality and dis-position of the mind. It comes mainly from personal experience. Education and training play some part in its development, but education and training cannot do it all. It is difficult to write a how-to book on fraud auditing; how-to books present their contents like cookbook recipes, but fraud involves so many variables in terms of fraud types, defrauder types, victim types, crime methods, techniques, tools, means, and instruments, that any effort to unify them into a comprehensive theory of causation or solution seems impossible. So it is more difficult to train fraud auditors in a methodical way. On-the-job training is perhaps the best method of instruction; one must experience fraud to know it best. But to some degree the experience can also be borrowed from others. The study of cases, especially those that have been the subject of books, is of particular value.

The knack of intuition can be acquired if one retains an open, objective, and inquisitive mind—not necessarily an analytical mind but one that can synthesize data and put it all together in some sort of scenario of what may have happened. Like jigsaw puzzles, data are easier to piece together after one develops the knack.

Mystery stories generally are exercises in deductive logic, and most lay-persons believe crimes can be detected and proven that way. Some *can* be. But crime or fraud discernment generally involves applying inductive as well as deductive logic. A recurring theme in most mystery stories is the solution of crimes through a brilliant flash of insight at some point in the investigation. Some minor or oddball thing happened or was found or observed that ulti-mately led to the crime's solution. A minor fact becomes the major fact in un-raveling the crime or identifying the killer.

It is not our habit to disagree with literary critics, but we do not believe that this language is correct. The process they call *deduction* is more like *synthesis.* It was not a missing piece in a jigsaw puzzle that solved the crime, but a missing link in the chain of evidence that brought the insight to the fore. It can be described as seeing the *whole* and the *hole* at once. The union of time, space, and energy caused the flash. That is intuition. But this knack of seeing the hole and the whole all at once comes with experience and the right mind-set. Mind-set is a predisposition to believe in the things you see, feel, taste, touch, smell, and experience—to believe in your own compe-tence. Some people call the latter arrogance, but it is not that at all. Good in-vestigators do not necessarily have a sixth sense. They are just open to their senses, open to suggestions, open to oddities. They can see both the dough-nut and the hole. Sherlock Holmes had this talent for seeing the oddity: the dog that did not bark.

In summary, the most accepted scientific methods for deriving truth in-volve using deductive and inductive reasoning. In deductive reasoning one proceeds from the general to the specific, whereas in inductive reasoning one proceeds from the specific to the general. Inductive reasoning involves an em-pirical approach to truth; that is, one takes a representative sample of the whole and predicts a probable outcome based on that sample. In deductive rea-soning one makes clinical observations, conducts physical examinations and interrogations; eliminates the extraneous; and draws inferences to arrive at certain generalizations or conclusions. Financial auditors tend to use the in-ductive approach, whereas investigators tend to use the deductive approach. Fraud auditors may have to use both approaches in developing their investiga-tive mentality.

THE FRAUD AUDITOR'S GENERAL MIND-SET

A maxim in the auditing profession is, "Most frauds are discovered by accident, not by audit or accounting system design." This has been repeated so many times by so many accountants and auditors that the general public accepts it as an axiom or a self-evident truth. Yet, many authors have written books about fraud auditing and most of them have found willing buyers and avid readers.

Most fraud audit books address the problem from an after-the-fact perspective. The fraud was discovered (usually by accident), and the author confirmed and corroborated it by certain methods. Discovery, not detection, is the main theme of the books. The authors of these books attribute their discoveries of fraud to chance, luck, or happenstance, never to statistics, probabilities, or scientific method. Neither deductive or inductive logic nor the rigors of science had anything to do with their success.

If fraud auditing has no scientific basis and most frauds are discovered by accident, what value can be assigned to the books that are written? Are they simply the memoirs and war stories of old men who stumbled or muddled through audits and got lucky? Yes, some are of that variety, but others are enlightening and useful. They catalog some of the more ingenious techniques the authors used to ferret out and prove fraud—techniques that by and large have worked well for them but have limited, not universal, application. So the search for a generally accepted methodology of fraud auditing goes on. To our knowledge, there is none to date. Instead, there are collections of anecdotes, a few useful gimmicks that may work under some circumstances, a number of commonly accepted myths, and a lot of hope that the future will provide more concrete and tangible solutions for the detection, auditing, and investigation of fraud.

Fraud auditing texts do disclose a common theme—that fraud is endemic and pervasive in some industries, locales, companies, and occupations, at some time. For example, railroad promoters in the 1870s raised more capital from less informed investors, based on more "water" in their stocks, than ever before. Samuel Insull did the same thing in the electric utility business in the 1920s. Insull sold millions of dollars of common stock in electric utility companies to unwary investors. The stock was greatly overpriced in terms of the utilities' real assets. When the stock market collapsed in 1929, it was apparent that Insull's holding company was insolvent and had been for some time. Only financial legerdemain had kept it afloat.

During the 1950s, more doctors were involved in more income tax frauds than ever before or since. Food franchisers, in the late 1960s, are another example of the fraud phenomenon. Some fast-food franchisers sold unwary small investors on untested restaurant concepts at over-valued prices. These half-baked concepts led to the bankruptcy of many of the franchisees. During the Watergate era of the early 1970s, more politicians were involved in corruption and fraud against taxpayers, and more corporations were involved in political and commercial bribery than ever before.

Are all of these events merely historical flukes? Did media attention create them? Perhaps. Media attention may have created the original public awareness, but the frauds and corruption were there all the time. What changed was the mind-set of the auditors. Nothing was taken for granted anymore. Suspicion fell on industries, professions, and various areas of government. The auditors' and investigators' undivided attention then led to wholesale charges of fraud, theft, and corruption.

Am I saying that mind-set is what brought these matters to light? Yes, I am—mind-set, not methodology. As indicated before, there is no commonly accepted fraud audit methodology. It is mind-set; but what particular mind-set do we address? Not mind-set of the paranoid who trusts no one and sees evil everywhere. The mind-set I speak of is one that suggests several things:

- Fraud can be *detected,* as well as discovered by accident.
- Financial audit methodologies and techniques come and go, but none are truly designed to ferret out fraud.
- Fraud detection is more of an art than a science. It requires innovative and creative thinking as well as the rigors of science.
- Doggedness, persistence, and self-confidence are more important attributes for a fraud auditor than a high IQ.

Every fraud has its own unique wrinkles. All thieves do not think alike. They tend to be opportunists. Given a set of circumstances that allow them to steal, they take the easiest way. Elaborate crimes make interesting reading, but they are committed only by characters in Agatha Christie novels. In the real world of corporate fraud, the culprits leave trails and make mistakes. Auditors must learn to look for these telltale signs. What are they? The authors hope to provide some insight to the reader—insight into the mind and behavior patterns of fraud perpetrators and the evidence they leave behind, from which their crimes can be reconstructed.

Fraud auditing, then, puts things together rather than taking them apart, as is the case in classic financial auditing or the modern method of systems analysis. The process of fraud auditing is also more intuitive than deductive, although both intuition and deduction play important parts. That is why the checklists and cookbook recipes of financial auditing do not seem to work as well in fraud auditing. Like financial auditing, fraud auditing and investigating have a planning phase, but it comes later. Checklists, questionnaires, patterned interviews, and canned audit programs may obscure the fraud problem if they are used too soon. Fraud auditors' minds must learn to wander about aimlessly and restlessly early on. Their curiosity should be piqued about everything. This is a new environment, with new people and new or different systems. To assume that past experience alone will solve the problem is specious reasoning. Frauds are like snowflakes—they have different sizes, shapes, and consistencies, and to concentrate on one type will not help much in measuring or weighing the next. All powers of concentration and attention must be given to the case at hand. Past experience may distract.

Sociologists tell us that criminal behavior is learned behavior; that is, learned from others. Fraud auditing, too, is learned behavior, but it is self-learning more than it is learning from others. So while you cannot be *taught* to become a fraud auditor, you can *learn* to become one.

Fraud auditing is not easy. It is often frustrating and grueling work. You will be surrounded with data, documents, reports, analyses, observations, and interview notes; and times, dates, places, people, procedures, and policies to remember. The pace of the audit effort is generally frantic and the working environment is hectic. The status of the audit may even seem chaotic at any point to the inexperienced observer. Often the fraud auditor does not know what to look for, or even why, other than that something looks suspicious or out of place. So to be overly organized when doing fraud audit work may be a handicap. You need a lot of freedom and space to let your imagination run wild. You need to poke holes into everything, including your own pet theories and biases.

Do not accept anything anyone says as the gospel truth. Do not assume that any document is what it purports to be. When conflicts between statements of witnesses occur, do not take sides or prejudge their veracity. Keep an open mind. The proof of fraud is rarely when and what you thought when you first began the audit. Preconceptions are dangerous. They invariably lead you down the wrong path. Do not assume the victim knows or understands what happened, either. Building your own theory based on the victim's preconceptions is equally dangerous. But do not discourage the victim or the victim's personnel from talking. They probably have an answer or two that will help you in the long run, an answer that they do not believe is relevant or significant at the time.

Management Fraud: Detection and Deterrence, edited by Robert K. Elliott and John J. Willingham,[1] is a compilation of papers Peat, Marwick, and Mitchell presented at a symposium in 1978. Peat, Marwick, and Mitchell commissioned the papers from a group of experts in relevant academic disciplines; for example, criminology, social psychology, auditing, and computer science. The book has a number of significant strengths and valuable insights. The chapter David R. Saunders contributed, "Psychological Perspectives on Management Fraud," offers one gem of wisdom that good detectives and fraud auditors have known for some time but have been unwilling to speak about in public: " . . . the ability to suspect fraud by some means that is better than pure guessing is an intuitive process, not subject to predictable forms of logical reasoning." We could not agree more. Good fraud auditors and investigators truly are a breed apart from their colleagues in auditing and law enforcement. They differ in personality, communication style, lifestyle, and beliefs and values. It is like comparing Columbo and Perry Mason:

- Mason, the articulate, clinically cold, calculating, brilliant, logical, deductive reasoner whose eternal questions are: Who did it? and Why?
- Columbo, the stumbling, bumbling, cigar chomping, eternally curious fool whose persistence and doggedness on questions like what, where, when, how many, how few, and how often always seem to end up proving the why and whom issues, too.

In simple, psychological terms, Mason is a left-brain thinker: logical, sequential, orderly, linear, deductive, analytical, and intellectual. Columbo, on the other hand, is a right-brain thinker: intuitive, creative, emotional, holistic, artistic, and inductive. In short, Mason analyzes, Columbo synthesizes. Mason takes it apart and Columbo puts it all together. Mason is the brilliant pathologist, and Columbo is the phenomenologist. What happened? versus Why did it happen?

A pessimist is often described as "someone who looks both ways while crossing a one-way street." The fraud auditor/investigator fits that verbal characterization and yet is not really a pessimist. In the realm of corporate fraud prevention and detection, it just pays to look both ways, and up and down, for that matter.

WHAT IS FORENSIC AND INVESTIGATIVE ACCOUNTING?

Although relatively new to the accounting profession, the role of a forensic expert in other professions has been in place for some time. Webster's Dictionary defines the word *forensic* as "belonging to, used in, or suitable to courts of judicature or to public discussions and debate" and the term *forensic medicine* as "a science that deals with the relation and application of medical facts to legal problems." Accordingly, the term *forensic* in the accounting profession deals with the relation and application of financial facts to legal problems. Forensic accounting evidence is oriented to a court of law, whether that court is criminal or civil. Furthermore, with its orientation to courts of law, the quality of the work forensic accountants must attain is subject to public scrutiny if the matter at issue goes to trial.

The involvement of the forensic accountant is almost always reactive; this distinguishes forensic accountants from fraud auditors, who tend to be actively involved in prevention and detection in a corporate or regulatory environment. Forensic accountants are trained to react to complaints arising in criminal matters, statements of claim arising in civil litigation, and rumors and inquiries arising in corporate investigations. The investigative findings of the forensic accountant will impact an individual and/or a company in terms of their freedom or a financial award or loss.

The forensic accountant draws on various resources to obtain relevant financial evidence and to interpret and present this evidence in a manner that will assist both parties. Ideally, forensic accounting should allow two parties to more quickly and efficiently resolve the complaint, statement of claim, rumor, or inquiry, or at least reduce the financial element as an area of ongoing debate.

WHO NEEDS FORENSIC ACCOUNTING?

The increased business complexities in a litigious environment have enhanced the need for this discipline. It is possible to summarize the range of application into the following general areas:

1. **Corporate Investigations.** Companies react to concerns that arise through a number of sources that might suggest possible wrongdoing within and without the corporate environment. From the anonymous phone call or letter from disgruntled employees and third parties, these problems must be addressed quickly and effectively to permit the company to continue to pursue its objectives. More specifically, the forensic accountant assists in addressing allegations ranging from kickbacks and wrongful dismissals to internal situations involving allegations of management or employee wrongdoing. At times, a forensic accountant can meet with those persons affected by the allegations, rumors, or inquiries; they may view the accountant as an independent and objective party, and thus be more willing to engage in discussion.

2. **Litigation Support.** Litigation support includes assisting counsel in investigating and assessing the integrity and amount relating to such areas as loss of profits, construction claims, product liability, shareholder disputes, and breach of contract.

3. **Criminal Matters.** White-collar crime has consistently used accountants and auditors in attempts to sort out, assess, and report on financial transactions related to allegations against individuals and companies in a variety of situations, such as arson, shams, fraud, kickbacks, and stock market manipulations. In criminal matters, accountants and auditors as expert witnesses are increasingly important in court cases.

4. **Insurance Claims.** Both the preparation and assessment of insurance claims on behalf of the insured and insurers may require the assistance of a forensic accountant to assess both the integrity and quantum of a claim. The more significant areas relate to the calculation of loss arising from business interruption, fidelity bond, and personal injury matters. Whereas certain of these cases require financial projections, many need historical analysis, on which to base future projections.

5. **Government.** Forensic accountants can assist governments to achieve regulatory compliance by ensuring that companies follow the appropriate legislation. Grant and subsidy investigations and public inquiries form a part of this service to government.

In generalizing the type of situation that requires a forensic accountant, it might be suggested that the forensic accountant is needed when there is a potential perceived or real financial loss or risk of loss. The responsibility of the forensic accountant is, in effect, to be a problem solver.

WHAT SHOULD A FORENSIC ACCOUNTANT BE ABLE TO DO?

1. **Identification of Financial Issues.** When forensic accountants are presented with a situation generated by a complaint, allegation, rumor, inquiry, or statement of claim, it is important that they clearly identify the financial issues significant to the matter quickly. They base these decisions on experience and knowledge, and any resulting recommendations must reflect both common sense and business reality. For example, if documents are needed from a foreign jurisdiction, although the most obvious recommendation would be to obtain these records, it is usually not practical to do so. Other alternatives must be considered.

2. **Knowledge of Investigative Techniques.** When the issues have been identified, it is imperative that further information and documentation be acquired in order to obtain further evidence to assist in either supporting or refuting the allegation or claim. Not only is it a question of knowing where the relevant financial documentation exists but also of knowing the intricacies of generally accepted accounting principles, financial statement disclosure, systems of internal control, and an awareness of the human element involved in the operation of a company.

3. **Knowledge of Evidence.** The forensic accountant must understand what constitutes evidence, the meaning of "best" and "primary" evidence, and the form that various accounting summaries can take to consolidate the financial evidence in a way that is acceptable to the courts.

4. **Interpretation of Financial Information.** It is unusual for a transaction or a series of events to have only one interpretation. The forensic

accountant must be extremely conscious of a natural bias that can exist in the interpretation process. It is important that transactions be viewed from all aspects to ensure that the ultimate interpretation of the available information fits with common sense and the test of business reality. A proper interpretation of information can only be assured when one has looked behind and beyond the transaction in question without any scope limitations.

5. **Presentation of Findings.** The forensic accountant must have the ability to clearly communicate the findings resulting from the investigation in a fashion understandable to the layperson. The presentation can be oral or written and can include the appropriate demonstrative aids. The role of forensic accountants in the witness box is the final test of their findings in a public forum.

Investigative Concerns

Investigative concerns must be addressed by forensic accountants at the appropriate time during the course of their investigations. For example, in dealing with criminal matters, the primary concern is to develop evidence around motive, opportunity, and benefit. Of equal concern is that the benefit of doubt is given to the other side to ensure that proper interpretations are given to the transactions. Other concerns, such as the question of method of operation and the issue of economic risk, must also be addressed.

Similarly, investigative concerns arise in litigation support. The accountant must ensure that a proper foundation exists for the calculation of future lost profits; that all assumptions incorporated into the work product are recognized and identified; that he or she understands where the expertise of the forensic accountant ends and the expertise of another starts; and that the issue of mitigation of damages is considered.

Investigative Mentality

Along with their accounting knowledge, forensic accountants develop an investigative mentality that allows them to go beyond the bounds set out in either generally accepted accounting or auditing standards. For example:

- Scope is not restricted as a result of materiality. Quite often, especially in the early stages of a management/employee fraud, the transactions are small and accordingly are more easily conveyed to the court to show a pattern of conduct that is deceitful. As the dollar value of the transactions and their complexity increase, the ability to convey the essence of the transaction is hampered, and the forensic accountant's task is made more difficult.
- The use of sampling is for the most part not acceptable in establishing evidence.

- The important difference affecting scope is the critical principle of the assumption of integrity of management and documentation, especially in corporate investigation and matters of white-collar crime.

The investigative mentality develops in the search for best evidence. In a recent case of secret commissions involving a purchasing agent for a large retail distributor and a major vendor, it was determined that the vendor was selling product to the purchasing agent's company through a company owned by their wives. At the time there was some concern as to how the plaintiff could overcome the documented evidence that placed ownership and control of the company with the wives. Bearing in mind alternative sources of information, the working papers of the accountant for the company were obtained, and an organization description confirmed that the shareholders were indeed the wives but the executive decision makers were their husbands. Thus, the best evidence no longer made it necessary to imply that notwithstanding ownership, control rested with the husbands.

Throughout the course of seeking evidence and information, the forensic accountant becomes involved in the interviewing process. This process is another art to master. The forensic accountant must be prepared to properly handle a confession in such a way that the evidence is admissible.

The investigative mentality is best developed by continued experience in the witness box. It is through this process that the forensic accountant's eyes are opened, because counsel for the opposing side raises issues and possibilities that the accountant may not have considered up to that point. Repeated experience as a forensic witness creates a greater awareness of what is relevant and must be considered, so that the witness can present financial evidence independently and objectively to reflect the reality of the situation.

SOME REFLECTIONS ON FORENSIC ACCOUNTING

When the author circulated a questionnaire among the staff members of Peat Marwick Lindquist Holmes, a Toronto-based firm of chartered accountants responsible for the forensic and investigative accounting practice, responses were insightful and should be of interest to the reader.

Q.1. *How would you distinguish forensic accounting, fraud auditing, and investigative auditing from financial auditing?*
A. The distinction is related to one's goals. Financial auditing attempts to enable the auditor to render an opinion as to whether a set of transactions is presented fairly in accordance with generally accepted accounting principles. The financial statements upon which the opinion is rendered are always the representations of management. The auditor is primarily concerned with

qualitative values (hence the concept of materiality comes into play), and generally is not concerned about whether the financial statements communicate the policies, intentions, or goals of management.

Forensic accounting, fraud auditing, and investigative auditing measure financial transactions in relation to various other authorities, such as the Criminal Code, an insurance contract, institutional policies, or other guidelines for conduct or reporting. The report is prepared by the accountant/auditor rather than by the client or subject, and does not necessarily include an opinion on the findings. In the investigation, one does not reject evidence as being immaterial; indeed, the smallest item can be the largest clue to the truth. Finally, where qualitative values are obviously an issue, even more important is the determination of the context—the mind and intentions of the criminal, the integrity of an insurance "accident," or the reasons for a particular occurrence.

However, in one important respect, these different practices must be identical. That is, the auditor/accountant must be skilled, experienced, and must maintain his or her independence and objectivity.

B. Forensic accounting is a general term used to describe any financial investigation that can result in a legal consequence.

Fraud auditing is a specialized discipline within forensic accounting, which investigates a particular criminal activity, namely fraud.

Investigative auditing involves reviewing financial documentation for a specific purpose, which could relate to litigation support and insurance claims as well as criminal matters.

The objective of financial auditing is to provide the auditor with a degree of assurance in giving an opinion with respect to a company's financial statements. The materiality level of an investigative auditing engagement is much lower and more focused than that of the normal financial auditing engagement.

Q.2. *How would you define what you do as a forensic accountant?*

A. I think of myself as one who seeks out the truth.

B. I would define my forensic accounting responsibilities as follows:

Investigation and analysis of financial documentation

Communication of the findings from my investigation in the form of a report, accounting schedule, and document briefs

Coordination of and assistance in further investigation, including the possibility of appearing in court as an expert witness

C. My role is that of an objective observer or expert. The final report that is issued as a result of my work will be used to negotiate some sort of settlement, be it financial or be it imprisonment. My role as a forensic accountant extends beyond the particular financial circumstances and seems to be one of an objective individual who provides the buffer between, in civil instances, the client and counsel, and in criminal instances, the investigator and the prosecutor. Therefore, I am considered an integral member of the team of professionals assigned to any given case.

Related to the specific work that I do, it has been described to me, and I agree, that the makeup of a given forensic accountant is one-third businessman, one-third investigator, and one-third accountant.

Q.3. *What qualities of mind and/or body should a forensic accountant possess?*

A. Creativity—The ability to step out of what would otherwise be a normal business situation and consider alternative interpretations that might not necessarily make business sense

Curiosity—The desire to find out what has taken place in a given set of circumstances

Perseverance—The ability to push forward even when the circumstances don't appear to substantiate the particular instance being investigated or when the documentation is very onerous and presents a needle-in-a-haystack scenario

Common sense—The ability to maintain a "real world" perspective

Business sense—The ability to understand how businesses actually operate, not how business transactions are recorded

Confidence—The ability to believe both in yourself and in your findings so that you can persevere when faced with cross-examination

B. As with any other pursuit, a healthy mind in a healthy body is a solid foundation. Beyond that, one should have generous proportions of common sense, inquisitiveness, skepticism, and an ability to avoid the natural tendency to prejudice—that is, to be fair and independent.

In addition, because forensic work ultimately can lead to court appearances, good posture, grooming, vocal projection, and stamina can all be valuable attributes.

C. The foremost quality a forensic accountant requires is independence, because a forensic accountant is often forced to balance conflicting opinions about the same piece of documentation.

The second major quality is an intense sense of curiosity coupled with a sense of order—a desire to put the puzzle back together.

D. Common sense/street smarts

Sensitivity/understanding of human behavior

Analytical/logical/clear

Ability to simplify complexities and delete jargon

Not be prone to lose the forest for the trees

Ability to identify and assess alternative explanations and interpretations

Ability to quickly assess cost-benefit of pursuing alternative avenues of investigation and reporting contents/formats.

E. The forensic accountant needs to be calm, cool, and collected; have good business judgment; and have a mind that can deal logically with esoteric issues and precise matters.

A forensic accountant involved in litigation must be physically fit to withstand the long days and long nights of investigation and preparation for trial and the trial itself. Forensic accountants need to have a pleasant appearance and demeanor so that they will not be offensive when in the witness box.

Q.4. *What skills are most important to the successful practice of forensic accounting?*

A. Solid technical accounting and financial skills—the basis of your "expertise"

Ability to quickly prioritize issues and map out a "game plan"—good judgment

Ability to communicate well—both verbally and in writing—is necessary to obtaining information, directing your staff, presenting your findings, and achieving your desired results. Even the best-planned and executed assignment can fail if you are unable to clearly and concisely present your findings

B. A forensic accountant needs to be precise, pay attention to detail, and be a broad thinker; that is, not suffer from tunnel vision.

C. When looking at a given forensic accounting engagement, there are two major areas that come to mind in the completion of a given case. First, there is the investigative aspect, and second, the communication aspect. I feel that investigative skills would include areas such as the ability to assimilate large volumes of information, general organization and administrative skills, use the microcomputer or understand the abilities of the microcomputer, and interpersonal skills. Communication skills would include the ability to write a comprehensive report understandably.

D. Communications skills: oral/written

Interpersonal skills

Listening skills

Ability to synthesize/integrate

Ability to identify/prioritize objectives/issues

TRAINING FRAUD AUDITORS

There are few, if any, college degree programs in fraud auditing. However, several professional associations provide fraud auditing training. The Institute of Internal Auditors provides periodic specialized training and conferences on fraud auditing, as does the National Association of Certified Fraud Examiners, which features a week-long course. The National Association of Accountants also sponsors frequent workshops and symposia for management accountants on fraud in books of account. These associations bring a substantial number of auditors to their programs. State CPA societies, on a selective basis, now provide one- or two-day fraud auditing programs.

Fraud auditing is a relatively new field in private-sector accounting. The public sector has had fraud auditing expertise for some time—at least since the Federal Income Tax Law was passed in 1913. Since that time, a host of federal regulatory agencies have been created with the power to review certain business organizations' records—for example, the SEC, FTC, Comptroller of the Currency, Federal Deposit Insurance Corporation, Wage and Hour Division of the Labor Department, and so on.

It seems that no junior accountants are in the field of fraud auditing. Those in this specialized field tend to be experienced in financial auditing, either in public accounting or fraud auditing in government agencies, before they venture into private practice.

Is there a way that academia can contribute to developing future generations of fraud auditors? Yes, it might at least expose college accounting majors to the idea that fraud in books of account is not only possible but highly probable when the risks are high, such as in organizations in high-risk companies (poor internal controls) with high-risk employees (compulsive personalities) or high-risk management (loose ethics).

Learning outcomes are the results a teacher hopes to achieve in a given course or subject matter: the specific skills the student should have acquired and the attitude, mind-set, and demeanor the student should have developed as a result of the course. In a fraud auditing course, an instructor might establish learning outcomes in knowledge domains such as legal, organizational, audit, investigative, and risk management.

Legal

1. Criminal, civil versus contractual fraud
2. Fraud versus theft and embezzlement
3. Material versus immaterial misrepresentation
4. Errors versus irregularities
5. Mistakes versus misstatements
6. Conspiracies versus individually perpetrated fraud

Organizational

1. Fraud committed for the company versus against the company
2. Insider versus outsider frauds

piracies with outsiders; i.e., customers, suppliers, com-
tors

low-level employee perpetrated frauds

short-term performance criteria

st versus low-trust organizations

xternal auditor's liability for detecting fraud

versus transaction frauds

3. Overstated versus understated profits, revenues, assets, losses, expenses, and liabilities
4. Diversion versus conversion of assets
5. Fake debits versus fake credits
6. Receipts versus disbursement frauds
7. Fabrication of accounts payable versus accounts receivable frauds
8. Front-end fraud (skimming receipts) versus rear-end frauds (disposing of assets)
9. On-book versus off-book frauds
10. Concealment, destruction, and alteration of records
11. Premature booking of sales versus delayed recording of expenses
12. Fraud auditing versus forensic accounting
13. Fraud auditing versus financial auditing
14. Left-brain thinking versus right-brain thinking
15. Columbo versus Perry Mason
16. Thinking like a thief versus acting like a thief
17. Fraud in manual versus computerized accounting systems
18. Input versus output versus throughput frauds
19. Altering input versus destroying or suppressing throughput

Investigative

1. Compromising controls versus compromising personnel
2. Psycho-social characteristics of thieves versus embezzlers
3. Greed versus need as motivations for fraud
4. Motivation versus opportunity as inducements to commit fraud
5. Detection versus prevention of fraud
6. Allegation of fraud versus discrepancy detection

Risk Management

1. Risk prevention versus risk transfer versus risk assumption
2. High-risk industries, companies, occupations, personalities
3. Red flags

The skill outcome of a course on fraud auditing might include demonstrated proficiency in

- Thinking like a thief.
- Designing fraud scenarios.
- Thinking creatively (right-brain) as well as logically (left-brain).
- Assessing the strengths and weaknesses of internal controls.
- Testing for compliance with control policies and procedures.
- Monitoring ratios and trends of key account categories (including sales to cost of sales, inventory, receivables, freight out, and commissions).
- Monitoring variances, exceptions, and oddities in accounting transactions and account balances—debit balances in payables, credit balances in receivables, out-of-cycle and out-of-pattern transactions, and so on.
- Following the flow of funds and supporting documents through the system and beyond.
- Locating hidden assets.
- Inspecting support documents for authenticity.
- Reconstructing transactions from outside sources when support documents are missing or destroyed.
- Determining the net worth and living expenses of suspects.
- Gathering and preserving evidence of accounting frauds; documents, correspondence, testimony, and so on.
- Documenting losses from fraud, theft, and embezzlement for criminal, civil, and insurance purposes.
- Estimating related damages from such losses.
- Testifying as an expert witness in accounting matters.
- Deterring fraud in books of account—creating awareness of the risk of fraud, establishing personnel policies, ethical codes, and loss prevention programs, conducting audits.
- Attitude, mind-set, and demeanor outcomes deal heavily with personal values and beliefs. Students of fraud auditing, after completing studies, for example, should assume that they are just beginning an adventure in a field of high interest and excitement in which they can match wits with

other accountants, lawyers, members of the media, and some of the most ingenious criminal minds in the world—white-collar criminals.

- The fraud auditor's mind-set suggests that internal fraud is possible in any organization. It is simply a matter of motive, opportunity, and the integrity of employees and managers. Therefore, if fraud is possible, it should be looked for; that is, audit programs should make sufficient provision for the review of internal controls and the testing of compliance therewith.

- Fraud auditors should place high among their personal and professional values such attributes as truth, honesty, accountability, fairness, and independence.

FRAUD AUDITING SOFTWARE TOOLS

The Information Technology Co., or Info Tech, developed a statistical and graphical suite of tools for exposing price collusion among companies bidding on local and state contracts for dairy products and other items. After uncovering rigged milk bids in Florida that robbed schools of $33.5 million, Info Tech's approach is being applied across the country.

The company's collusion detection system originated in the late 1970s when Info Tech helped Florida's attorney general develop automated tools for spotting suspicious patterns in highway construction bids. The results were so good that Info Tech built a mainframe-based package called Bid Analysis and Management System (BAMS).

Paying duplicate bills can cost U.S. companies $3.5 billion or more a year, reports Robert Fields. He founded the Burlingame, California-based business, Fields & Associates, by correcting their carelessness.

Shatwell, McLeod Software Group, Inc., 83 Pine Street, Peabody, Massachusetts 01960, (508) 535-0206, offers *Banc-Audit,* an integrated EDP bank product containing a fraud-detection module intended to spot oddities, errors, and irregularities in accounting transactions. A number of the fraud-detection routines follow.

- Employee Transaction Monitor highlights employees, especially tellers, entering transactions against their own accounts.

- Deposit and Loan Interest Accrual Recalculations recompute interest period-to-date for deposit instruments and produce exception reports that highlight improper and spurious interest accrual adjustments not supported by principal balance or current balance at any time.

- Dormant Activity Analysis highlights improper transaction activity on dormant accounts.

- Dormant Recalculation highlights accounts that should be classified as dormant and are not properly classified. Misclassifying accounts allows improper activity to take place without an audit trail.

- Negative Balances Report examines all dollar account balances on customer account records for evidence of negative values; for example, unapplied insurance, partial payments, withholdings, and so on. Fields are drawn below zero and monies are applied to another field within a single account record to make monies available for illegal withdrawal, removal, or transfer.

- Internal Transfers Analysis examines the movement of monies between two or more customer account records for evidence of skimming or removal of funds from dormant or inactive customer account balances. This routine highlights movements to unrelated accounts and groups recipients by common keys, such as similar address.

- Loan Rollover Analysis detects the payoff of one loan with proceeds from another loan. Rollovers are used to hide spurious loans, seriously delinquent loans, and as a method of permitting perpetual nonpayment of interest or principal. This is almost impossible to detect if accounts are not related within the same customer information file. The product detects occurrences based on parameters set by users and keys, which the accountant develops.

- Payment Lapping Analysis detects lapping frauds in which a payment to one account is applied to another. Because lapping must use transaction-effective dating, the product performs independent, transaction-effective dating and highlights out-of-pattern occurrences. Forward lapping is also detected through this routine by which effective dates of financial transactions are allowed to be moved forward. A multimillion-dollar embezzlement in securities inventory was highlighted through analysis of forward-dated transactions.

- Suspect Duplicate Addresses are used in a number of fraud detection routines. Address analysis is done to report similar addresses and related addresses that have been changed in a minor way so that they will not be detected as duplicates through normal sort operations. For example, regardless of how post office box numbers are represented, this routine will relate to them. Second and third address lines are flip-flopped, minor differences in street names are ignored, temporary and secondary addresses are matched, and so on.

- Account Maintenance Monitor routines build files of account maintenance activity, which bypass transaction controls. It is typical to allow changes to nonfinancial fields to be handled through account maintenance transactions. This product detects these and builds records of them. It automatically highlights out-of-pattern and out-of-sequence changes to records used to manipulate accounts, high defalcations, and so on. This is a highly useful parameter-driven routine that allows dynamic auditing based on activity over any time period.

- Transaction Monitors allow the user to create parameters that highlight out-of-pattern and unusual financial transaction activity including irregular supervisory overrides, activity against accounts on "hold," and unusual error corrections. This routine is used to independently recreate transaction-based reports and G/L postings. It is a valuable routine for uncovering report manipulations and G/L manipulations.

- Loan Extension Recalculations recompute extensions given to loans that are used to defer payments until a later period. Improper extensions allow loans to appear paid up-to-date and allow deferral payments. Payments are applied elsewhere.

- Loan Current Balance Recalculations recompute current or principal balances of loan accounts and are used to highlight manipulation of loan balances.

- Reports highlighting exceptions in service charges, delinquent charges, production of account and customer notices are a series of routines that perform independent audits and computations to highlight exceptions and out-of-pattern and out-of-norm conditions of various types. These routines are used to detect coverups of illegal actions. For example, detection of an out-of-pattern reversal of late loan charges uncovered a large defalcation driven through the issuance of loans to employees.

  These are just a few of the automated menu and parameter-driven routines available through the product. The company is constantly adding new routines. One of the more important for the banking industry is a very sophisticated parameter-driven Kiting Suspect Analysis routine. This routine is directly integrated to the data files of the systems on which it is installed.

- Code Review is an artificial intelligence-based program that scans medical bills for coding errors and abuses. Sold by Health Payment Review, Inc., of Boston, the program applies 55,000 rules developed by 50 doctors. Caterpillar Tractor helped to finance its development and saved itself 10 percent to 15 percent on its medical claims, or $1.2 million in 1989 alone.

Clinton Financial Services of Davis, California, has introduced a software program for personal computers to assist internal auditors, supervisors, and senior management in detecting organizational fraud—the Fraud Detection Matrix.

Developed by accounting and audit professionals, the Fraud Detection Matrix helps businesses detect, diagnose, and remedy potential and existing fraud in their financial operations. The program is useful for:

- Assisting companies in preparing their risk-assessment and annual audit plan
- Training junior auditors and non-auditing supervisors in the analysis and documentation of fraudulent situations, while strengthening guidelines for internal controls
- Improving the overall efficiency of a company's financial operations

The program uses a step-by-step process that (1) indicates exposures in accounting and security systems, (2) defines symptoms of possible fraud, and (3) outlines a series of audit steps to identify and correct a fraudulent exposure. The steps used are in compliance with AICPA and IIA audit standards. Users can customize information according to the unique nature of their operation, or can use the Fraud Detection Matrix's standard features for 18 departments or functions. This program was designed for both small businesses and large corporations, with special emphasis on financial, insurance, and government entities.

The Fraud Detection Matrix runs on all IBM PC compatibles, is completely menu driven, and includes help screens and full documentation. For further information or to order the Fraud Detection Matrix, contact Arthur Clinton, Clinton Financial Services, 1595 Notre Dame Drive, Davis, California 95616.

INSIGHT Consulting, Inc., a wholly owned subsidiary of Software AG, has developed the Fraud Identification, Neutralization, and Deterrence (FINDER) Program, a unique combination of technology and services for identifying and eliminating commercial fraud. FINDER combines the data visualization and analysis features of NETMAP(R), from Alta Analytics, with powerful, intuitive investigation methods to speed fraud detection. The system allows investigators to review a higher volume of suspicious activities and successfully prosecute more fraud cases.

Commercial fraud includes such criminal activity as financial fraud, insurance fraud, credit-card fraud, embezzlement, contract fraud, retail fraud, investment fraud, and computer fraud. Current methods for detecting commercial fraud typically involve time-consuming manual research and analysis. Automation of these activities using artificial intelligence (such as neural networks and rule-based systems) requires significant initial investments and often produces disappointing results.

FINDER is an automated method that extracts data from a company's database(s), allowing investigators to analyze the data for patterns or relationships that may reveal collusion and other signs of fraud. For example, when applied to insurance fraud, FINDER can detect repeated relationships between a provider, such as a mechanic, and an appraiser. These two parties may also have a pattern of connections with a particular claimant revealing a "triangle" of potentially collusive activity. Currently, investigators must manually compare data on hundreds of claim forms to detect such activity.

INSIGHT Consulting is offering a no-risk customized demonstration program to companies. This program allows the customer to view and analyze its own data files on a trial basis. If FINDER does not achieve the projected results after a predetermined trial period, no payment is due for the software system.

"Elimination of fraud represents a huge opportunity for performance improvement in today's corporations," says Jonathan Church, general manager of INSIGHT Consulting, Inc. "The potential for bottom-line improvement from cost-effective fraud reduction programs can only be realized with the introduction of comprehensive data analysis methods and technology. The FINDER program uses expert methods and proven technology."

The Federal Bureau of Investigation estimates that fraud in health insurance alone costs $80 billion each year. The National Insurance Crime Bureau says that 10 percent of all auto insurance claims, 15 percent of auto theft claims, and 20 percent of workers' compensation claims involve some form of fraud. In the credit-card fraud area, Visa International's 1992 cardholder fraud losses were $689 million, up 28 percent from 1991. Overall, fraud has increased in recent years, causing companies to look for new ways to fight fraudulent activity.

INSIGHT Consulting worked with John Naveau, a retired agent for the U.S. Treasury Department who has over 25 years of fraud investigation experience, to ensure that FINDER's functionalities meet the demanding needs of fraud investigation units. "FINDER will be as valuable to fraud investigators as fingerprints, ballistics, and DNA are to traditional criminal investigators," said Naveau. "FINDER substantially reduces the time it takes for an investigator to spot suspicious activity. FINDER allows you to review and match, from the desktop, at least five times the number of suspicious items as current methods allow. This capability alone dramatically increases the amount of fraud that an investigator can detect and successfully prosecute."

FINDER is available today. Pricing starts at $30,000 and depends on the number of investigators and the complexity of data structures to be analyzed.

NETMAP, the technology underlying the FINDER program, is a data visualization tool that simplifies complex databases by finding patterns, groupings, and consistent relationships within databases of any size and displaying them in a logical, intuitive format. NETMAP operates on UNIX-based platforms with ANSI-C, X-Windows, and OSF/Motif. It is available on HP 400/700 series, SUN SPARCstations, DEC workstations, and the IBM RS/6000. INSIGHT Consulting distributes NETMAP under an agreement with its developer, ALTA Analytis Inc., of Dublin, Ohio.

NETMAP's crime-fighting capabilities have been proven by several U.S. Government agencies that use it to detect fraud and other illegal activity. NETMAP has also been used by the State of Arizona Department of the Attorney General, the Western States Information Network, and Scotland Yard's Serious Fraud Office.

Software AG, with primary locations in Reston, Virginia, and Darmstadt, Germany, is one of the largest independent software firms in the world. The company develops and markets open, multiplatform product solutions including: ADABAS for database management, NATURAL for application engineering, ENTIRE for developing and deploying distributed computing solutions, and ESPERANT, a state-of-the-art SQL query and reporting tool.

Founded in 1969, Software AG has customers in over 79 countries, and reported revenues of $510 million (U.S.) in 1993.

Sales information can be obtained by calling 703-391-6696. NETMAP is a registered trademark of ALTA Analytics Inc.

BankWatch, the information security division of BankRisk, Inc., is a risk-analysis software product for banks and financial institutions. BankWatch addresses both information security and EDP audit. In addition, it contains question sets dealing with Electronic funds transfer security, and ATM network security. BankWatch automates the process of risk analysis, vulnerability assessment, and EDP audit. It includes a report feature that uses dollar values and threat frequency to create cost–benefit ratios for each potential safeguard. BankWatch automatically surveys remote sites electronically and is customizable. Price: $4,900.

AuditorPlus, from Brain Tree Technology, Inc., is an Open VMS security management and auditing system that exposes security vulnerabilities, reports on networkwide security policy compliance, monitors and notifies of security breaches and intrusions as they happen, and simplifies UAF and password management. It automates Open VMS security management including automatic correction of security weaknesses, enforcement of site-specific Open VMS security policies, and unattended real-time response to security breaches and intrusions. AuditorPlus has menu, command-line, and graphical user interfaces. It features access control, optional password synchronization and either centralized or distributed configuration operation. Price: $1,000–$15,000.

BreachComber, from BrainTree Technology, Inc., is an open VMS security management utility that gives full control over VMS Audit Journal reporting. It can select and report on any field in the VMS Audit record by overcoming the selection and output limits of VMS Analyze/Audit. BreachComber offers the flexibility to summarize selected information from the range of data produced through VMS's Expanded/Full record format. It allows networkwide security audit reporting from a central point with a single command, to produce concise reports detailing audit events. Price: $1,000–$10,000.

CA-Examine, from Computer Associates International, Inc., performs MVS operating-system integrity verification and auditing. CA-Examine helps identify and control security exposures, viruses, trap doors, Trojan horses, and logic bombs. The software identifies potential problems, makes suggestions, and answers questions. It supports the new Product Verification Interface that establishes traceability of system software products and identifies proper installation requirements for a number of Computer Associates products. Price: NA

CA-PanAudit Plus, from Computer Associates International, Inc., is a file-interrogation audit solution based on the CA-Easytrieve Information-retrieval and data-management system. CA-PanAudit Plus contains more than 100 audit-specific applications for interrogating application files. The administrator can produce detailed reports of the distribution characteristics of a file, search for integrity issues within a file, or perform file comparisons. CA-PanAudit Plus can also perform statistical functions, such as dollar unit sampling, combined attributes/variables sampling, and multiple regression with correlation analysis. Price: NA

A tool kit from the Institute of Internal Auditors covers nine areas of telecommunications fraud. A diskette contains audit programs and preliminary survey questions. Price: $200.00.

USING COMPUTERS AS INVESTIGATIVE AIDS

The advent of the PC brought with it some very useful applications for investigators. For example, locating witnesses and assets in the manual era took hours and hours and wore out one's shoe leather, eyesight, and patience. These searches are now much shorter and less painful on the feet and eyes. To do investigative data base research, the following resources are needed: (1) a PC, (2) modem, (3) communication software, such as Procomm, (4) knowledge of data base research methods (most providers of on-line data bases have tutorials and are usually menu driven), (5) a gateway; that is, a local network service like Tymnet to keep long distance costs down, (6) a subscription to relevant data bases such as TRW, D&B, and others.

You are now ready to dig into files. The procedure is to (1) turn on the PC; (2) insert the communication software diskette in the A: drive; (3) when the program is loaded, dial up the data base provider; (4) when connection is made, sign on with your user ID and then with your code name; (5) when the menu is displayed, select an area of interest and follow the instructions. (It is a good idea to sign up with Compuserve or Prodigy to gain some practical knowledge and develop confidence in doing data base research.)

Investigative data bases come in two major varieties: private and public. Private data bases contain credit, medical, and educational histories, competitive intelligence, proprietary information, and so on. Access to these data bases is restricted to users with certain legal privileges; for example, employers, bankers, employees of insurance companies, and others with a right and a need to know.

Public data bases are generally accessible by all because they are public records. They generally show ownership of real estate, cars, boats, airplanes, and office and industrial equipment. They also contain criminal and civil litigation records, voting records, birth and death records, liens, bankruptcies, name changes, address changes, assumed names, incorporations and partnerships. Other public nongovernmental records include telephone and city directories.

The names and locations of a few selected investigative data bases include:

- CBI/Equifax, Brea, California
- Transunion, Fullerton, California
- TRW, Orange, California
- Dun & Bradstreet, Van Nuys, California
- Metronet, Lombard, Illinois
- CDB Infotek, Orange, California
- IRC, Fullerton, California
- Super Bureau, Monterey, California
- Prentice-Hall, Monterey, California
- Damar Corp, Los Angeles, California
- Data Quick, San Diego, California
- Redloc, Anaheim, California
- Redi Real Estate, Miami, Florida
- Mead Data Central, Dayton, Ohio
- NCI Network, Jackson, Michigan
- Compuserve, Columbus, Ohio
- Dialog, Louisville, Kentucky
- Dow Jones, Princeton, New Jersey
- Vu/Text, Philadelphia, Pennsylvania
- Western Union, Upper Saddle River, New Jersey
- Westlaw, St. Paul, Minnesota

Contract data base researchers include:

- Information on Demand, McLean, Virginia
- Research on Demand, Berkeley, California
- Savage Information Service, Torrance, California

Data base directories include:

• Directory of On-Line Data Bases, Cuadra-Elsevier Publishing, Los Angeles, California
• National Directory of Bulletin Boards, Westport, Connecticut

Data base wholesalers include:

• U.S. Datalink, Baytown, Texas—represents 250 information brokers

One call access to public documents in all fifty states:

• NCI (Jeff Kirkpatrick), Jackson, Michigan. (Skip tracing and credit data)

These data bases provide a wealth of valuable information. They search the following records:

• State and local public records (generally available to everyone)
• State and local records that permit only limited access
• Federal records that are publicly available, e.g., SEC, 8-K and 10-K reports
• Federal records that are accessible for limited purposes to limited persons; e.g., IRS.
• Privately owned data sources for which a fee is paid

A list of available information from these data bases includes:

• Notices of birth, marriage, divorce, death, and name change
• Real estate ownership, mortgages, liens, and taxes
• Chattel mortgages on cars, boats, airplanes, and trailers
• Civil litigation, voting records, adoptions
• Criminal conviction, driver's licenses; auto ownership
• Driving record, assumed names; incorporations and partnerships
• Bankruptcy, military service, phone directories, city directories, cross indices, corporate financial data—D&B, S&P, SEC; credit histories, bank account
• Stock and bond ownership, school records, medical records
• Life insurance, annuities, credit-card ownership
• Safety deposit box rental, address changes
• Address of post office box owners, newspapers
• Magazines, books, information gathering agencies
• On-line data bases

Most of these items can be accessed by a phone call to an information gathering agency or an on-line data base. In the case of an on-line data base, some are wholesalers. They provide access to a number of data bases for a fee, and you may do your own research. However, you must have a PC, modem, communication software, and a gateway.

One on-line data base is the NCI Network, P.O. Box 1021, Jackson, Michigan 49204. Business phone is (800) 783-4567. If you wish to demo the service, dial in via your own PC to (513) 521-4420. At the user name prompt, type DEMO 198 and press return. Then follow the prompts.

Today an investigator does not have to leave home to do research. A new on-line ordering feature introduced by Mead Central, Inc., gives Lexis-Nexis subscribers quick and easy access to public record filings from any jurisdiction—state or local—in the country.

With the LEXDOC™ feature, subscribers can electronically place an order for a manual search or for certified or uncertified copies of public record filings.

The LEXDOC feature allows users to order searches for or copies of a variety of public records documents, including articles of incorporation, certificates of good standing, annual reports, Uniform Commercial Code (UCC) filings, tax liens, judgments, and pending suits. LEXIS customers may order one document or several from any state or local jurisdiction in the country, all in a single session.

Technical Advisory Service for Attorneys (TASA) provides attorneys, insurance companies, and government agencies with information on independent experts for case evaluation, litigation preparation, and testimony.

TASA's data base includes information on nearly 15,000 experts in 4,000 categories. Being listed in the data base is one way of becoming known as a CPA expert witness. For more information on TASA's expert data base, contact Technical Advisory Service for Attorneys, 1166 DeKalb Pike, Blue Bell, Pennsylvania 19422-1844, (215) 275-8272.

Martindale-Hubbell has provided the legal profession with information on lawyers and law firms for more than a century. It has released the *Martindale-Hubbell Law Directory* on CD-ROM, which is accessed through a personal computer and a compact disk drive. The CD-ROM format enables users to access, in a matter of seconds, detailed information on over 700,000 lawyers, law firms, banks, and services and supplies to the legal community, contained in the *Martindale-Hubbell Law Directory.*

INVESTIGATIVE DATA BASE RESOURCES BIBLIOGRAPHY

Carroll, John M., *Confidential Information Sources: Public and Private,* 2d ed., Boston: Butterworth-Heinemann, 1991.

Data, Al, *Investigator's Guide to Information Resources,* P.O. Box 922169, Sylmar, CA 91392, 1991.

Iapin, Lee, *How to Get Anything on Anybody,* San Mateo, CA: ISECO, Inc., 1991.

Kramer, W. Mitchell, *Investigative Techniques in Complex Financial Crimes,* National Institute on Economic Crime, Vienna, Virginia, 1990.

Financial Investigative Techniques. Department of Treasury, Internal Revenue Service, 1978.

Online Database Selection: A User's Guide to the Directory of Online Databases, New York: Caudra/Elsevier, 1989.

U.S. Department of Justice, *Basic Considerations in Investigating and Proving Computer-Related Federal Crimes,* Nov. 1988.

REFERENCES

1. Elliott, Robert K. and John J. Willingham, *Management Fraud: Detection and Deterrence,* New York: Petrocelli Books, 1980.

Chapter 3

Auditor Liability for Undetected Fraud

Financial auditors (internal and external) are still in doubt as to the extent of their legal and professional responsibility for fraud detection when conducting routine financial audits. But courts do not seem to be of a similar mind. Nor does the investing public. There is a growing public perception that auditors by the nature of their education, intuition, and work experience can sniff out fraud wherever and whenever it exists in books of account. That standard is far higher than anyone in the audit professions has ever advocated. In fact, the public's perception of auditor responsibility for fraud detection is highly unrealistic. No auditor could ever afford to relax in the face of such a strict standard of care. Nor could any auditor afford the premiums for professional liability insurance if the public's perception of the standard became a legal reality. What, then, *is* the fraud auditor's legal standard of care, and what is his or her responsibility for detecting fraud?

ARE AUDITORS LIABLE FOR FRAUD DETECTION?

One source for insight on the external auditor's standard of care and responsibility for fraud detection is *American Jurisprudence.*[1] Under the general heading "Accountants," that volume offers this:

> It is generally recognized that a public accountant may be held liable on principles of negligence, to one with whom he is in privity, or with whom he has a direct contractual relation, for damages which naturally and proximately result from his failure to employ the degree of knowledge, skill, and judgment usually possessed by members of that profession in the particular locality.

But Section 17, page 366, reads as follows:

> An accountant is not an insurer of the effectiveness of his audit to discover the defalcations of frauds of employees but may be found liable for fraudulent or

negligent failure to discover such defalcations because of lack of compliance with proper accounting procedures and accepted accounting practices or by his contract in the light of circumstances of the particular case. . . . And the employer may be precluded from recovery because of his own negligence when it has contributed to the accountant's failure to perform his contract and to report the truth.

The second excerpt gives auditors a breather. Obviously external auditors should not be held liable for not detecting fraud when their clients deceive them.

In 1984 the Institute of Internal Auditors issued its Statement on Internal Auditing Standards, which deals with deterrence, detection, investigation, and reporting of fraud.[2] The Standard makes a number of interesting points in its Foreword and Summary. To quote from the Foreword:

Fraud is a significant and sensitive management concern. This concern has grown dramatically in recent years due to a substantial increase in the number and the size of the fraud uncovered. The tremendous expansion in the use of computers and the amount of publicity accorded computer-related frauds intensifies this concern. The issue of the internal auditor's responsibilities for deterrence, detection, investigation, and reporting on fraud has been a matter of much debate and controversy. Some of the controversy can be attributed to the vast differences in internal auditing's charter from country to country and from organization to organization. Another cause of the controversy may be unrealistic—nevertheless increasing—expectations of the internal auditor's ability to deter and/or detect fraud in some circumstances.

Generally accepted accounting standards (GAAS), as promulgated by the American Institute of Certified Public Accountants (AICPA), assign the "independent auditor . . . the responsibility, within the inherent limitations of the audit process, to plan his or her examination to search for errors or irregularities that would have a material effect on financial statements."[3] It would seem by that statement that external auditors are not liable for detecting immaterial fraud. The cost of attempting to do so could become enormous in corporations like IBM, GM, AT&T, and Exxon. And even though the external auditor is duty bound to evaluate internal controls, management may override such controls.

But in *United States v. Arthur Young & Co.* (March 21, 1984),[4] the Supreme Court tried to define *professionalism* in the accounting profession in the loftiest terms. In a unanimous decision the Court stated:

By clarifying the public reports that collectively depict a corporation's financial status, the independent auditor assumes a *public* responsibility *transcending any employment relationship* with the client. The independent public accountant performing his special function *owes ultimate allegiance to the corporation's creditors and stockholders,* as well as to the investing public. This "public watchdog" function demands that the accountant maintain *total independence from the client at all times* and requires *complete fidelity to the public trust.* To insulate from disclosure a certified public accountant's interpretations of the client's financial statements would be to ignore the significance of the accountant's role as a *disinterested analyst charged with public obligations.* [*Emphasis added*]

The Court continued:

It is therefore not enough that financial statements *be* accurate; the public must also perceive them as being accurate. *Public faith* in the reliability of a corporation's financial statement depends upon the *public perception* of the outside auditor as an independent professional. [*Emphasis added*]

The Auditing Standards division of the AICPA summarized auditors' responsibilities regarding fraud and illegal acts under current GAAS in the July 1985 newsletter *In Our Opinion,* as follows:[5]

The auditor's responsibility to detect and report fraud is set out in Statement on Auditing Standards (SAS) No. 16, The Auditor's Responsibility for the Detection of Errors or Irregularities, (1977) and SAS No. 17, Illegal Acts by Clients, (1977). The standards were developed as a direct result of problems in the business community in the mid-1970s. The disclosure of client frauds, such as Equity Funding, and questionable payments, primarily in foreign countries, stirred the profession to adopt more specific standards in the area of client misconduct.

SAS No. 16 establishes an affirmative requirement for auditors; the auditor is required to plan the examination to search for material errors and irregularities and to carry out the search with due skill and care. The auditor's responsibility with regard to illegal acts is less distinct; because auditors are not lawyers trained to recognize illegal acts, they are not expected to search for illegal acts, but rather to be aware that some matters that come to their attention during the examination might suggest that illegal acts have occurred. If auditors discover an error, irregularity, or illegal act, they are required to report it to management, and depending on its significance, possibly to the board of directors or its audit committee. Auditors are also required to assess the effect on the financial statements and, if material, to insist on adjustment or additional disclosure in the statements or to qualify the audit report.

Auditors recognize that although there is an affirmative responsibility to search for material errors and irregularities, there is a chance that they will not be found. They test selectively; that is, usually accounts are sampled rather than examined 100 percent. Thus, if the sample does not identify a fraudulent transaction, the auditor will be less likely to suspect one in the unsampled portion of the financial statements. Auditors, of course, control this sampling risk, but to eliminate it would require them to examine all of the entity's transactions for the year, which would result in astronomical audit costs, and still would not necessarily detect cleverly forged or unrecorded transactions.

The public furor in North America about the liability of external auditors for detection of fraud is not yet over. In fact the pressure for imposing more stringent requirements on public accountants for fraud detection appears to grow with each passing day. The Canadian Institute of Chartered Accountants (CICA) has established a commission to examine this issue. In the United States, the Financial Fraud Detection and Disclosure Act of 1986 is a manifestation of the public's concern. The congressional history and details of that bill follow:[6]

Background

The regulatory system established by the federal security laws is based on the concept of complete and fair disclosure of important information to investors and other users of corporate financial reports. This regularity system is administered by federal agencies, such as the Securities and Exchange Commission (SEC) working in concert with private, independent auditor firms, which check corporate financial records and certify the reports given to the public. Over the past several years, numerous cases of massive financial fraud have occurred where the independent auditors failed to either detect or to report the fraudulent activities at the companies being audited. These include E.F. Hutton, United American Bank, General Dynamics, E.S.M. Government Securities, Inc., Home State Savings and Loan of Ohio, American Savings and Loan of Florida, Saxon Industries, San Marino Savings and Loan of California, and many others. The costs of these frauds have been enormous both financially and in terms of public confidence in the soundness of the nation's economic system. The American Institute of Certified Public Accountants (AICPA), a private trade organization, establishes the generally accepted auditing standards (GAAS), which are used by independent auditors and accepted by the SEC. Under present GAAS rules, independent auditors do not include as part of their audit significant procedures to detect management fraud, and their consideration of fraud is restricted to its material impact on a corporation's financial statements. In a large corporation, financial fraud amounting to millions or even hundreds of millions (of dollars) could go unreported because such amounts would not be considered material to the total financial condition of the corporation.

Even when actual fraud and illegal acts are discovered, the GAAS rules only say that the auditor should inform the company's management and consider resigning from the audit account. There is no requirement that auditors report fraud or illegal acts to the appropriate government authorities. In addition, auditors rely on the internal control systems of a corporation, but do not issue an opinion regarding the adequacy of management's internal controls. Thus, financial fraud has occurred in many corporations which have been allowed to operate with substandard or nonexistent internal controls because the independent auditor did not report on the adequacy of internal controls.

The AICPA and the SEC were criticized on this issue 10 years ago by the Senate Subcommittee on Reports, Accounting and Management. That subcommittee's final unanimous report stated that auditors should look for illegal acts and report them to government authorities. The AICPA appointed its own study group, the Cohen Commission, which failed to recommend active detection and reporting of illegal acts. The SEC and the AICPA did nothing further until the Subcommittee on Oversight and Investigations began its accounting hearings on February 20, 1986.

At the March 6, 1985 hearing, Chairman Dingell was joined by other members in expressing his concern about an audit rule that merely suggested that the auditor, as the public watchdog, only consider leaving the premises if he or she found a criminal, instead of reporting the criminal to the proper authorities. In response, the AICPA established a new group, the Treadway Commission, to further study the issue. Neither private accounting organizations nor the SEC have the authority to grant independent auditors immunity from legal action that could arise as a result of fraud detection and disclosure responsibilities, so legislation is the only way to fully protect auditors performing their duties in good faith.

Chairman William Seidman of the Federal Deposit Insurance Corporation, who formerly headed a large audit firm, agreed with Chairman Dingall and Congressman Wyden at the Subcommittee's April 28, 1986, hearing that auditors should look for fraud and report it to regulators.

Legislative Proposal
The Financial Fraud Detection and Disclosure Act of 1986 (the Act) amends the federal securities laws to provide reasonable assurance that fraudulent activities at companies covered by these laws will be discovered and reported to the proper authorities. The Act will not apply to small businesses or other companies that are exempt from the securities laws. The Act is necessary now because the SEC and the accounting profession lack the authority to provide full legal protection for auditors who report fraudulent activities.

The Act strengthens the present regulatory system of federal agencies working with private audit firms by establishing clear standards for the detection and reporting of financial fraud, as well as the tools necessary to meet those standards and fully protect auditors performing their duties. The Act does not create a new federal agency or regulatory burden, but instead assures that audits conducted under the present system will meet the legitimate concerns of Congress and the public that major companies are not operating fraudulently. The incremental audit costs of meeting the standards established by the Act are minuscule when compared with the lost billions of dollars resulting from frauds and the decline of public confidence in the integrity of the nation's economic system. The Act has several basic provisions as described below:

1. The Act requires that auditors include specific and substantive procedures for detecting financial fraud as part of the audit plan. Present audit standards regard fraud detection as incidental to the financial audit. Therefore many auditors either fail to recognize indications of fraudulent activities, or else convince themselves that such activities are not within the scope of the audit and that the auditor has no responsibility to act on such matters.

2. The Act requires that auditors evaluate the internal control systems established by corporate managers in order for the auditor to determine whether those internal controls assure that corporate assets are being handled properly and lawfully. Present audit standards on reviewing internal controls are not strong enough in this regard.

3. The Act requires auditors to issue a written report that: (a) gives the auditor's opinion regarding the adequacy of internal control systems; (b) identifies any weaknesses in those systems; and (c) states that the audit was conducted in a manner that provides reasonable assurance that fraudulent activities have been detected and reported.

   The auditor's written report is the place where the auditor gives opinions on the results of the audit. Present standards do not require that the auditor issue an opinion on fraud detection or the adequacy of internal controls.

4. The Act requires that the individuals actually responsible for the audit sign the audit opinion on behalf of the firm conducting the audit. Present audit opinions only bear the name of the audit firm conducting the audit, even though the firms auditing most SEC registrants are giant organizations with hundreds of partners and thousands of staff. This provision in the Act is a no-cost, common sense way to enhance personal accountability to help assure that the audit was conducted properly. It also provides personal recognition for the individuals doing good work, and enables the public and regulatory authorities to determine if auditors identified with problem audits are being made responsible for other audit engagements. The practice of individuals signing work product personally on behalf of their firm is commonplace in the legal profession and others.

5. The Act requires public disclosure of known or suspected fraudulent activities, and gives the auditor a responsibility for assuring such disclosure. Present standards do not provide adequate disclosure of fraudulent activities, and auditors have no responsibility for assuring disclosure. Under existing rules the corporate managers who are often involved in the fraud are given sole responsibility for reporting to the public. The Act requires disclosure of activities that, in the auditor's view, may be fraudulent so that users of financial reports and corporate managers will be able to take appropriate actions without the delay inherent in complete legal proceedings to reach conclusions which satisfy every requirement of law and evidence. In most cases losses are magnified and irrevocable by the time legal

proceedings are completed. This provision meets the requirement of the securities laws to give fair and complete disclosure of important information to the public in a timely manner, so that the financial markets will operate efficiently.

6. The Act requires that auditors report known or suspected illegal activities to the appropriate government, regulatory, or enforcement authorities. Present standards only require that auditors report such activities to corporate management (who may be involved), and then consider resigning the audit engagement if the corporate managers do not take appropriate action. Auditors are employed to be the public watchdog, and the public is not served by the present standard, which only suggests that the watchdog leave the premises if he finds a criminal. This provision also improves the efficiency of government regulatory and enforcement authorities by giving them the information which can only be found through the work of on-site auditors.

7. Finally, the Act provides complete legal protection for auditors who perform their duties under the Act in good faith. Although the public expects auditors to report known or suspected fraudulent activities, auditors could suffer legal liability for honest reporting of their findings. This provision is consistent with the legal protection given to officials acting in good faith on the public's behalf in other areas. While the Act establishes clear standards to meet the public's expectations of auditors, it also protects the men and women who will implement its provisions.

Authorities in business management insist that the audit function, both internal and external, is a visible deterrent to fraud and accounting irregularities. This pious assumption is predicated on a theory held by police authorities, who suggest that the visible presence of a uniformed police officer or marked police car on regular patrol deters crime. Since the passage of the Foreign Corrupt Practices Act in 1977, many corporations have established internal and EDP audit functions or bolstered the staffs of these organizational units only to discover no decrease in the number of defalcations—frauds, thefts, and embezzlements—by corporate users. In "Perception of the Internal and External Auditor as a Deterrent to Corporate Irregularities," Wilfred C. Uecker, Arthur P. Brief, and William R. Kinney, Jr., tested the hypothesis that an increase in the perceived aggressiveness by internal and external auditors in detecting corporate irregularities would function as a deterrent.[7] The study concludes that managers contemplating acts of management fraud are not deterred by the presence of internal and external auditors; neither does an increase in the perceived aggressiveness of the internal or external auditor significantly decrease the occurrence of corporate irregularities.

So one may have to make one's own case for a viable fraud-reduction strategy. Should it be:

- More and better laws?
- More and better auditors and auditing?
- More and better audit training?
- More and better internal controls?
- More honest senior managers?
- All of the above?

FRAUD DETECTION AND DISCLOSURE: ARE NEW TEETH NEEDED?

On June 23, 1986, John Shad, Chairman of the Securities and Exchange Commission, in testimony before the House Subcommittee on Oversight and Investigations, made the following apologies for the nation's financial reporting system (i.e., the U.S. Congress, the SEC, and the accounting profession):[8]

1. The evidence concerning alleged audit failures suggests that the system is working well.
2. There are 11,000 publicly owned companies that file reports and registration statements with the SEC.
3. During the past three years, the SEC has taken action against 100 issuers or their employees for disclosure violations. In 43 other cases, the SEC has taken action against public accountants for alleged misconduct.

As Chairman Shad explains:

> The Commission's primary concern of course is with fraud that materially impacts the public financial reports of registrants. While the Commission has been unable (and it is unaware of any study that has been able) to quantify the nature and impact of such fraud, it is clear that fraudulent accounting or disclosure practices, however isolated, can cause substantial harm to investors, creditors, and others.

To add emphasis to Chairman Shad's concerns, we note the recent collapse of E.S.M. Government Securities. That celebrated fraud shook the world's confidence in the United States banking system. When news of the enormity of the E.S.M. debacle (the waiting lines of depositors in Ohio) reached the world media, gold prices jumped $30 an ounce, and the American dollar plummeted on international money markets.

The significance and long-term impact of the E.S.M. case can be likened to that of the Three Mile Island nuclear disaster. The ripple effects of E.S.M.

will be felt for many years to come. Trust in the financial system has been severely damaged by that fraud.

This is no longer the time for damage assessment and control. This is the time for risk reduction and risk prevention. There are obvious and serious risks and perils out there. At least 95 cases exist of public companies and regulated financial institutions in the United States in which stockholders, creditors, or regulatory authorities alleged that audit failures by major public accounting firms occurred during the past 15 years.

WHAT ABOUT AUDITORS' EXPECTATIONS?[9]

by Ron E. Ellis, MBA, CA and David C. Selley, FCA

Is it possible that the expanded role of the Macdonald Commission report envisaged for auditors could in some instances actually diminish their effectiveness by opening up even more gaps?

Overall, we find [that] the *Report of the Commission to Study the Public's Expectations of Audits* provides the accounting profession with a unique opportunity to lead the way in improving financial reporting and enhancing corporate accountability.

The commission displays great confidence in its recommendations. Of all 50 of them, it says: "There are no throw-aways, and every recommendation is intended to be acceptable in principle, workable in practice, and to meet a cost–benefit test." Its report makes "here-and-now recommendations to deal with issues that are with the profession now and to which the profession must respond with a sense, not of panic, but of urgency."

That's the real challenge issued by the commission. Its report, intentionally we presume, makes it extremely difficult for the profession and, to a lesser extent, others charged with implementing its recommendations, to find good excuses not to do so without contradicting its stance regarding their rectitude.

We find that stance somewhat presumptuous, implying the commission obtained, during its deliberations, all the knowledge necessary to make an unchallenged decision. Counterbalancing this, a number of the more controversial recommendations appear in the form of statements proposing a move in a particular direction but indicating the matter should be studied before being implemented. We believe it is important to distinguish between the commission's recommended conclusions and its recommendations on how to achieve them.

The commission concludes, correctly in our view, that the present financial reporting structure is fundamentally sound but that certain potentially serious gaps exist between the public's expectations of audits and what an auditor should reasonably be expected to accomplish—what it calls the "audit expectation gap."

The commission's recommendations are not radical. For example, there were rumors at various times that it might recommend a ban or at least a severe restriction on providing management consulting services to audit clients, or recommending rotating audit appointments, joint audits, or setting up an independent standard-setting body such as the U.S. Financial Accounting Standards Board (FASB).

Instead, the commission believes that an effective job can be done if a number of specific changes are made in the existing structure, but warns that if these are not made, the consequences for the profession could be serious.

Objectives and Premises

The commission's 50 recommendations to close—or at least narrow—the audit expectation gap result from three broad objectives, and one "defensive" objective:

- Strengthen auditor independence.
- Buttress the professionalism of auditors.
- Improve the quality of present financial disclosure and extend financial and financially related disclosure.
- Take steps (the commission calls them "defensive" steps) to lessen public misunderstanding of the auditor's role.

Three basic premises underlie the recommendations on the auditor's role in financial reporting:

1. The commission recognizes that corporate governance, accountability, and good financial reporting are shared responsibilities; auditors don't work in a vacuum. They, along with directors, management and regulators, all share responsibility and have a role in improving financial reporting. This explains the apparent anomaly of a commission set up by the public accounting profession producing a report in which about half the recommendations are aimed at parties other than public accountants.

   We think the commission's view is entirely appropriate. Furthermore, we believe there are other parties who, though not mentioned, also play a role in corporate accountability and effective financial reporting: lawyers (including corporate counsel), investment bankers and internal auditors. The commission does not discuss the role or responsibility of the first two and, except with respect to financial institutions, makes no significant reference to internal auditors.

   In the executive summary, it notes how important it is to set an appropriate tone at the top for corporate governance and accountability:

   > We also believe that more will be expected of corporate directors in general. They, along with chief executive officers, are responsible for setting the overall tone for corporate behavior, including the attitude towards financial disclosure.

2. The audit committee should play a pivotal role in managing and strengthening relationships between the parties responsible for improved financial reporting, and its role and responsibilities should be significantly expanded to strengthen auditor independence.

3. The roles of the auditor and management with respect to financial reporting should be better communicated, because financial statement users and the public have misconceptions about them.

The commission focuses on the financial accountability of public companies and does not consider nonprofit corporations, nor, except in the case of regulated financial institutions, privately owned corporations.

The fact is, though, the profession's accounting and auditing standards are intended to apply to all business corporations, large or small, public or private, and it has generally been considered impractical to set different standards for public and private enterprises, except for certain financial disclosure requirements (segment reporting, earnings per share data, and so on). Consequently, recommendations to improve accountability and financial reporting for public companies may also, if implemented, be forced on small private companies where no such need may exist. The CICA obviously will have to address this issue.

A final point to note is that the audit expectation gap is a major concern in the United States and the United Kingdom as well as in Canada. The recent Treadway commission report in the United States deals with a number of the issues addressed by the Macdonald Commission and arrives at similar conclusions, including the need for stronger corporate governance and for strengthening the position of auditors through more active audit committee involvement.

The Recommendations: An Overview

The commission's recommendations, outlined in five chapters, deal with: strengthening auditor independence; financial reporting; professionalism; fraud, illegal acts and auditor charges; and regulated financial institutions. They can be better understood, however, when grouped under the three broad objectives and one defensive objective noted earlier.

Strengthening auditor independence   Twenty-one recommendations are designed to improve auditor independence, 11 of which focus on improving relationships involving the auditor, principally through the audit committee. Seven recommendations cover strengthening professional standards—the essential bulwarks, in the commission's view, of the profession. Finally, there are three on strengthening the profession's code of conduct and enforcing its independence.

Strengthening auditor's professionalism   There are 12 recommendations designed to strengthen professionalism: Six focus on increasing the profession's responsiveness to public concerns, principally by expanding the auditor's role somewhat; four focus on the need for renewed recognition of the vital role of professional judgment; and two are designed to improve self-regulation.

Extend and improve financial disclosures   Thirteen recommendations would expand accounting standards and improve financial disclosures, and two call for greater auditor responsibility for those disclosures. The commission clearly believes (as do we) that there is a significant accounting component to the audit expectation gap.

Lessen public misunderstanding of the auditor's role   The commission concludes, correctly in our view, that a public advertising and educational campaign would not be effective in explaining the role of the auditor or in reducing public misunderstanding. It points out, however, that published financial reports might better explain the respective roles of the auditor and management. Two recommendations are designed to achieve this.

First, a statement of management's responsibilities for financial reporting and the financial statements would be included in the annual report; and, second, a more explicit audit report, similar to that recently adopted by the American Institute of Certified Public Accountants, would better explain the auditor's role. In addition, one of the recommendations grouped under the first objective, that audit committees report annually to shareholders, should also help to explain the respective roles of management and auditor.

The Danger of Apathy

Although we do not agree with all the commission's recommendations, we support most of them and believe they should be implemented. The commission cautions the profession not to be too complacent because serious concerns about auditor independence and professionalism exist both inside and outside the profession. What's more, it urges the CICA to revamp its standard-setting process to prevent accounting standards from lagging unacceptably behind the pace of changing events.

The profession's future, it says, will be determined mainly in two places: in the user marketplace, which depends on how users view the cost-effective value added by audits; and in the realm of regulatory bodies, governments, legislatures, and courts, where the profession's standards will be applied and ultimately established and its continued independence and scope determined.

Some in the business community regard the profession as being resistant to change and slow (if not unwilling) to react to criticism—a concern voiced by Terence Corcoran in his *Financial Post* column "CA's Report Card Points to Failures," June 3, 1988:

> There is the ability of the profession to sit on reports of its own failings until hell freezes over. For the sake of users of financial statements audited by the profession, let us hope that this fate does not

befall the *Report of the Commission to Study the Public's Expectations of Audits.*

The commission's report is balanced and points out the profession's strengths as well as its problems. Unfortunately, as Corcoran notes, the positive points could give the profession "a screen behind which to duck." In other words, there's a danger we might choose to focus on the positive to derive the message that all's well and change really isn't needed.

As Corcoran notes, "Over the years several reports on the role of the auditor have been produced by the profession, but very few substantial changes were made, which in part explains why the Macdonald commission had such a heavy load of subject matter to review."

While we don't agree with many of Corcoran's remarks (he has exaggerated the problem), his message should be noted nevertheless: the accounting profession must take the lead and respond to the report—and quickly.

As noted earlier, the commission requires changes by regulators, directors and management, as well as by auditors. It would be easy for them to take the view that auditors are trying to make other parties, rather than themselves, responsible for fixing their own problems, especially if the auditing profession doesn't lead the way in responding to the report and implementing change.

In our view, the CICA should take the lead and demonstrate its strong commitment to the need for change by appointing a senior, well-respected member of the profession to play a coordinating role in overseeing the overall implementation of the recommendations.

We live in an environment marked by constant change. Business and financial reporting are all affected by growing internationalization, computerization, the development of innovative and sophisticated financial instruments, and increasingly complex transactions.

To maintain its important role in aiding the efficient operation of the capital markets, the accounting profession needs to improve our accounting and auditing standards at a faster pace. If we don't, we will become obsolete and lose our public standing and credibility. Moreover, we will leave ourselves open to the possibility of increased legal liability as the public's expectations continue to grow and the gap widens between what we provide and what they expect of us.

The Need for Better Accounting Standards

The commission says its main messages are addressed to the CICA and the provincial institutes, whose cooperation is necessary if they are to be implemented.

Most of its recommendations pertaining to the CICA deal with the standard-setting process and the significant gaps it sees in the *CICA Handbook's* accounting standards. Relying on due process to set those standards is time consuming, it says, and fails to provide timely authoritative guidance on emerging issues.

Too General   One of the main problems with accounting standards, the commission says, is that they permit too wide a range of alternative treatments, resulting in widely diverging reported figures, and they are often stated only in terms of general principles and not as more specific guidance. (This is seen as a weakness because it makes it possible to take advantage of their flexibility in managing reported financial results, while at the same time it leaves auditors in a weak position to object.)

The commission notes that the philosophy of the CICA's Accounting Standards Committee has been to express its recommendations in terms of general principles. This "broad approach," it acknowledges, has been seen to have the advantage of providing room for different accounting methods when professional judgment suggests that differences in circumstances warrant them.

It does, however, require that professional judgment and steadfastness be applied to match the appropriate accounting alternative to the circumstances, which should differ widely enough to justify alternative methods.

We agree with the commission that the problem with the broad approach is that, while it permits flexibility, neither the CICA nor the provincial institutes monitor financial reporting to see that flexibility isn't abused:

> We consider that, if the Accounting Standards Committee has a policy of encouraging adaptability of accounting methods to circumstances, it has a corresponding obligation to see that the resulting flexibility in accounting standards is not abused. The profession cannot retain its credibility if it is inconsistent, especially if the inconsistency is perceived by the public to facilitate management-dominated reporting objectives at the expense of fair and unbiased financial reporting to the shareholders. The profession cannot stress the importance of judgment in the application of standards, and then permit auditors to claim they cannot effectively exercise judgment to arrive at conclusions that differ from those of management because the standards do not entitle or enable them to do so.

The real challenge is how to resolve this problem.

No Monitoring Mechanism   To the commission, effective standards are essential to safeguarding auditor independence. Standards provide little leverage and protection, however, unless their application is monitored and followed up, and those who deviate from them are disciplined.

Unless the profession quickly moves to implement an effective monitoring system, regulators will step in to fill the gap. For example, the Ontario Securities Commission has, within the past year, started to review financial statements filed with it and to follow up instances of questionable accounting.

The Macdonald Commission is recommending a more specific, detailed approach to standard-setting to resolve these problems. Specifically:

1. The CICA should speed up the standard-setting process without sacrificing due process.
2. It should identify and provide guidance on issues where the accounting standards are unstated or unclear—the message is to close gaps quickly.
3. Efforts should also be made to eliminate accounting alternatives not justified by substantive differences in circumstances.
4. The CICA should sponsor a separate committee or task force to express opinions on emerging accounting issues and give quick, practical advice in order to curtail bad accounting practices.
5. There should be greater emphasis on ensuring that the accounting policies adopted properly reflect the economic substance of the transactions.
6. The CICA and the provincial institutes should improve the professional conduct, discipline, and practice inspection processes by ensuring countrywide uniformity.
7. Financial statement disclosures should be improved, especially of risks, uncertainties, commitments, and estimates.

We agree with the commission's concerns and the thrust of its recommendations, while recognizing that there will be practical problems in their implementation. Accounting standards are increasingly being challenged as a result of the inflow of new sophisticated financial instruments and complex transactions. Often the form of a transaction differs from its substance.

If, in these situations, the *Handbook* is viewed like the Income Tax Act, the substance of its recommendations may be forgotten. Instead, recommendations may be seen as rules to be exploited and examined for loopholes, with the accounting following form rather than substance and focusing on the letter, rather than the spirit of the recommendations.

A broad approach to standard-setting cannot withstand this process unless that is a mechanism to review financial statements to uncover abuse of accounting standards and to follow up and mete out discipline whenever appropriate. Its absence, together with the changing business environment, suggests we must move toward a more detailed approach to standard setting. But there are serious problems with that approach, too.

A Veritable Cookbook   Detailed standards, though they can provide more security and better leverage for the profession and improve consistency, would require enormous efforts and resources in both personnel and money to keep pace with the changing business environment and financial developments. Further, if the more specific standard-setting process is carried out badly, it can lead to rigid uniformity when circumstances really do differ and different accounting treatments are called for. A more detailed approach would also lead to concerns about "standards overload" and a "cookbook approach" and to complaints from financial statement preparers.

We do, however, support the commission's recommendations for improved accounting standards. Standards need to be expanded and made more explicit, and, when necessary, issued on a more timely basis. But the profession can and should avoid the cookbook approach to standard setting, provided:

1. Broad principles set out in the standards are carefully linked and related to more specific guidance for dealing with the complexities of modern business transactions.

2. The profession renews its emphasis on the ethical dimension of standard setting—the need for a strong commitment to professionalism, independence, and accounting for substance over form.

3. An effective process is implemented for monitoring the application of standards and, where abuse occurs, disciplining those deviating from them.

The Squeeze on Money, Time, and People   The commission suggests [that] the CICA, because of limited resources, consider using task forces made up of informed professionals; adopting, on an unmodified basis, certain FASB standards; appointing full-time standard-setting committee members; and obtaining additional financial support from sources other than CICA membership fees.

In our view, the commission fails to adequately recognize the resource problem the CICA faces. An enormous increase in financial and human resources would be required to implement all its recommendations on standard setting. Indeed, there is a real danger the commission may be increasing the audit expectation gap because it is setting up an expectation for a greatly enhanced standard-setting process that cannot reasonably be met, given available resources.

The recommendation that the timeliness of releasing accounting standards be improved but that due process be preserved seems at first to be rather naively contradictory, since it is the need for due process that creates the timeliness problem (at least when it comes to *Handbook* pronouncements). The commission does, however, suggest certain approaches to improve timeliness (such as adopting FASB pronouncements).

We believe timeliness could indeed be improved [in Canada] by adopting selected foreign standards (U.S., international accounting or auditing standards, U.K. standards) with virtually no changes. In this case, due process could start with an exposure draft prepared from the foreign pronouncement. At least this would eliminate most of the time incurred prior to the exposure period might be shortened; and last, but by no means least, printing and translation time should be drastically reduced.

Companies can agree on, translate, and print prospectuses within days. The CICA at present deals in terms of months—from the date of approving a *Handbook* pronouncement to [the date it is released] to members. In our view, this is unacceptable, though we recognize there will be increased costs in accelerating the translation and printing processes.

One of the stumbling blocks to narrowing accounting alternatives and additional disclosures may be the composition of the CICA's Accounting Standards Committee. At present, only one member could with certainty be classified as primarily a "user" of financial statements. Of the other 20, eight are from public practice, seven are preparers, four are academics, and one is from government. With this makeup, and recognizing that a two-thirds majority is required, the financial statement preparers could be in a position to veto any move to narrow alternatives or increase disclosures, provided they can gain the support of one or two other members.

Serious thought will have to be given to the composition of the Accounting Standards Committee if the commission's recommendations are to work. In particular, there should, if possible, be a more balanced ratio of users to preparers.

Alternatively, the appointment of full-time paid committee members would help ensure [that] the committee can devote the time and effort required to properly deal with the complex issues facing the profession today and [it] would also enhance the committee's independence. We believe this may be the only practical answer, but recognize that it will be expensive.

The commission raises the funding question. We think it is essential the CICA assess, as soon as possible, the cost of implementing the commission's recommendations for strengthening the standard-setting process, to establish whether the profession is able to finance an expanded standard setting process, and consider whether other sources of funding are needed, including assessing the potential risks to the independence of the process associated with funding from outside the profession.

The larger public accounting firms and major corporations should also be prepared to second, on a full-time basis for significant periods, senior skilled professionals to the CICA so it can meet these increased standard-setting demands. Consideration should be given to compensating those who contribute more than their fair share.

Are Three Heads Better Than One?   One persistent and rather large problem is the need to change the structure and role of the CICA and the provincial institutes. The commission recommends the creation of interprovincial bodies to ensure uniform codes of conduct, discipline, and practice inspection processes.

We are concerned, however, about the excessive bureaucracy that might result if, when national issues come up that are not currently within the

CICA's jurisdiction, an intermediate level, in the form of interprovincial committees separate from the CICA is set up.

If our profession has to contend with a national issue, it should logically be dealt with under the auspices of the CICA, and a provincial issue likewise should be dealt with at a provincial institute level. We therefore strongly support the Macdonald Commission's views that codes of conduct, practice inspection and disciplinary processes be standardized; but to the extent legally possible, we would like to see more national uniformity when needed, even if it means the provincial institutes transferring some of their present responsibilities to the CICA. Times have changed: many businesses are now national and international in scope and the profession needs to operate more efficiently on a national level.

We support the commission's conclusions that the provincial institute's disciplinary process should be modified to apply to firms as well as to individuals. This simply recognizes the reality that it is the firm that signs the auditor's report, accountant's comments, or notice to reader; and certainly in large client situations, the audit opinion is often a collective decision made with a number of partners in the firm.

There is one standard-setting area not considered by the commission: the need for the international harmonization of standards. We believe the growing internationalization of business and financial markets means there is an increasing need for accounting standards that are compatible on an international basis. This area should be of concern to the CICA.

Demanding More from Auditors

Half the commission's recommendations relate primarily to the public accounting profession—to the responsibilities of the auditor, the role of the profession's governing bodies to strengthen independence and professionalism and auditor responsiveness to user expectations. In particular, there are specific recommendations covering:

- Changes in the auditor's standard report, including going-concern disclosures.
- Auditor association with information other than audited financial statements.
- Standards dealing with the auditor's responsibilities with respect to employee and management fraud and illegal activities.

The audit recommendations are, with one or two important exceptions, consistent with the AICPA's new auditing standards, and they could probably be implemented with only minor changes to present practice.

The Auditor's Standard Report   The commission believes a standard report should be provided because, without standard wording, it may be difficult to tell whether an auditor is rendering a clean opinion, a qualified opinion, or no opinion at all. The present standard report is not understood by users and fails to adequately explain the nature and extent of the auditor's work and the degree of assurance it provides. Accordingly, the commission rejects the preference of the Adams Committee (a special committee appointed in 1977 by the CICA to examine the role of the auditor) for a shorter, simplified form of standard report, but recommends that:

- The report should, while remaining standard in form, be made more explicit in content.
- The CICA should adopt wording that, to the extent possible, conforms with that used in other major industrial countries (a strange recommendation, since there is considerable divergence among such countries!).

The commission appears to favour Canada adopting the revised standard report recently developed by the auditing profession in the United States, which more explicitly describes the audit and the auditor's role than [Canada's] does.

The commission also concludes that the present Canadian requirement to disclose a going-concern uncertainty only in the notes of the financial statements does not meet the expectations of users, who want such uncertainty to be given a special flag or emphasis.

It also concludes that it is inappropriate to qualify the auditors report for a going-concern uncertainty when that uncertainty is properly disclosed in the financial statements. Accordingly, its position is that a going-concern uncertainty should be emphasized or highlighted by being disclosed in an additional paragraph to the standard audit report. In our view, that is a good, pragmatic solution to the problem. Note that, unlike the new U.S. standard, this recommendation does not apply to other types of uncertainties.

Information in Annual Reports   The commission believes the public doesn't always distinguish between the auditor's responsibility for information in the audited financial statements and that which appears elsewhere in the annual report. Accordingly, it recommends the CICA adopt clearer, more positive standards concerning the auditor's responsibility for financial disclosure— disclosure that is not part of the audited financial statements.

What's more, it recommends an auditor not accept an engagement to report on financial statements without also having the right to examine and comment on the document in which those statements are to be included, and to refuse consent to the audit report being published in it if he or she seriously objects to the other financial disclosure.

But in our view, the present standards concerning the auditor's responsibility for reviewing other information in an annual report (*CICA Handbook* Section 7500) are quite clear and need not be expanded. The test of withholding the auditor's report should continue to be based on the existence of a material inconsistency with information in the financial statements or of a material misstatement of fact. It is unrealistic to expect the auditor to withhold his or her report in any other circumstances.

Fraud and Illegal Acts   The commission regards the present standards concerning the auditor's responsibility for fraud detection deficient because they don't clearly differentiate between fraud and error, nor do they focus sufficiently on the auditor's responsibility to look for fraud indicators.

It is particularly concerned with respect to management fraud since management prepares the financial statements and is usually in a position that "the auditor is the first line of defense, along with the directors, against management fraud."

As a result, it recommends that the CICA set standards requiring the auditor to consider fraud, especially management fraud (for which it provides a set of red flags), and that the auditor test the controls intended to prevent material employee fraud.

We believe the auditor can and should consider fraud, especially management fraud, specifically and separately from error, but that the report's list of red flags is too long (there are over 50) and ineffective as a guide to practice. This list is so extensive that it's unlikely any company doesn't already have many of the conditions it pinpoints. The problem is, it doesn't differentiate the "real" fraud indicators from the "merely possible." To the best of our knowledge, fraud research suffers from the absence of a control group to isolate the incremental factors present only in fraud situations.

The evidence suggests that part of the expectation gap is a misunderstanding on the part of the public (and perhaps the commission) concerning the role of internal control in the financial reporting process. Apart from some regulated entities, there is no statutory or professional requirement for companies to meet any particular standard regarding internal control. Nor is there any requirement for an auditor to obtain a detailed understanding of, or to test, specific internal control procedures unless doing so is thought to be the most efficient way to gain the assurance necessary to express an opinion.

The sole statutory responsibility of companies in this area is to produce annual financial statements that are fairly presented, and the sole duty of the auditor is to express an opinion on whether such financial statements are fairly presented in accordance with an appropriate, disclosed basis of accounting (usually GAAP).

As a separate engagement, an auditor may also be asked to express his or her views on the adequacy of a company's internal control system—now the case in a few regulated entities and sometimes requested by the client. It is, however, an assignment separate from the financial statement audit assignment.

If it's decided that the existence of adequate internal controls is so important to shareholders that management, with some kind of endorsement from the auditor, needs to inform shareholders about them, then it should be established as a separate objective. Indeed, the commission recommends this be done with respect to financial institutions (noting, correctly in our view, that it should be done only when proper guidelines and criteria are in place).

In many cases, substantive procedures are likely to produce a more satisfactory result to the auditor within a reasonable materiality range, and provide better evidence for management that material employee fraud has not occurred, than carrying out the additional procedures on internal controls.

If management or anyone else wants separate assurance about the existence of proper internal controls, can ask the auditor to provide it; such a report might usefully serve as ongoing assurance to management (who would be aware of any subsequent system and personnel changes that might affect the conclusion), but is risky to provide to the public (because they may inappropriately project the assurance into the future).

While we think the commission has overemphasized internal controls in the context of auditor detection of fraud, we agree with the commission's emphasis on the greater importance of internal controls in financial institutions because of their special fiduciary responsibilities, which require effective internal controls.

The commission recognizes [that] an auditor may encounter illegal activities other than management fraud and concludes the audit cannot be relied on to uncover these since the auditor is not a legal expert. It believes, however, that the CICA should provide the auditor with additional guidance on reporting any discovered illegal actions. This recommendation will need to be considered carefully since disclosing such actions may have material financial consequences for a company.

Other Auditor Responsibilities   The commission has three important messages for public accounting firms concerning the auditor's role and professionalism:

1. **A renewed dedication to professionalism.** The quality of the audit should not be compromised by commercial pressures. Note that the commission concluded that providing appropriate consulting services is not incompatible with the auditor's role and need not impair independence if properly considered.
2. **The vital importance of remaining independent,** a virtue to be prized and carefully guarded. "Unswerving independence and impartiality in the face of a difficult structure of relationships and strong commercial pressures is the pearl beyond price and the indispensable shield for the profession."

3. The importance of standing back and exercising common sense and judgment. The commission cautions, "Perhaps the biggest single risk and source of danger for the profession in terms of both public expectations and liability exposure, apart from failures of independence and impartiality, is too literal an approach or cast of mind."

Two other measures recommended to strengthen auditor independence, which we support, are constraints on opinion shopping and a better flow of information with regard to changes in auditors.

The Central Role of Audit Committees

We agree with the commission's emphasis on the key role of the audit committee in public companies. It recommends:

1. All public companies have an audit committee made up entirely of outside directors.
2. Boards of directors draw up and publish for shareholders a formal statement of responsibilities assigned to the audit committee.
3. Audit committees report annually to the shareholders on how they have fulfilled their mandate.
4. Audit committees review annual and interim financial statements before they're published. (Note the Treadway Commission exposure draft recommended that audit committees review interim financial statements—a proposal changed in the final report to an oversight role.)

We believe the commission's recommendations will help strengthen auditor independence and the relationship between audit committees and the auditor. For some public companies, implementation will require a few changes in existing practice; for others, significant changes. Audit committees would need to meet more frequently (at least quarterly to review interim financial statements), putting much greater demands on directors' time. Expansion of the audit committee's role would also require a clear definition of the lines of authority and responsibility between it and management. Requiring interim financial statement preissuance reviews may also cause logistical problems.

Regulated Financial Institutions

The commission devotes a lot of its attention to regulated financial institutions (RFIs) such as banks, trust companies, insurance companies and investment brokers, because they are extensively regulated, broadly exposed to the public, highly leveraged and, as part of their normal business, undertake risks that require strong accounting systems and internal controls.

RFIs receive and hold the public's money and are vulnerable to the loss of public confidence, which could lead to withdrawals and severe liquidity problems. Furthermore, the spillover effect from the failure of one RFI could lead to failures in others and could adversely affect the Canadian economy.

Accordingly, the commission believes auditors of RFIs should have broader responsibilities, particularly to depositors. We agree, but note that in taking on additional responsibilities, the various recommendations for strengthening the system need to be implemented on an integrated and not a piecemeal basis, as the commission correctly points out.

It recommends:

1. Communications between regulators, auditors, management and directors should be improved.
2. All financial institutions should have audit committees made up of outside directors only.
3. Shareholder financial statements should be in accordance with GAAP.
4. There should be enhanced disclosure regarding risks, liquidity, and asset and liability valuation.
5. The auditor should report on internal controls.

We are in favour of those recommendations, but we think the first and last two warrant some comment. The commission recommends [that] auditor should be able to report directly to regulators on "matters of great moment" if he or she cannot persuade the institution to do so. The commission notes that the provincial institutes' confidentiality rules presently create a roadblock to this recommendation and should be amended to permit this kind of reporting.

It will also be necessary to enact standards defining "matters of great moment." If these turn out to be vague, not only will the auditor's task be difficult, but he or she will be exposed to later condemnation (and the legal consequences) if, for example, an RFI collapses and hindsight suggests a matter of great moment wasn't properly communicated—which will likely be very easy to allege in the absence of clear standards for reporting such matters.

The commission favours the auditor reporting to the regulator (but not necessarily every year) on the adequacy of internal controls, but only if appropriate standards are developed. It recommends the CICA take the lead in pursuing this aim together with regulators and representatives from RFIs. There are already some standards in place for internal control reporting, and *Handbook* Section 5900 ("Opinions on Internal Accounting Control") would be a good starting point for developing specific standards. We support the issuance of such standards.

We do, however, have the following concerns about this recommendation:

1. At present, the auditor is usually able to rely to a great extent on internal auditors with respect to testing the internal controls of some RFIs. It may be necessary to rework that relationship (at some cost) since it would be necessary to maintain greater control over the internal audit function if

the auditor were to be directly responsible for reporting on internal controls.

2. The auditor will, in most cases, need the assistance of highly trained special staff to understand and test the major internal control systems at large RFIs, and this will be costly. The benefits, however, may be well worth it.

3. Internal control reporting may not flow easily from existing audit approaches in RFIs, necessitating major changes in the audit approach. Some of the large RFIs, such as banks, have extremely complex systems understood by few individuals on either the inside or outside. The auditor presently may have no cost-effective choice when dealing with such a highly complex situation but to devise appropriate substantive procedures to provide the evidence needed to express an opinion on the financial statements. It may be a big step from there to expressing an opinion on controls in such systems.

There is also the need to carefully weigh and consider the impact increased disclosure of risk and liquidity can have on a particular RFI and, indeed, the entire financial system. The loss of confidence produced by such a disclosure could result in the failure of the institution and pose a significant problem for the entire system.

Moving to Close the Gaps

Although the commission concludes that the present reporting structure and the public accounting profession are fundamentally sound, potentially serious gaps exist between the public's expectation of auditors and what an auditor should reasonably be expected to accomplish.

Most of the commission's recommendations are fundamentally sound. It is vital that the profession lead the way in implementing the recommendations if we are to maintain our public credibility and set the appropriate tone and example to regulators, management and directors who are also being called upon to make changes.

The CICA must lead the way by improving the standard-setting process. The provincial institutes should find better ways of enhancing needed national conformity in key areas. If the profession does not take the lead, nobody else will, except possibly the regulators, and we might not like the result.

As individual chartered accountants, we should re-emphasize traditional standards of independence, objectivity and professionalism and be prepared to pay larger annual fees to fund an enhanced standard-setting process. The major firms and corporations should be prepared to provide skilled resources to the CICA so that it can undertake an enhanced standard-setting process.

The business and financial environment is changing rapidly, and we as a profession must change and adapt more rapidly than we have done in the past if we are to continue to play a useful role in society and maintain public confidence.

"WHAT LIABILITY CRISIS?"[10]

by Mindy Paskell-Mede

I have been asked many times recently whether liability suits against Canadian accountants are getting worse: Are they more frequent, for higher amounts and costlier to defend? Are we, in Canada, facing a "liability crisis" similar to that in the United States? Perhaps it's the recent American experience—and the media's fascination with massive lawsuits—that have renewed interest and concern here. In late 1993, for example, a Texas jury awarded more than $70 million (U.S.) in punitive damages to a plaintiff in a lawsuit against auditors before reaching *any* decision as to how much, if anything, should be paid in compensatory damages. Unfortunately for American members of the profession, awards in the $100-million-plus range are not all that rare. At the end of 1993, pending suits against auditors totaled between $20 billion (U.S.) and $30 billion (U.S.). It's easy enough to see why the situation in the United States is referred to as a crisis.

Do we have a problem of the same magnitude in Canada? I don't believe so. Nor do I believe that we're likely to see damages reach those lofty heights anytime soon. There are probably no more than a half-dozen pending claims in Canada that seek in excess of $100 million from auditors. Nonetheless, when one considers the smaller size of our economy, the accounting profession and the pool of available insurance, there is cause for concern about moving any closer toward the American model. A Canadian bankruptcy, such as the one in 1990 of the U.S. firm Laventhol & Horwath, is not inconceivable.

In my view, some significant differences between the Canadian and American legal systems provide Canadian auditors with greater comfort. Of course, comparisons of this nature necessarily overlook the many differences among Canadian provinces and those among American states. That said, however, the following five differences between the two legal systems generally prevail, and provide two very different legal contexts for litigation.

1.   Jury trials. While certain Canadian provinces still theoretically permit jury trials in civil cases involving the use of expert testimony, the jury is virtually extinct for auditor liability suits in Canada. This is not the case in the United States, where almost every major award is determined by a jury. As a lawyer, I shudder to think of the amount of work (and additional cost) it must take to educate a jury in the issues involved in an auditor liability suit. Not only must the decision-maker understand (with the help of conflicting expert testimony) highly technical, complex and often dry accounting and auditing issues in order to determine whether a negligent error was committed, but he or she must also appreciate the economic, regulatory and business context, which is also relevant. At the same time, the defence will often invoke the contributory negligence of the plaintiff or will point to other causes of the plaintiff's losses. Obviously, many jurors lack the experience or background necessary to render predictable judgments. In Ontario, the move to a special list of commercial judges for cases involving auditors (and other business disputes) indicates a policy to favour more, rather than less, relevant experience in the decision-maker.

One advantage that the American plaintiff no doubt enjoys when he or she selects a jury trial is the sympathy factor. Although judicial sympathy is also a significant factor in Canadian cases, judges are less likely to be impressed by high drama, simply because they are more apt to have heard a similar story before and will be more conscious of how a decision in any given case can influence the outcome of future cases where the sympathies lie differently.

2. Punitive damages. Both the predictability and affordability of judgment awards are affected by the different uses of punitive damages in the two jurisdictions. In the United States, it's often the punitive damage component (which is not always insurable, depending on the law in each state and the wording of the insurance policy) that pushes the total into the stratosphere and fuels high settlement offers.

In Canada, punitive damages are not as readily available. Indeed, I can think of no such award ever rendered against auditors. That's because Canadian judges do not award punitive damages for mere negligence. For a judge to be sufficiently outraged or scandalized to make such an order, he or she usually requires evidence of a deliberate, high-handed or malicious act. Moreover, when punitive damages have been awarded in Canada, the amounts have tended to be symbolic, representing only a fraction of the compensatory damages assessed.

3. Costs sanctions. We appear to have much more effective costs sanctions in Canada than those that exist in the United States. The general rule here is that the unsuccessful party pays a portion of the costs incurred by the winner, plus his or her own legal fees. The higher those costs (known as "taxable costs"), the more effective they are in reducing frivolous suits and encouraging responsible settlement offers. (Perhaps it's the lottery-type size of potential gains to American plaintiffs that renders this element less relevant in the United States.)

Individual provinces have increased the efficacy of taxable costs from the fairly unimpressive "party-and-party" tariff that might result in taxable costs of no more than 5% of the successful party's actual legal expenses. In British Columbia, for example, the tariff was revised so that a successful party can realistically expect to recover as much as 50%–60% of the actual legal fees. In many provinces, out-of-pocket disbursements (often including expert witness fees) are fully or almost fully recoverable. In Quebec, a special rule applies to all amounts claimed in excess of $100,000: The unsuccessful plaintiff must pay, in addition to the taxable costs assessed by ordinary tariff, 1% of the amount claimed. Finally, in many Canadian jurisdictions, a formal offer that equals or exceeds the ultimate judgment triggers additional cost sanctions against the party who rejected the offer (the most effective sanction being the payment of all actual costs incurred after the offer was made).

4. Class actions. With few exceptions, representative actions (a procedural precursor to the class action, which is unwieldy for both sides) have not been used against auditors. In provinces without class-action legislation, the rules might permit an individual to take suit on behalf of others if the impracticability of taking individual action and the similarity of suit(s) could be demonstrated. The rules, however, are not explicit as to the procedure to be followed, nor is there a clear way to impose a settlement on all plaintiffs. Quebec has had class action legislation for many years and Ontario has recently introduced such legislation, but, once again, the mechanism has not been used successfully against accountants. In one of the first Ontario cases to test the new class action legislation, the action against the auditors was dismissed at a preliminary stage partly because the class action procedure was held to be inappropriate: Each plaintiff would have relied on the accountant's work differently and might have suffered losses as a result of different causes.

In the United States, however, shareholder class action suits have become commonplace. Sometimes different plaintiffs' lawyers in different states have launched the same action using different class representatives, who then must fight among themselves for control. The potential earnings are high enough to have created a specialized plaintiffs' class action bar, something unknown in Canada.

5. Regulatory environments. Even a cursory examination of the two countries' legislative and regulatory systems reveals substantial differences. For example, American securities legislation (which is of federal jurisdiction in the United States, but dealt with on a province-by-province basis in Canada) has created the "fraud on the market" theory, unknown to Canadian law, which increases the exposure of auditors of publicly traded companies. According to this theory, purchasers of shares on the secondary markets (that is, not those buying from new company issuances) can sue the auditors, even if they have not read or relied directly on the financial statements. The underlying assumption is that the marketplace efficiently uses the information and that the share price was therefore affected by any false or misleading information allowed to circulate by the auditor.

In addition, American regulators (the SEC or FDIC, for example) appear to be more active in suing accountants than their Canadian counterparts, although it is difficult to determine whether this is due to any underlying philosophical difference or whether it's simply a matter of time before the trend moves northward. There appears to be no compelling reason to conclude that Canadian regulators would not respond to significant losses suffered by the public in the way that their American counterparts have.

Faced with the differences mentioned earlier, however, it seems safe to assume that Canadian accountants will not face lawsuits of the same magnitude and frequency as those withstood by American accountants, so long as no fundamental changes are made to our legal system. On the other hand, lawsuits are getting larger and it's no longer inconceivable for Canadian accountants to be sued for amounts in excess of their insurance limits. Since accountants cannot practice in limited liability corporations, one must therefore ask whether, despite out differences, it's simply a matter of time before we, too, face a liability crisis.

REFERENCES

1. *American Jurisprudence,* 2d ed., Vol. 1, Sec. 15, Rochester, N.Y.: The Lawyers Cooperative Publishing Co., 1962, pp. 365–366.

2. *Statement on Internal Auditing Standards,* Institute of Internal Auditors, 1984.

3. "Generally Accepted Accounting Standards," *AICPA Professional Standards,* Vol. 1, AV Sec. 327, New York: American Institute of Certified Public Accountants, pp. 322–323.

4. *U.S. v. Arthur Young & Co.,* March 21, 1984.

5. *In Our Opinion,* July 1985, Vol. 1, No. 2.

6. Financial Fraud Detection and Disclosure Act, H.R. Doc. No. 4886, 99th Cong. 2d Sess.

7. Wilfred C. Uecker, Arthur P. Brief, and William R. Kinney, Jr., "Perception of the Internal and External Auditor as a Deterrent to Corporate Irregularities," *The Accounting Review,* (July 1981), pp. 465–478.

8. John Shad, Chairman of Securities and Exchange Commission, testimony before House Subcommittee on Oversight and Investigations.

9. From "What about Auditor's Expectations," *CA Magazine,* September, 1988. © the Canadian Institute of Chartered Accountants. Reprinted by permission. The authors are Ron E. Ellis, MBA, CA, a partner in Clarkson Gordon's National Accounting Standards Department, Toronto; and David C. Selley, FCA, Clarkson's national director of auditing and the CICA's auditing standards director from 1983 to 1985.

10. Mindy Paskell-Mede, BCL, LLB, Nicholl Paskell-Mede, Montreal, "What Liability Crisis?," *CA Magazine,* May 1994, pp. 42, 43. © the Canadian Institute of Chartered Accountants. Reprinted with permission.

Chapter 4

Forensic and Investigative Accounting: A Case Approach

Accountants and auditors can develop fraud awareness and the investigative mentality through a case-study approach. This chapter gives a brief review of the potential for white-collar crime within the accounting system, followed by case studies, first, relating to the purchases, payables, and payment system; and second, to the sales, receivables, and receipts system. There are a variety of ways individuals might fraudulently steal or embezzle company assets:

- Through the purchase, payables, and payment system (using such tools as false expense reports, false supplier invoices, and other false information)
- Through the sales, receivables, and receipts system (using, for example, front-end fraud, lapping, and false sales invoices)

But such fraud, theft, and embezzlement can be proven by uncovering evidence that establishes:

- The job role of the accused within the accounting system.
- The control the accused person exercises on the accounting system.
- The knowledge by the accused of the accounting system.
- The systematic pattern used in covering up the fraud.
- The extent of the fraud.
- The personal financial position of the accused, which can be relevant to motive and can illustrate benefit.

To establish credibility and prove the case beyond a reasonable doubt, it is wise to give the benefit of the doubt to the accused. When establishing the situations and the extent of the fraud, select only those examples or specific items of theft, fraud, or embezzlement that are unassailable.

It is often essential in crimes against a business to obtain evidence from company employees and those who had access to the assets that were allegedly misappropriated. It has to be established for each and every person who had access that he or she did not take the assets in question.

FRAUD WITHIN THE PURCHASES, PAYABLES, AND PAYMENTS SYSTEM

The purchases, payables, and payments system is the accounting system that records and controls a company's acquisition of assets and its incurrence of expenses. It records, for example, the purchase of fixed assets and inventory and the payment of salaries and sales-promotion expenses. False entries in books and supporting documents for purchases and payments can be used to perpetrate a fraud on a company. The main attack falls into three categories:

1. False expense reports
2. False supplier invoices
3. False information

False Expense Reports

Expense reports prepared and submitted for payment or reimbursement to the company are false if they contain:

- Nonbusiness items
- Inflated items
- Fictitious items
- Duplicate items

A company credit card can be used for personal items. If the entire amount of the account is paid and expensed by the company, then fraud may be occurring.

The issues are as follows:

- Is the expense item an allowable business-related expense?
- Is the expense amount the actual amount incurred?
- Is the expense ultimately charged to the business? If yes, is there evidence of any reimbursement by the employee?

To address the first issue, it is necessary to determine the company's policy regarding allowable business expenses. To address the second issue, it is necessary to obtain the supplier's copies of the original expense vouchers and compare them with those submitted in support of the expense report. It is also necessary to understand the approval-and-payment system that was in effect. Who approved the expense reports? How were the expense reports categorized in the accounting records? Were they adjusted through a journal entry at a later date to reflect their personal nature? Was there any pattern in the submission, approval, and/or recording of the fraudulent expense reports?

False Supplier Invoices

Suppliers' invoices prepared and submitted for payment to the company are false if:

- No goods have been delivered or services rendered.
- The quantity or price is inflated.
- The quality has been compromised.

The delivery of goods or services to a location other than a business location (for the use and benefit of the perpetrator) is a common technique, as is the payment to a "friendly" supplier when no goods or services were actually provided. Payments of inflated amounts to suppliers often reflect the existence of secret commissions (bribes).

The issues the investigative accountant should address are as follows:

- Were the goods and services actually provided?
- Did the company receive the benefit?
- What was the approval-and-payment system?

It is necessary to learn, first, whether the supplier company actually exists and, next, whether such goods or services were in fact provided. If they were provided, one must determine for whom.

It is often necessary to obtain the bills of lading, that is, the freight companies proof-of-delivery slips, to confirm the location where goods and services were delivered.

As with false expense reports, one must understand the approval-and-payment system.

False Information

A business receives vast amounts of information, and, subject to the existing systems of internal control, relies on it in making decisions and in initiating, executing, and recording transactions. If this information is false, a business can be deceived, resulting in deprivation and hence placing the company at economic risk.

Examples of false information that businesses may rely on include:

- False financial statements
- Overstated accounts receivable listings
- Overstated statements of income and net worth
- False general journal entries
- Altered internal company records
- Fictitious customer credit information
- False asset valuations

Some of the issues to be addressed are as follows:

- Is the summary information presented (accounts receivable listing, financial statements) consistent with the underlying books and records?
- Are the entries in the general journal properly approved? Are they appropriate and consistent with the facts?
- Can transactions be confirmed with third parties?

To address the first issue, it is necessary to determine the representation made by the person or company under investigation and the understanding reached. Once this has been done, the books and records supporting the summary financial information in question can be examined from the appropriate perspective.

To address the other issues, it is necessary to understand the accounting systems in effect. It is important to contact third parties to review and discuss their books and records, and then to compare that information with the information represented to the victim.

FRAUD WITHIN THE SALES, RECEIVABLES, AND RECEIPTS SYSTEM

This part of the accounting system records the company's sales and revenue collections. Various fraudulent activities can occur with this system, primarily in three categories:

1. Front-end fraud
2. False sales invoices
3. Lapping

Front-End Fraud

Company revenue may be diverted before it ever reaches the sales, receivables, and receipts system, thus circumventing the accounting system entirely. This is commonly called a *front-end fraud*. A front-end fraud occurs when company products are sold for cash, the sale and the receipt of cash are not recorded, and the cash is diverted—usually directly into the pocket of the perpetrator. A front-end fraud occurs when a company's customers are improperly directed to take their business elsewhere, thus depriving the company of business and profits it could otherwise have earned. A front-end fraud occurs when special or unusual revenues and cost reductions, such as purchase rebates, are received and misappropriated. The questions to ask in front-end fraud are:

- Do recorded sales represent all company sales?
- Has the company unexpectedly experienced reduced sales from some of its oldest and best customers?
- Are all revenues recorded?

Generally, front-end fraud is characterized by management override of internal controls. In the situation in which no sales have been recorded, there is nothing in the sales accounting system to red-flag an unpaid or overdue account. As a result, unrecorded sales are difficult to detect. However, actual inventory on hand has been depleted. If the company has a good inventory accounting system, the unrecorded sale may be detected.

Service businesses, such as a ferry service and the theater and movie business, operate primarily with cash sales and have no inventory systems. Front-end fraud in these types of businesses is extremely difficult to detect.

Benefit may be established through a review of personal bank accounts if they reveal unexplained cash deposits. Otherwise, the net-worth approach may be necessary to establish benefit.

The sales records and other supporting documents of both the victim and the customers (assuming they can be identified) should be analyzed for the period before the date of the alleged front-end fraud to determine business in the normal course.

False Sales Invoices

A company sales invoice can be altered to show a lower sale amount than was actually the case. The difference between the real sale amount and the adjusted lower amount can then be misappropriated without the accounting system showing a red flag.

Questions to ask include:

- Are recorded sale amounts the actual sales amounts?
- Can sales be confirmed with customers?
- Are sale amounts reasonable in the circumstances?

It is important to obtain and examine all original copies of an invoice and all the related books of original entry. Again, the investigator must become familiar with the accounting system and understand the person's position within the system. Did the person have the necessary authority to perpetrate this crime? Did the person have the opportunity?

Lapping

When cash receipts from customer A are misappropriated and the misappropriation is subsequently covered up by recording the receipt of monies from customer B to the credit of customer A (to the extent of the earlier misappropriation), lapping is occurring.

Approximate questions include:

- Are the amounts recorded as owing to the company actually still owing to the company?
- Are deposits from Peter being used to cover Paul's debts?

To deal with these issues it is necessary to understand the system in effect for receiving customer payments, making bank deposits, and preparing entries to customer accounts.

Who first received the payments? Who prepared the company bank deposit? Who updated the customer accounts? Have any accounts been written off? Who approved the write-off? It is also often necessary to contact customers and obtain their records of payments, including paid checks and remittance advices. Do their records show payment of specific invoices that are shown as unpaid in the victim company's records?

MANAGEMENT FRAUD WITHIN THE PURCHASES, PAYABLES, AND PAYMENTS SYSTEM

Regina v. Lipsome

This case is an example of management (the president) exercising influence over its suppliers to obtain a secret commission. The deceitful document was the supplier's invoice bearing the name "Fashion Coordinators, Inc." The supplier's billing to the customer was inflated by the amount of the secret commission paid to the president.

The customer, an agent for a major retail department store, purchased the goods from suppliers in foreign countries. The president took an active interest by personally participating in arranging contracts between foreign suppliers and the company. The foreign suppliers realized that contracts could be obtained only because they agreed to pay to the president's personal bank account in a foreign jurisdiction an amount equal to two percent of the value of the business to be transacted with their new customer. This additional fee, included as a cost of the product, was billed to the customer. In order to ensure that the higher cost would not be detected or questioned by anyone in the purchasing department, the president approved all of these invoices for payment.

One day, the foreign supplier, confident that he could retain the company's business, informed a director of this arrangement. In the end both parties lost.

The fact that the president was performing a clerical function—reviewing suppliers' invoices for approval of payment—was an indication of the activity. In any investigation, departures from a normal business practice should be questioned.

Regina v. Barter

Don Barter entered into an agreement with Norgard to start a construction business. It was agreed that Norgard would finance the company and Barter would manage and operate the business, to be known as Norgard Construction. Barter agreed to accept a salary plus expenses and to share the profits equally with Norgard. The business mainly consisted of constructing service stations. The operation progressed and the business showed a profit for the first three years of operation.

Norgard did not take an active part in the construction business. He continued to operate his own plastering company. The new business, Norgard Construction, operated as a division of his company, P.L.R. Plastering Limited. Norgard, the sole check-signing officer and absentee owner, visited the office regularly to sign checks, some of which were blank.

Barter tendered and obtained contracts, hired subcontractors, hired and fired employees, and purchased goods necessary to operate the business without interference or direction from Norgard. Barter could also purchase material he required through the construction business and charge this amount to himself on the business books as a form of salary.

Norgard was aware that over the years Barter had erected a barn on his farm and renovated other buildings, including his residence. Barter informed Norgard that he had obtained a grant from the government for $100,000 to finance the renovations and improvements.

Gradually Norgard Construction began to have difficulty paying its suppliers and was eventually petitioned into bankruptcy by a creditor. The company's debts exceeded $100,000 at that time. Barter gave no explanation for the shortage of funds except to say that he had miscalculated the actual cost of the various construction jobs. An examination of the books of account, canceled checks, and available supporting documentation revealed that Barter had defrauded Norgard Construction of $287,000 by various means.

As general manager of Norgard Construction Company, Barter was responsible for the day-to-day operations. The owner was usually absent and the general manager was afforded a degree of trust. At the same time, the absentee owner retained signing authority over all checks and control over all policy decisions.

In his private capacity as a farmer, Barter incurred debts with suppliers who also dealt with him as general manager of Norgard. Barter personally owed one of these suppliers, United Cooperatives of Ontario, more than $9,800. In June 1970, Barter purchased a $4.30 item, documented by invoice #512403, from the supplier and made out in pencil. Later, the penciled information on this invoice was erased. Information was typed in, indicating instead that the company, Norgard, had purchased $3,500 worth of material for a job then in progress. On the strength of this typed document, the absentee owner signed a check for $3,500 to the supplier, believing, of course, that the disbursement was to the benefit of the company. When the supplier received the check, he credited Barter's *personal* account, reducing the debt to $6,300 on Barter's instruction. (Exhibits 4.1 and 4.2).

The alteration of documents (erasures and/or information stroked out) is at times the only indication of fraudulent activity. It discloses the state of mind (intent) of the person making the entry. Such alterations frequently occur in the earlier stages of a fraud when the perpetrator has yet to perfect the scheme.

In another example, G&M Forest Products invoiced Norgard for the sale of "Roof Trusses," with delivery scheduled for a construction site. However, the back of the invoice disclosed a notation that described the route to Barter's farm. The building of his barn required roof trusses. A review of the bill of lading confirmed the redirection.

These two major proofs went a long way toward convincing the trial judge of Barter's guilt.

EMPLOYEE FRAUD WITHIN THE PURCHASES, PAYABLES, AND PAYMENTS SYSTEM

Regina v. Down and Out

It is obvious that most perpetrators of illegal activity wish to remain hidden and anonymous. If they own companies engaging in illegal activities, they will wish to, and indeed strive to, remain in the background. They may wish

Exhibit 4.1   United Co-Operatives of Ontario Invoice

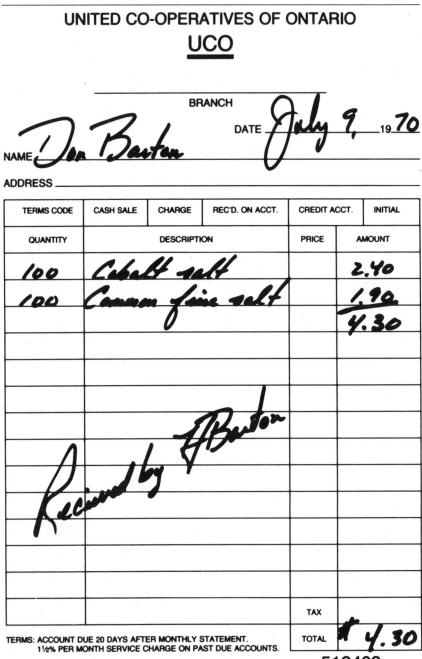

UNITED CO-OPERATIVES OF ONTARIO
<u>UCO</u>

BRANCH

NAME *Don Barton*

DATE *July 9,* 19 *70*

ADDRESS

TERMS CODE	CASH SALE	CHARGE	REC'D. ON ACCT.	CREDIT ACCT.	INITIAL

QUANTITY	DESCRIPTION			PRICE	AMOUNT
100	Cobalt salt				2.40
100	Common fine salt				1.90
					4.30
	Received by *F Barton*				
				TAX	

TERMS: ACCOUNT DUE 20 DAYS AFTER MONTHLY STATEMENT.
1½% PER MONTH SERVICE CHARGE ON PAST DUE ACCOUNTS.

TOTAL **$ 4.30**

512403

I HEREBY CERTIFY THAT THE GOODS ARE PURCHASED FOR FARM USE

Exhibit 4.2 United Co-Operatives of Ontario Invoice. Typewriter remarkably similar to United Co-Op's typewriter.

UNITED CO-OPERATIVES OF ONTARIO

UCO

Uxbridge, Ont.

BRANCH

DATE May 30, 19 70

NAME Norgard Construction Co.

ADDRESS 485 Kennedy Rd., Scarboro, Ont.

TERMS CODE	CASH SALE	CHARGE ✓	REC'D. ON ACCT.	CREDIT ACCT.	INITIAL

QUANTITY	DESCRIPTION	PRICE	AMOUNT
	For the supply of steel posts		
	and farm type fence for the		
	Gulf Oil. Belleville, Ont.		$3,500.00
	6204 9444		
	CD June/70		
		TAX	
		TOTAL	

TERMS: ACCOUNT DUE 20 DAYS AFTER MONTHLY STATEMENT.
1½% PER MONTH SERVICE CHARGE ON PAST DUE ACCOUNTS.

512403

I HEREBY CERTIFY THAT THE GOODS ARE PURCHASED FOR FARM USE ______________ to create official records showing that someone else owns the business making that other person appear as the directing mind.

It is often useful for perpetrators to geographically separate their various corporate activities from each other (if they have several companies) and from their home turf. This may in part be due to a belief that an investigator will have to expend significantly more energy to identify the true owner. Others may believe that appointing their lawyer as the nominal owner will prevent disclosure.

Within a corporate setting, employees will attempt to hide their ownership in another company that is doing business with or stealing customers from their employer. This results in employees taking for their own benefit a rake-off or commission from the employer.

The main focus of an investigation into suspected hidden ownership is an attempt to identify the directing mind of the company. Who has authority? Who appears to report to whom? Who received information, particularly financial information? Who signs legal documents or banking agreements? Do suspected owners receive commissions, bonuses, or loan advances? In *Regina v. Down and Out* the chief purchasing agent for a municipality and the town engineer together set up a phony supplier company. The dummy company, Sparks Engineering and Drafting Supply, ostensibly was providing the town with certain office supplies, to the tune of some $320,000 from 1975 to 1982. In fact, no supplies were ever delivered.

The fraud surfaced when two accounts payable clerks began to wonder why they had never seen anyone from the vendor organization call on the town's purchasing agent. Sparks did not even send the town a Christmas card despite the amount of business ostensibly placed with it. Then one day one of the clerks decided to dial the telephone number printed on Spark's invoice. To her surprise an auto body shop in Toronto answered her call. She reported her concerns to Douglas Down, the chief purchasing agent. After this incident the clerk noticed that the telephone number on Sparks' invoices had been changed. She called repeatedly. Each time she heard the following tape-recorded message, "Sorry, we're not in right now. Please phone back later." She discussed her concerns with the other clerk, who had also noticed some unusual things about Sparks; for example, the invoice had a post office address (Exhibit 4.3). She also noticed that all of the Sparks invoices were for amounts under $500 (the town had a policy that all orders for goods in excess of $500 had to be put out for bid), and that checks issued in payment for Sparks's invoices were always under $2,000 (the town's policy was that checks issued in amounts over $2,000 were to be approved by the town treasurer, who signed the checks by hand). Checks under $2,000 were signed by a check-signing machine after being approved by Douglas Down.

One clerk also noted that Douglas Down insisted on delivering the checks to Sparks himself, rather than having them mailed, as were all other suppliers'

Exhibit 4.3   Sparks Invoice to Municipality

SPARKS Equipment Service
& Drafting Supplies
P.O. BOX 2704, STATION 'F'
SCARBOROUGH, ONTARIO, M1W 3P3
416-498-5237

INVOICE NO. 3749
DATE Oct. 13.1982

Sold To:

Town of Markham
8911 Woodbine Ave.
Markham, Ontario
L3R 1A1

QUANTITY	DESCRIPTION	PRICE	AMOUNT
2 doz.	Black 3–Ring Binders	$12.95	$310.80 √
	Less 5% Discount		15.54 √
			$295.26 √
	Prov. Tax 7%		20.67 √
	Total		$315.93 √
			======

SUPPLIER #   VOUCHER # *123548*

DATE *Oct. 13/82*   AMOUNT *315. 93*

INVOICE # *3749*   P.O. #   LOT. PURCH. REQ.

ACCOUNT # *0300   0300   00001   0*

PRICES CHECKED   EXTENSION CHECKED   BATCH

DEPARTMENT HEAD APPROVED   WEEK

checks. Checks for Sparks were never issued when Douglas Down was on vacation, and Richard Out had ordered most of Sparks's purchases for the town engineering department.

The clerks then reported their concerns to the town treasurer. He talked to the receiver in the warehouse, who informed him that to the best of his recollection no Sparks truck had ever delivered goods.

Then Richard Out was interviewed. He admitted that he and Douglas Down had set up Sparks to defraud the town.

The investigative accountant retained in the case performed the following tasks:

- Prepared a listing of invoices rendered by Sparks and paid by the town
- Analyzed the activity in Sparks's bank account, to help determine whether Sparks was carrying on business in the normal course
- Analyzed the activity in the personal bank accounts of the two accused, to assist in identifying financial benefit
- Prepared a schedule setting out Sparks's purchases from suppliers and subsequent resale at the 20 percent markup to the town, to quantify the amount of the alleged abuse

The analysis of Sparks's bank account records indicated that the only source of company funds were the checks received from the town. The only uses of funds were checks issued to Out and to Out's friend, and during the last few months to Down. There were no disbursements for such items as purchases from suppliers, payroll, overhead, or other normal business expenses.

The analysis of the activity in Out's personal bank accounts indicated that Out's income was heavily augmented by amounts transferred from Sparks. It also revealed many checks issued to Down and many written to cash. The analysis of Down's bank accounts also indicated that large amounts had been deposited in excess of his known sources of income.

Out was confronted with this information. He admitted that Sparks had not delivered any supplies to the town, but had simply rendered invoices that were duly paid. He also admitted that the profits were split, with 45 percent going to Down and the remainder to himself.

VENDOR FRAUD WITHIN THE PURCHASES, PAYABLES, AND PAYMENTS SYSTEM

Another of the more common frauds are scams perpetrated against a company by its vendors, contractors, and suppliers. These frauds are even more difficult to detect during a financial audit than those that management commits. The outsider often has an inside confederate who steers him or her clear of control-system snags, or greases the way. That combination is hard to beat so long as the co-conspirators do not have a falling out.

But sometimes ingenious vendors perpetrate frauds by themselves with no help from insiders.

Regina v. Kotowski

Kotowski, president of Central Fuel Company Limited, defrauded a school district by charging it for fuel that had not been delivered to a high school in Fort Frances, Ontario.

For three years Central Fuel Company submitted the lowest bid to the school board for the delivery of fuel oil to the school, even though one of the other bidders was the same major oil company that supplied fuel oil to Central Fuel Company for its sale to the school. Because Central Fuel offered the lowest price per gallon (14.5 cents), the school board accepted its bid. It was later established that the company was able to charge the lower market price per gallon because it billed the school board for oil that had not, in fact, been supplied. The meter on the company's oil truck was rigged to continue running after the oil was shut off. The gallons of fuel oil ostensibly delivered were subsequently billed to the school district.

Before the documentary evidence could be collected, the premises of the Central Fuel Company were destroyed by fire. Since the documents required to complete the fraud investigation were no longer available, the forensic accountants had to seek documentation from various third parties.

The sales invoices submitted by Central Fuel Company were available from the school board's Department of Supply and Services, as were their canceled checks and their agreement with Central Fuel Company. Documents concerning Central Fuel Company's supply of oil were obtained from the major oil company. Their invoices to Central Fuel and their statements of account, indicating the payments received from Central Fuel for the purchase of the oil, were reviewed. From this information schedules were prepared to show the total number of gallons invoiced and the invoiced dollar amount of those gallons for each of the three school years. This information, however, was useless without evidence from an engineer who could calculate how many gallons of oil the high school heating system should have consumed.

The engineer analyzed the capacity of that system by determining the number of heating degree days during each of the school years, making the extremely conservative assumption that the doors and windows of the school were open all winter long. The number of gallons of oil the school required, according to the engineer, was much lower than the number of gallons Central Fuel invoiced to the school for each of the three years.

Color graphs were prepared for each of the three years to show the contrast between gallons invoiced and the expert engineer's assessments. These visual aids enabled the court to readily grasp the meaning of the financial data

Exhibit 4.4 Gallons Delivered versus Maximum Gallons Required According to Engineering Study

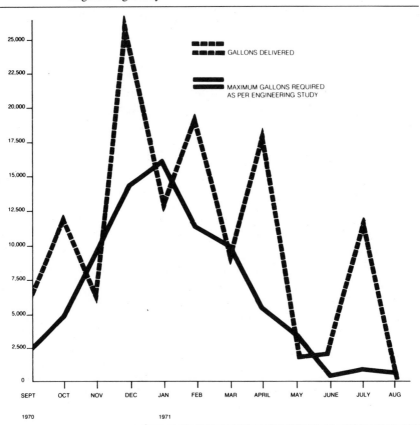

presented in evidence. (See Exhibit 4.4). To further support the engineer's evidence, the forensic accountants produced a schedule to show the number of gallons delivered in the year following Kotowski's dismissal (see Exhibit 4.5). It was less than the engineer's assessment.

MANAGEMENT FRAUD WITHIN THE SALES RECEIVABLE RECEIPTS SYSTEM

United States v. Goldblum, Levin, Lewis et al.

This case involves the Equity Funding Insurance Company of America and was popularized in the videotape "The Billion Dollar Bubble."

Exhibit 4.5 The Number of Gallons of Oil Central Fuel Company Delivered
Compared to the Number Gulf Canada Delivered

	1969—1970		1970—1971	
	Number of Degree Days	Number of Gallons Delivered	Number of Degree Days	Number of Gallons Delivered
December	1,561	12,916	1,908	26,959
January	2,106	25,555	2,239	12,447
February	1,694	18,595	1,550	18,618
	5,361	57,066	5,697	58,024
Deliveries by:	Central Fuel Company		Central Fuel Company	
Maximum number of gallons required per Engineering Dept.		38,599		41,018

	1971—1972		1972—1973	
	Number of Degree Days	Number of Gallons Delivered	Number of Degree Days	Number of Gallons Delivered
December	1,745	18,883	1,893	14,691
January	2,195	9,953	1,720	11,467
February	1,848	18,475	1,561	6,000
	5,788	47,311	5,174	32,158
Deliveries by:	Central Fuel Company		Gulf Canada	
Maximum number of gallons required per Engineering Dept.		41,674		37,253

On January 1, 1978 the shares of Equity Funding Corporation of America
were trading on the New York Stock Exchange in moderate volume at about
$37. Three months later, on March 28, trading in Equity Funding shares was
stopped by the SEC after a week of fevered activity had reduced their price to
$14.

Despite its spectacular growth and earnings history, Equity Funding had
not actually earned a penny of profit in the preceding four years—it had lost
money. The fraud was not a sophisticated computer operation run by a small
group, as was first suspected. Instead a large number of employees had sys-
tematically developed and maintained a completely false picture of sustained

growth and prosperity that pervaded the company's operations. Using the inflated values of the shares of the company, they were able to acquire a small empire of other companies with real assets. As one method of extending the fraud outlived its usefulness, the conspirators turned to another.

Art Lewis, the chief actuary, had access to the computer facilities and was also responsible for preparing the corporation's annual financial statements. In 1969 the preparation of the financial statements was delayed. Necessary information was unavailable from the computer facility, primarily because certain computer programs had not been completely debugged. As a result, the executive vice-president, Fred Levin, suggested that a net income figure be chosen and the sales be estimated using this number.

It was discovered soon after that the actual results fell far short of the reported (and estimated) results. Art Lewis and Fred Levin took steps to create false insurance policies to inflate actual revenues and profit to the levels of those reported. This maintained the stock price of the corporation on the market. These policies were input on the computer as "99" policies so that they could subsequently be identified. In addition, if a request was received from an auditor to confirm a policy, the "99" policies were automatically excluded from being selected for confirmation by the computer. At this time, Levin and Lewis considered their actions a temporary expedient in order to maintain the company's stock in the market.

Unfortunately, because this revenue was fictitious, there was no corresponding cash flow to the company, and the company soon experienced cash shortages. Stanley Goldblum, the president, asked Levin and Lewis to obtain cash to subsidize the insurance and other operations related to the corporation.

This necessitated selling the false insurance policies to insurance underwriters for approximately twice the annual premium. The phony policies were sold to the underwriters and this brought cash into Equity Funding Insurance Company. What Levin and Lewis did not consider at the time was that after the initial payment on the insurance policy to the underwriter, Equity Funding would have to make the yearly payments for the imaginary people they had insured. (Eventually, they even began to kill the phantoms to collect real proceeds.)

The payments on the fictitious policies caused an even worse cash-flow problem and necessitated the creation of even more fictitious policies and their sale to the insurance underwriters. At one point, Lewis and Levin calculated that by the end of 10 years they would have sold more insurance policies than there were citizens in the United States.

Astonishingly, with dozens of people intimately acquainted with the details of the fraud and with audited financial statements, the secret was kept for a decade. Only when Equity Funding fired the "wrong" employee, Ron Secrist, did the story begin to unfold. Publicly, the stock price plunged. Huge blocks changed hands at the last minute, resulting in an endless series of lawsuits as buyers and sellers tried to conclude or renege on transactions. Eventually, twenty-two employees and three auditors were indicted for fraud. The fraud had grown in a few short years to the following proportions:

- Assets were overstated by over $100,000,000.
- Fictitious funded loans to policyholders totaled $62.3 million.
- Fictitious bonds totaled $24.6 million.
- Fictitious commercial paper totaled $8 million.
- In 1972 Equity Funding listed assets of $737.5 million and a net worth of $143.4 million.
- The subsequent investigation and audit showed actual assets to be worth only $488.9 million and actual net worth was negative $42 million.
- Over 200 people (insiders) were aware of some aspect of the fraud before its exposure.
- Thousands of fictitious insurance policies were generated by company computers.
- Stock certificates were counterfeited in the company's own print shop.

EMPLOYEE FRAUD WITHIN THE SALES, RECEIVABLES, AND RECEIPTS SYSTEM

Regina v. Harvey

Smith Transport Company operated a trucking terminal in Belleville, Ontario. Its accounts receivable clerk, Ms. Harvey, had been a loyal and faithful employee for over eight years. The terminal manager often complimented her for the effort she put into the business, evidenced by the amount of work she frequently took home.

Ms. Harvey began part-time employment with Smith Transport, Belleville Terminal, as a rating and billing division office clerk. She later took over as accounts receivable clerk and seemed to digest the instructions easily, showing a keen interest. She was able to train new rate clerks and billers and answer all rate requests from customers through the day.

Ms. Harvey soon learned to handle compensation reports, refund or overcharge claims, interline accounts payable, intermediate terminals procedure, terminals engineering reports, and payroll work, and was able to replace any office staff members while they were on vacation. She was well liked by the office personnel, drivers, and customers, and seemed to be a real asset to the company.

Harvey's primary function each day was to balance the cash received with the primary sales invoices and prepare a cash deposit for the bank and a cash report for processing in the computer. She processed all incoming checks from charge-account customers by matching checks to the applicable invoice copies and preparing a deposit for the bank and a receivable report for processing in the computer. She presented the cash and receivable reports to the manager for his signature, along with the customer checks and cash.

The supporting sales invoices were always in sealed and stapled envelopes for each report. The manager did not open the envelopes and verify the contents. If the total of the bank deposit agreed with the total of the sales invoices, he signed the report.

Harvey worked on the accounts receivable aged analysis, a list of all outstanding pro-bills prepared in Toronto. (Pro-bills are outstanding invoices.) She questioned certain delinquent accounts for payment, and often took the analysis home because she said she was too busy to do it during the day.

The manager looked at the Accounts Receivable Aged Analysis monthly and questioned certain delinquent customer accounts. Harvey informed the manager of checks that arrived after her contact with the delinquent customer. She advised her manager that a major customer had had serious problems converting to a computer accounting system, and as a result requested that Smith Transport be patient with the amount of old, outstanding receivables.

Harvey became ill; her house was listed for sale. Smith Transport decided to hire a new person to replace Harvey.

The new person began the collection work on the two largest charge account customers because successful collection of these accounts would immediately reduce the 60- and 90-day totals on the accounts receivable aged analysis. She asked one of the companies, if it was having computer problems, and the response was negative. The customer told the manager that the receivables had, in fact, been paid. When Smith Transport checked its deposit slips and reports, it found checks from its major customer deposited and applied to older sales invoices and to other customer sales invoices, not to the specific sales invoices the customer had specified with the check.

Through investigation it was determined that the accounts receivable clerk had conducted a lapping scheme over a period of six years. The lap grew so large during this period that she had to take the aged receivable analysis home in the evenings, along with the paid and unpaid sales invoices, in order to set aside those invoices for payment the next day, thus ensuring a favorable aged receivable analysis the following month. As the lap grew, the daily cash receipts were no longer sufficient to cover the previously misappropriated funds. Accordingly, the clerk began to apply checks received from the company's larger customers to cover up other customers' already-paid invoices.

In attempting to establish benefit to the accused, the known personal bank accounts of the accused and her husband were examined. An amount of $35,000 in cash was found deposited to these bank accounts over and above

Exhibit 4.6   A statement of the apparent sources of deposits to the known bank account in the name of Richard and Lois Harvey.

Total Deposits		$113,227.04
Less-known nonpayroll deposits:		
Family allowance	$ 232.00	
Family finance plan loan	23,103.14	
Transfer from A/C 1012	232.00	
Smith Transport Credit Union	1,049.35	
Bancardchek	920.00	
Tax refund	217.57	
Not sufficient funds	2,906.42	
Loan	1,450.00	
Ontario Credit Union	1,000.00	
Miscellaneous	10.11	31,220.59
		82,106.45
Less-known payroll deposits:		
Richard Harvey payroll checks	29,570.08	
Lois Harvey payroll checks	8,971.73	38,541.81
Balance of deposits whose source unknown		$ 43,564.64
Composed of:		
Cash		$ 35,477.19
Checks		8,087.45
		$ 43,564.64

personal income during the relevant period (Exhibit 4.6). Had the terminal manager examined any one deposit and report, lapping could have been detected much sooner.

CUSTOMER FRAUD WITHIN THE SALES, RECEIVABLES, AND RECEIPTS SYSTEM

Planned bankruptcy occurs when management has converted the assets of a business to its own benefit and then tries to conceal the conversion through formal bankruptcy proceedings. Characteristics include the following:

1. The business has established a reputation for trustworthiness in the business community.
2. It sells tangible and highly salable products such as furniture.
3. The business has little net worth.
4. It has not been a financial success.

5. A new person is introduced in a senior position.
6. The business departs from its normal business practices with regard to purchasing, payments to suppliers, sales, and the granting of credit to customers.

These changes in business conduct are likely to be followed by these manifestations:

1. The volume of inventory ordered from existing suppliers increases significantly. The suppliers will probably extend credit up to 60 days, largely as a result of their wish to retain the business and because of the established reputation of the company.
2. The unsuspecting suppliers will receive little or no payment. The scam probably will be completed within 60 days of the date of purchase of the inventory. After that time the suppliers are likely to become suspicious and might take action of some kind.
3. The company refuses to sell its inventory on credit and sells only on a COD basis. To get customers to pay cash, the selling price per unit may be at or below the company's cost as shown on supplier invoices.
4. If inventory remains on hand after the usual customers have been approached, it may be sold to new customers. Such sales usually tend to be for cash. (Although the sales invoices may indicate the payment was made in cash, the deposit of the cash into the corporate bank account does not necessarily follow.)
5. If, after all these efforts to sell, inventory is still left at the site, it will be physically removed. The trail of the goods will be covered up to prevent detection.

A planned bankruptcy is designed, of course, to benefit those in control of the planned bankrupt. However, it is essential that no trail be left behind to enable the trustee in bankruptcy to retrieve the proceeds of the crime and return those proceeds to the bankrupt company. The techniques employed to block the path of the trustee are limited only by the perpetrator's imagination, and will vary according to the circumstances.

Regina v. Rosen

This case illustrates the changes in purchasing and payment activity that occurred just before the company declared bankruptcy. Brittany Antiques Limited was incorporated in October 1970. Rosen was the president of the company that sold antique furniture by auction and on a wholesale basis. For the fiscal year that ended October 31, 1973, the company reported sales of $122,090, merchandise purchases of $90,265, and a net loss of $3,740.

In the fall of 1974 John Mac joined Rosen's firm. In January 1975 Brittany changed its buying habits to include large purchases of merchandise. Rosen and Mac went to various furniture and gift shows in January and February 1975, in Toronto, to become personally acquainted with the many dealers. They explained that they were in the business of buying and selling by auction, and mentioned that they had a contract to supply furniture to two new motels in the Northern Ontario towns of North Bay and Kapuskasing.

In fact, Brittany's new purchasing policy resulted in the acquisition of merchandise during the period of January 1975 to May 31, 1975, totaling $411,586.13. However, by June 24, 1975, Brittany's new payment policy resulted in only $10,248.86 being paid to these suppliers.

A key ingredient in a successfully planned bankruptcy is being able to blame someone for the failure of your corporation. Equally important, the transactions the trustee normally examined in the search for corporate assets should not leave a trail of evidence—especially when it becomes apparent to the trustee that there is a large inventory discrepancy.

In May 1975 Brittany advertised the position "bookkeeper . . . chance for advancement to managerial position." The real Mr. John Peter Geslak, a Toronto accountant, called Brittany to apply for the position. He was advised by Brittany's office to send in his resume. Because he was applying for several positions at this time, he had prepared several copies of his resume and simply sent one to Brittany. This was the last he heard from them about the position.

On April 9, 1975, Rosen went to see his bank manager to introduce a John Geslak as Brittany's new accountant. Rosen stated that Geslak would handle all of the firm's financial affairs and would have full signing authority for the firm (thus solving the problem of access to assets). A banking resolution was drawn up to this effect, and the authorized signature card was changed to show the name of John Peter Geslak.

With the changed policies, the new people, and an inventory of furniture boosted to its highest levels in the company's history, the planned bankruptcy was now ready for the next stage, the quick disposal. To document these activities, the investigative accountant had to reconstruct the sales and cash receipts of Brittany.

Based on the available documentation, known sales of $245,222 occurred between April 15, 1975 and May 17, 1975. This amount included four invoices marked "paid in cash—John Geslak" dated April 28 and May 2, 12, and 15. But the bank records for Brittany did not disclose the deposit of *any* cash to the company's account.

Thus, the introduction of a John Geslak into the operation of Brittany Antiques, along with the sales invoices marked "paid in cash—John Geslak," enabled Rosen to claim that John Geslak must have taken this cash from the customer and, instead of depositing the cash in the company account, had stolen it.

This technique was employed to block the trustee's access to the furniture. It initially prevented the trustee from attacking Rosen, because Rosen could blame his plight on the theft of the sale proceeds by his accountant John Geslak.

In a planned bankruptcy, time is of the essence. Most creditors allow 30 to 60 days for payment, especially for more significant orders. They are, after all, in business to do business, and granting credit is an accepted practice and an accepted risk in business. With most of the purchases having occurred in March and April 1975, it was not surprising that in the latter part of May some of the suppliers would be pressuring Brittany for payment of account.

One of the better ways of buying time, from Brittany's viewpoint, was to issue checks to the suppliers. This began on May 20, 1975. Checks totaling $65,285.33 were issued to 12 creditors between May 20 and May 26, 1975, although the bank balance as of May 20 was $1,209.20. Of course all of these checks were returned subsequently marked NSF (not sufficient funds).

On May 30, 1975, Rosen wrote to the suppliers saying, in part, "Our accountant has absconded with all deposits, placing our firm in a terrible position." (Exhibit 4.7)

On June 16, 1975, the landlord of Brittany's business premises had a bailiff lock the place for nonpayment of rent.

On July 15, 1975, Rosen filed an assignment request in bankruptcy for Brittany Antiques Limited.

At the time of bankruptcy Rosen believed that the trustee's path had been blocked, and with John Geslak having returned to his home country with the proceeds of crime, it appeared initially that a planned bankruptcy had in fact succeeded.

However, when investigation commenced, it was determined that the real John F. Geslak in Toronto, Ontario, had had no relationship to Brittany Antiques Limited. The question of the real identity of the person who had claimed to be John Geslak then arose. Eventually investigation revealed that the accountant who had absconded with the firm's money was living in Hyannis, Massachusetts—after, of course, sharing the benefits with Rosen.

INVESTIGATIVE ACCOUNTING IN MURDER, ARSON, AND COMMERCIAL BRIBERY CASES

Murder

Forensic accounting skills may be applied to homicide investigations for the following purposes: (1) to analyze and determine a possible financial motive for murder; (2) to analyze financial documentation relating to a murder for

Exhibit 4.7 A Further Attempt by Management to Stall Creditors

---

BRITTANY ANTIQUE LTD.
AUCTION HOUSE

30 Baywood Rd. Unit 9
Rexdale, Ontario M9V 3Z1

Tel. 749-9791
749-9391
May 30, 1975

Dear Sir or Madame:

It is our sad misfortune to inform you at this time that for reasons beyond our control, our payment to you shall be somewhat delayed.

Our accountant has absconded with all deposits, placing our firm in a terrible position. However, the police are presently looking for him and seem quite optimistic about his apprehension.

We have full intentions of meeting our obligations as soon as possible and beg your indulgence in this matter.

We remain very truly yours,

Brittany Antique Ltd.,
Carl Rosen
President

---

possible investigative leads; and (3) to identify possible payments on a contract for murder.

In determining financial motive, the accounting analysis is directed primarily toward establishing any financial benefit to the accused as a result of that person's association with the murder victim. Benefit may be shown in various ways:

- Payments by the victim to the accused (extortion)
- Assets such as stocks, bonds, real estate, or collectibles transferred to the accused before or after the murder
- Insurance proceeds paid to the accused as beneficiary under a policy
- Other benefits, such as obtaining an interest in a business

When analyzing the financial affairs of the victim, the forensic accountant may seek to determine the following to assist a police investigation:

- The victim's business relationships and the identity of people with whom he had dealings
- Whether the victim had any debts and whether there is evidence to suggest that the victim was either resisting or had an inability to pay them
- Whether any debts were owed to the victim and whether there is evidence to suggest that the debtor was resisting payment on them
- Whether a financial motive can be eliminated as a direction to pursue in the investigation
- Whether other motives may exist

Regina v. Serplus   In *Regina v. William Serplus,* it was alleged that Serplus had murdered Muriel MacIntosh, an aging prostitute with whom he had lived for two years, for the purpose of appropriating certain of her assets to his own use. Those assets included a collection of Royal Doulton figurines valued at over $100,000, MacIntosh's private home in Toronto, which had an equity of $35,000, and certain jewelry items.

Serplus had met MacIntosh at the Warwick Hotel in Toronto during the fall of 1979. MacIntosh used the hotel as her point of solicitations. She and Serplus became friendly and MacIntosh confided that because of her age (54), she felt she couldn't work much longer as a prostitute. She wanted to become involved in another line of work. Serplus installed a security system in MacIntosh's home at 151 Gilmour, and shortly thereafter he moved in with her.

Throughout the next two years, Serplus derived a number of financial benefits from his relationship with MacIntosh. He apparently convinced her to invest her money in his new venture, the Triple S Holding Company. From time to time during their cohabitation, MacIntosh also advanced money to Serplus for either investment or other purposes. A schedule of such benefits and the documentation used as proof at the trial of William Serplus are shown in Exhibits 4.8, 4.9, 4.10, and 4.11.

Sometime during the evening of November 18, 1980, or the early morning of November 19, 1980, Muriel MacIntosh was beaten, tied, and strangled with an electrical cord. Friends told the police that she was missing, and about two months later her body was found in a garage at the rear of her home, frozen solid, inside a blue steamer trunk. She was dressed in a nightgown with a wool sweater over it, and around her upper body was a green Glad bag that matched a package of trash bags found in the kitchen of her residence. Paint on the electrical cord matched the paint in the back bedroom of the house, and the string used was matched to a ball of string in one of the kitchen cupboards.

Exhibit 4.8   Transactions in Schedules I, II, and III that Benefit William Serplus

Date		Schedule Number		Amount
1979				
December	27	I	CIBC cable of funds	$ 5,000.00
1980				
January	7	I	CIBC cable of funds	1,491.00
March	25	I	Cash value from insurance	1,700.00
September	17	I	CNCP money transfer	350.00
September	25	I	CNCP money transfer	165.00
June	27	II	Cash deposit to Triple S Holding	6,000.00
November	11	II	Equity transferred on 151 Gilmour Avenue	35,000.00
November	18	III	Cash from Royal Doulton figurines	550.00
November	20	III	Cash from Royal Doulton figurines	2,500.00
November	21	III	Cash from Royal Doulton figurines	9,225.00
				$61,981.00

On November 20, 1980, Serplus had rented a van and a hand dolly from Sommerville Rental at Bloor and High Park in Toronto. Around noon, two witnesses saw Serplus coming from 151 Gilmour Avenue with a blue steamer trunk on a hand dolly. The van was parked opposite the house. It appeared to the witnesses that Serplus was unable to load the trunk into the rear of the van. He was seen wheeling the trunk north on Gilmour Avenue and around the corner toward the alleyway leading to the garage at the rear of 151 Gilmour. The Canadian Centre for Forensic Sciences found blood and paint from the steamer trunk on the hand dolly. On that same day, Serplus received $2,500 in cash from Charlton's as a partial payment on the Royal Doulton collection of figurines.

On Friday, November 21, 1980, Serplus went to Ivan's Jewelry Store on Bloor Street West and spoke with Teresa Bellovits, the owner of the store. He ordered a wedding ring he said was for a niece who was getting married in the States. He also purchased a Bulova wristwatch for himself. He showed Bellovits seven rings he had in his possession and a very expensive watch he was trying to sell. Bellovits purchased two of the rings and a set of earrings from Serplus for $3,500.

On November 22, 1980, Serplus met with a Mr. Cross from Charltons and was paid $9,225 as the final installment for the Royal Doulton collection. Serplus later went to his office and showed his secretary the money. That evening Serplus met Bellovits for supper and then went back to her house and spent the night.

Exhibit 4.9　Documentation of Transactions that Benefit William Serplus

Date		
1979		
December 27	A Canadian Imperial Bank of Commerce payment by cable #CT0270007 in the amount of Canadian $5,000.00 from Miss Muriel Macintosh is paid to the benefit of William Serplus via Canadian Imperial Bank of Commerce, Nassau, Bahamas.	$5,000.00
1980		
January 7	A Canadian Imperial Bank of Commerce payment by cable #CT0270008 in the amount of Canadian $1,491.00 from Miss Muriel Macintosh is paid to the benefit of William Serplus via Canadian Imperial Bank of Commerce, Nassau, Bahamas.	1,491.00
March 25	Independent Order of Foresters check #1-0152186 in the amount of $1,700.00 is payable to the order of John McCrady. The back of the check bears an endorsement by a John McCrady and a bank stamp dated March 26, 1980, indicating a deposit to Royal Bank account #5921028 in the name of William Serplus. The Royal Bank statement for account #5921028 in the name of William Serplus indicates a deposit of $1,700.00.	1,700.00
September 17	CNCP money transfer #X4950475 in the amount of Canadian $350.00 is made by Muriel Macintosh payable to William Serplus, Scranton, PA.	350.00
September 25	CNCP money transfer #X4951019 in the amount of Canadian $165.00 is made by Muriel Macintosh payable to William Serplus, Scranton, PA.	165.00

A week later on November 29, 1980, Serplus married a school teacher in Scranton, Pennsylvania. They honeymooned in Puerto Rico, and on their return to Scranton lived together in her apartment until his arrest. Meanwhile, in Toronto, several of Muriel MacIntosh's friends contacted the police to file a missing person report. On December 30, 1980, the police received a call from a man who identified himself as William Serplus calling from New York City. He informed the officer that MacIntosh had gone to the East Coast to visit her brother. He also said that he would be in Toronto January 6 and would come to see the officer on January 7. He failed to show up. The police arrested him a few days later. He was subsequently tried and convicted of homicide.

Exhibit 4.10 Documentation Regarding 151 Gilmour Avenue, Toronto, Ontario

Date		

<u>1980</u>

June	19	A real estate appraiser's report indicates an appraised value for the land and building at 151 Gilmour Avenue of an amount of $70,000.00.
June	27	A Muriel Macintosh obtains a mortgage in the amount of $35,000.00 from the Premier Trust Company secured by the Gilmour Avenue property.
June	27	A "Statement of Trust Distribution" prepared by Nakelsky, Barrister and Solicitor, sets out the disbursement of the $35,000.00 mortgage proceeds notes "paid to Muriel Grace Macintosh $9,839.13."
June	27	A trust check #4078 for $9,839.13, drawn on the account of David Nakelsky, Barrister and Solicitor, is issued to the order of Muriel Macintosh. The back of the check bears the endorsement Muriel Macintosh. The deposit of this check could not be identified in any of the known bank accounts of Muriel Macintosh.
June	27	A Guaranty Trust deposit slip for account #900357 in the name of Triple S Holding Company indicates a deposit of $6,000.00 cash composed of six $1,000.00 bills. A review of the accounts payable listing and the bank statement in the name of Triple S Holding Company appears to suggest that the funds were applied to cover the following disbursements: $6,000.00

Sources:

June 24	Beginning bank balance	$ 153.05
June 27	Deposit	6,000.00
		$6,153.05

Applications:

June 30	Cash (June 30)	$2,000.00
June 30	The Bay (June 28)	300.00
July 3	Cash (July 3)	500.00
July 3	Public Optical (June 27)	40.50
July 3	Noia Tax & Accounting Services re rent (July 1)	185.00
July 3	Public Optical (June 27)	76.50
July 10	Cash (July 4)	500.00
July 10	Toronto Hydro (June 25)	25.19
July 15	Cash (July 14)	1,500.00
July 15	Ind. Order of Foresters (July)	119.52
July 15	S/C	1.28
July 15	Ending bank balance	905.06
		$6,153.05

Exhibit 4.10   (*Continued*)

Date

1980 (*Continued*)		
November 11	A deed of land indicates a conveyance by Muriel Macintosh of the property identified as 151 Gilmour Avenue to Triple S Holding Company Limited in consideration for "monies paid or to be paid in cash $35,000.00," with a further notation "gift from shareholder to corporation." It would appear that the amount of $35,000.00 represents the difference between the appraisal value of the property and the amount of the existing mortgage with Premier Trust Company.	$35,000.00
November 12	Triple S Holding Company Limited is incorporated, with William Serplus noted as the company's first director and shareholder, holding 304,000 shares.	
1980		
November 17	Charlton International Publishing Inc. purchase order #NP1390 indicates a purchase from William Serplus of Royal Doulton figurines for $11,725.00. Notations on this document indicate payment in cash as follows:	

	November 20, 1980	$ 2,500.00	$ 2,500.00
	November 22, 1980	9,225.00	9,225.00
		$11,725.00	

November 18	Charlton International Publishing Inc. purchase order #NP7108 indicates the purchase of "6 figurines" for $550.00.	550.00
November 25	A loan ledger of the First National Bank, Dunmore, PA indicates a loan of $3,000.00 granted to William Serplus and bears the notation: "$9000 Canadian money collateral."	

Arson for Profit

Arson for profit and planned bankruptcy share some similar characteristics. In both situations, business problems exist and are acknowledged to exist by management. Arson, like planned bankruptcy, can become the means for making the best of a bad situation.

The role of the forensic accountant in arson-related matters is to determine the present business position of the company and its owners. Although

Exhibit 4.11   Documentation on the Royal Doulton Collection

Date		
1980		
May	14	A Tippet—Richardson Limited storage order form in the name of Mr. M. Constantineau c/o Miss Muriel Macintosh indicates the storage of 200 pieces of Royal Doulton and an insurance value of $100,000.00.
June	2	A Tippet—Richardson Limited invoice #3962 to Mr. M. Constantineau makes reference to nine large china packs.
September	30	A Tippet—Richardson Limited document indicates delivery of the nine cartons to Miss Muriel Macintosh at 151 Gilmour Avenue in Toronto with the move to occur on October 2, 1980.
November	11	A document signed Miss Muriel Grace Macintosh under the date of November 12, 1980, states in part, "I, Muriel Grace Macintosh, hereby do assign to be used for capitalization, Triple S Holding Co. Ltd. for one share, at no par value, Two Hundred and Twenty-five Thousand Dollars of Royal Doulton figurines . . ." Listed thereafter are the names of the Royal Doulton figurines collection.

the financial position may have a considerable bearing on motive, motive is better understood in the context of the business itself and the owners through a review of all aspects of the operations and ownership of the business. Accordingly, it is usually appropriate to obtain as much background information as possible. A starting point might be the date of acquisition of an established business or the commencement date of a new business venture. A review of the annual financial statements and associated working papers since acquisition may disclose the company's yearly performance and any underlying business problems.

Any review of the status of a business must be objective. It should identify not only matters unfavorable to management and the owners of the company, but also matters that are favorable. The unfavorable matters may well be obvious (steady decline in sales, worsening creditor relations, or a significant withdrawal of funds immediately before the fire). On the other hand, the owner may have put a substantial amount of his or her own money into the business shortly before the fire.

A review of the recent court cases shows that the main characteristics to consider and establish as evidence of arson are:

- Ownership
- Final motive

- Existence of an insurance policy
- The establishment of exclusive opportunity
- The origin of the fire as incendiary

Accountants can assist with investigation of the first three of these issues and, in particular, ownership and financial motive. They can analyze information from several sources to construct a chronology of the financial records of the owner, the business, and third parties; and demonstrate the company's position at the time of the fire compared to earlier periods. The initial sources of documents are the financial and accounting records of the business that were not destroyed. Beyond this, the accountant should seek information from others directly or indirectly connected with the business. Such sources may include the company's banker, lawyer, accountant, customers, suppliers, insurers, and government agencies and realtors. Business owners should always be given the opportunity to volunteer any personal or business records they might have.

Key questions forensic accountants should consider and documents they should examine are:

- Who maintained the accounting records?
- What accounting records were kept that would have been available if not destroyed in the fire?
- What is the ownership structure and form of organization?
- Is the financial position of the owner solid? How about the entity itself?
- Does the business support the owner?
- Does the owner support the business?
- Has the owner had any past connection with failed business ventures?
- What is the history and pattern of earnings?
- Could ownership benefit from "selling out" to the insurance company?
- Did any significant events relating to the owner or the business occur at or around the time of the fire?
- Who are the major suppliers and what were the business's relations with them?
- Who are the major customers and what were the business's relations with them?
- Who are the bankers and what were the business's relations with them?
- Who is the external accountant?
- Who is the corporate solicitor?
- Has the business recently been offered for sale or had negotiations to sell that failed?
- Have there been any recent changes in insurance coverage?

Third party documents that should be sought include:

- Filings for incorporation, partnership, or assumed names
- Deeds, mortgages, and liens on real estate
- Chattel mortgage filings
- Accountant's working paper files
- Tax returns
- Correspondence with customers and suppliers
- Bank credit files
- Credit files from other creditors
- Bank statements, deposit slips, credit/debit memos (paper or microfiche records)
- Bank statements and canceled checks not mailed out
- Payroll information from employees
- Attorney's closing files and trust ledger sheets (escrow accounts)
- Real estate listings

Commercial Bribery (Secret Commissions)

Simply defined, secret commissions (or bribery) represent payments or the provision of goods, services, advantage, or benefit of any kind in return for actual or perceived advantage, benefit, or preferential treatment. The relevant section of the Criminal Code of Canada (383) does not require that a secret commission be given; it need only be offered or demanded. (Cases cited herein are violations of Canadian law but typical of U.S. cases, as well.) In any event, essentially two parties are involved: the payor and the recipient. The payor, through actual or potential relationships with the recipient's principal (employer), has or wishes to obtain a benefit, advantage, or preferential treatment. For example, Company A (the payor) wishes to sell its product to Company B (the principal). The recipient is a person in a position of authority or influence in the affairs of the principal (employer), or is perceived to be in such a position. The payor wishes to obtain the benefit of preferential treatment through the recipient. The recipient may be a senior officer, a purchasing manager, or someone with control over company assets, including their acquisition or disposal.

Many companies today issue codes of ethics to which employees must adhere. Employees usually must acknowledge these by signing a copy. These codes often prohibit the employees from accepting gifts and gratuities, or permit them to accept only those below a certain value. Employees may also be prohibited from taking actions that constitute a conflict with the employer's interests.

The payor may rationalize the offer or payment of a secret commission as necessary to obtain new business or to maintain the status quo in existing business relationships. Thus, the payor may view the transaction as being in the normal course of business. The recipient will rationalize receipt of the payment, especially if he or she had recently been denied a promotion or pay raise. The secret commission may be part of a larger criminal act. A secret commission may be offered or paid to gain the cooperation or acquiescence of the recipient so that a fraud can be perpetrated on the recipient's principal.

The secret commission may be a straightforward cash transaction directly between the payor and the recipient, or goods and services such as travel or gifts, at no cost or reduced cost. The commission could also be paid indirectly through related companies or businesses owned by the payor and/or recipient, often in foreign jurisdictions. The indirect route is taken to lend the appearance of legitimacy or to disguise the transaction.

Investigative accountants must resolve several issues. They must:

- Determine the nature of the relationship between the payor and the recipient and the principal. This is crucial to establishing the motive for paying the alleged secret commission.
- Determine the recipient's relationship with the principal and with the alleged payor, to establish whether and how the recipient could influence the affairs of the principal.
- Identify all related companies or businesses of the payor and the recipient. The payor may not necessarily be the person or company receiving the advantage, benefit, or preferential treatment the recipient grants; it may be a subsidiary company. Also, the recipient may not receive the secret commission directly.
- Determine the form and the purpose of the alleged secret commission. Usually, this involves reviewing the accounting and banking records of both the payor and the recipient.

The accounting records are extremely important when investigating the issues discussed earlier. The investigative accountant can assist in several ways, including the following:

- Examine the financial records of the payor and the principal to establish the nature of the relationships (e.g., supplier/customer) and the extent of their dealings. The records may disclose the bid process or other purchasing process.
- Investigate the personal financial affairs of the recipient to help establish a motive. Analysis of the records may help to establish a life-style inconsistent with income and hence a need for personal gain.

- Establish whether the recipient has any power to authorize transactions, and what the power is. He or she may be authorized to sign checks, authorize purchases, or grant credit; for example, up to a certain limit. Has the limit been strictly observed?
- Uncover loans or advances related to the principal or to the payor by examining audit work and tax returns.
- Establish whether the alleged secret commission takes the form of cash or payments to the benefit of the recipient (e.g., travel, car, etc.). The books of account of the payor or of the appropriate related company will have to be reviewed for supporting documentation, such as checks or supplier invoices. The review should also disclose how the payor recorded such payments.

For example, if the payment is recorded as an expense, the auditor will:

1. Establish the nature of the expense (e.g., promotion, travel, etc.) and whether such payments reflect the normal course of business or indicate an unusual transaction.
2. Obtain documents such as an invoice, purchase order, contract, or shipping document that describes the goods or services being paid for.

If the payment is recorded as a loan to the recipient, the investigator should consider the following:

1. What was the purpose of the loan?
2. Does a promissory note exist?
3. Has any interest been charged on the loan, and has any interest been collected?
4. What are the terms of repayment, if any, and have any payments been made?
5. If the loan has been repaid, was a check presented for payment, and did it properly clear the banking system?

If the alleged secret commission is in the form of cash, recipients' bank records should be reviewed to identify, if possible, unaccountable deposits to their accounts. It would also be useful to review the recipients' known assets. How and when were they acquired and what documentation is available in support? It is possible that payment was made to a bank account in a foreign jurisdiction.

The alleged secret commission may appear to be a normal business transaction for normal business purposes. However, the substance of the transaction must be determined. In addition, does the alleged secret commission coincide with an event or transaction that, because of the relationship between the payor and the recipient and his or her principal, results in an actual or potential benefit?

Red Flags in Commercial Billing   The accountant should be aware of those situations that might disclose possible kickbacks. Here are some examples:

- Unaccounted-for cash; assets such as a house, cottage, or car; the recipient's life-style—expensive vacations, gambling.
- Unusual transactions or unusual changes in the activity of the *principal* of the recipient: Unusual transactions are those that deviate from normal business practice or price; changes might include a switch of major suppliers for which price or quality cannot account.
- Payments to a business or company the recipient owns or controls, or to a non-arm's-length partner, such as a spouse.
- Acts by employees beyond the scope of their normal responsibilities, to approve or influence the approval of transactions.

Regina v. Campbell and Mitchell   At a social function in 1983, the director of a major retailer was told that there were possible irregularities in the retailer's purchasing function. The director was told that certain toy suppliers were having considerable difficulty in presenting their products for consideration by the retailer.

As a result of the retailer's preliminary investigations, it was suspected that Campbell, its buyer for toys and related products, possibly had an ownership interest in companies that sold products to the retailer. These companies were apparently operated by Mitchell, a supplier of toys and an agent for several toy manufacturers.

Police searches were executed on Campbell's office at the company, the business premises of Mitchell's companies, Campbell's personal residence, Mitchell's personal residence, and the offices of the various accountants and lawyers related by Mitchell's companies.

Campbell had signed annual conflict-of-interest statements that did not disclose transactions with or ownership interest in companies that dealt with the retailers. Twelve companies were owned to some extent by some combination of Campbell and his wife and Mitchell and his wife. These companies reported approximately $6 million in sales for the period from 1976 to 1983. More than 50 percent of this amount was attributable to transactions with the retailer. Campbell and his wife received over $500,000 and Mitchell and his wife received over $700,000 in cash and benefits from Mitchell companies.

The report of the forensic accountant, supported by multivolume briefs of documents, included:

- Corporate structure charts that outlined the ownership history and relationships between the Mitchell companies
- Summarized chronologies by each individual Mitchell company outlining corporate ownership, transactions with the retailer, and benefits received by Campbell and Mitchell and their wives

The defense counsel concentrated on the following activities:

1. Confirming that the books and records of the Mitchell companies were reasonably maintained and complete.
2. Confirming that the wives of Campbell and Mitchell were inactive in the operations of the Mitchell companies.
3. Confirming that the income and benefits those persons received from the Mitchell companies were properly and fully disclosed in their personal tax returns.
4. Establishing that the number of companies and the changing interrelationships were primarily for tax planning purposes.
5. Establishing that there was no evidence that Mitchell knew that Campbell had not disclosed to the retailer Campbell's ownership interest and benefits related to the Mitchell companies.
6. Establishing that there was no evidence of any financial loss to the retailer related to its transactions with the Mitchell companies.
7. Establishing that Campbell was not active in the Mitchell companies.
8. Establishing that the buyers reporting to Campbell, not Campbell himself, were responsible for the retailer purchases from the Mitchell companies.
9. Establishing that the financial records indicated that Campbell had little responsibility for purchases the retailer made from the Mitchell companies on reorders rather than initial orders.

The trial judge concluded that Campbell and Mitchell were guilty as charged. The judge outlined the rationale for the law related to secret commissions. In brief, it is to protect the principal (in this case, the retailer) from secret and dishonest acts of its agents (in this case, Campbell). The judge concluded that a principal-and-agent relationship clearly existed in this case. The judge then concentrated on the following matters:

1. The offense requires that benefits/considerations pass from the offeror to the acceptor in a corrupt or *mala fide* manner. (In this matter the Court must conclude whether corrupt intent existed, if only "reasonable inference" is submitted as evidence.)

2. There was no direct evidence that the benefits were passed corruptly. All consideration and benefits were recorded in the books and records of the Mitchell companies and in the personal tax returns of the Campbells and Mitchell.

3. Further, there was no direct evidence that Campbell routed the retailer's business to the Mitchell companies. Also, there was no direct evidence that Mitchell knew of Campbell's nondisclosure to the retailer of his conflicts of interest.

But the trial judge concluded that Campbell's opportunity and motive did support the reasonable inference that Campbell routed the retailer's business to the Mitchell-related companies. The trial judge further concluded that Campbell's and Mitchell's long-standing social and business relationships, and the nature and extent of business the Campbell–Mitchell companies ·had done with the retailer, allowed the reasonable inference that Mitchell understood Campbell's role and responsibilities as the retailer. Together with Campbell's nondisclosure to the retailer of his conflict of interest, these reasonable inferences led the trial judge to conclude that benefits were passed to Campbell in a corrupt or *mala fide* manner.

Chapter 5

Prevention and Detection of Fraud

Preventing fraud is what this book is about. Our primary goal is to reduce the number of accounting-type frauds. Our secondary goal is to reduce the amount of the losses attributable to such frauds. With those goals in mind, we offer the following "invitations to fraud" for whatever instructive value the list contains.

INVITATIONS TO CORPORATE FRAUD, THEFT, AND EMBEZZLEMENT

- Make profit the only corporate objective and the only criterion for performance appraisal.
- Create a corporate culture in which everyone knows the cost of everything but not the value of integrity.
- Create a corporate culture in which profit and economic incentives are the only motivators.
- Fail to establish and to communicate an effective code for corporate conduct.
- Create strong and authoritarian management controls but do not monitor them for compliance.
- Ignore complaints from customers, stockholders, or employees.
- Fail to monitor management override of internal controls.
- Make internal communication a one-way process—top down.
- Fail to enforce or monitor non-arm's-length transactions.
- Ignore the importance of effective personnel policies.
- Assume that competitors are less than ethical, in order to rationalize a competitive behavior as fair and justified.

LANDMARK CASES IN CORPORATE FRAUD

Internal Environment Red Flags

What factors in an organization's internal environment lead to fraudulent behavior by executives, middle managers, and lower-level employees? Let us examine the following cases as examples:

1. *SEC v. McCormick & Co.,* Civil Action No. 82-3614 (D.D.C. 1982)
2. *SEC v. AM International, Inc.,* Civil Action No. 83-1526, (D.D.C. May 2, 1983), Litigation Release No. 9980, (February 27, 1984)
3. *SEC v. U.S. Surgical Corp.,* Civil Action No. 84-0589, (D.D.C. 1984), Litigation Release No. 10293, (February 27, 1984)

In the *McCormick* case, the Securities and Exchange Commission's complaint alleged that McCormick inflated the reported current earnings by deferring recognition of various expenses and increasing reported revenues; this was achieved by accounting for goods ready for shipment as current sales, even though they were not shipped until later. These irregularities occurred in autonomous divisions and involved a number of employees in middle-management roles. These employees believed the improper practices were the only way to achieve the profit goals set arbitrarily by a distant, centralized corporate management. Several employees said they viewed their activities as a team effort, all for the benefit of the company. There was no evidence that corporate funds were diverted for the personal benefit of any McCormick employee.

In *AM International,* the commission alleged that AMI grossly overstated its results of operations, assets, and shareholders' equity, understated liabilities, and misstated statements of changes in financial position.

How did AMI accomplish this? Inventory losses were deferred and ending inventory overstated; books were kept open after cutoff dates to increase reported sales and earnings; sales were recorded although products were not shipped; sales were inflated by deliberate double-billing; operating leases were recorded as sales; allowances for losses were arbitrarily reduced without any basis whatsoever; sales were recorded although the products were shipped only to branch offices and a public warehouse, not to customers; accounting policies were changed to increase earnings without disclosure of the changes in policy; known errors that caused increased earnings were ignored; intercompany accounts were out of balance and the differences arbitrarily reclassified as inventories; known inaccuracies in books and records were not investigated, let alone resolved; costs of sales were manipulated; and accounts payable simply were not recorded.

The organizational environment aired in the AMI complaint made a highly negative impression on the commission. Two excerpts from the SEC complaint exemplify this environment:[1]

> During the course of the 1980 fiscal year AM International's financial position deteriorated and its management then applied increasing pressure on the divisions to meet performance goals. Such pressure consisted of, among other means, threatened dismissals, actual dismissals, and character attacks on certain of the division's senior management. This pressure was in turn applied by the division's senior management to middle management. These pressures were motivated in part by the desire of AMI to have a public offering of its securities in the fall of 1980, and the belief that a pretax profit of $10 to $12 million for the 1980 fiscal year was necessary in order to proceed with the offering. . . .
>
> In response to the pressure . . . various divisions . . . engaged in widespread and pervasive accounting irregularities . . . in order to present results of operations which conformed to budget performance objectives. Throughout the 1980 fiscal year AMI's corporate headquarters learned of many instances of accounting irregularities employed by its divisions. Despite this knowledge, AMI continued to pressure its divisions to meet projected operating results.

The Commission's complaint in *U.S. Surgical* alleged that Surgical:

1. Issued falsified purchase orders to vendors who, in turn, submitted untrue invoices so that Surgical's reported cost of parts was decreased and its reported costs of materials was improperly capitalized by over $4 million.
2. Shipped significant quantities of unordered products to customers and recorded them as sales.
3. Improperly treated shipments on consignments to its dealers, salespeople, and certain foreign entities as sales, resulting in a cumulative overstatement of income by over $2 million.
4. Improperly failed to write off assets that could not be located or had been scrapped, and capitalized certain operating costs as overhead, increasing earnings by millions of dollars.
5. Improperly capitalized approximately $4 million of legal costs, purportedly for the defense of certain patents, when those costs did not relate to the defense of patents but were recurring operating expenses.

Internal Environment Red Flags

1. Do employees have an economic reason to cheat?
   Are salaries and fringe benefits equitable and competitive with other similar firms in the same market?

Are pressures for production and profitable performance so great that people are burning out or becoming disgruntled?

Are employee evaluations and salary reviews based on fair and objective criteria?

Are promotions based on merit and contribution, and administered fairly, impartially, and openly?

Are job-related goals and objectives imposed on subordinates rather than negotiated with them?

2. Does the company suffer from a "we–they" syndrome: Management versus nonmanagement personnel or middle management versus top management?

3. Do conflicts abound among the top-management group over issues that involve corporate philosophy, purpose, direction, or ethics?

4. Is there evidence of spite, hate, hostility, or jealousy among the firm's top-management group?

5. Do employees feel oppressed, abused, exploited, or neglected by top management?

6. What is the company's past history with respect to:

Labor-management relations?

Turnover of top executives?

Moonlighting and conflict of interest by employees and executives?

Vandalism, theft, and sabotage by employees?

Corruption of customers?

Corruption by vendors or competitors?

Corruption of labor leaders, regulatory authorities, and political officials?

Association of executives with organized-crime figures?

High living by executives?

Lack of concern for truth in advertising or marketing its products or services?

Convictions for business-related crimes?

7. What is the history of the firm and the industry regarding regulatory compliance?

8. What is the past, current, and future profitability of the firm?

9. Are there litigation and complaints pending against the firm by regulatory authorities, vendors, customers, creditors, and competitors?

HOW CAN MANAGEMENT AND CORPORATE FRAUD BE DETECTED?

Detecting fraud is a matter of acknowledging:

1. That fraud exists
2. That any organization can become either a victim of fraud or a perpetrator of fraud
3. That certain weaknesses in internal controls and human character can be conducive to fraud.
4. That certain tests of internal controls and tests of the organization's motivational environment can provide some insight on the possibility of fraud in that environment.
5. That the key to fraud auditing is training the mind to see both the doughnut and the hole.

The hole we speak of consists of errors and irregularities, but of the type that seem to be beyond the normal bounds of human error and inconsistency. Perhaps "oddity" would be a better word to describe the anomalies one looks for in fraud auditing.

An oddity is something different from what is expected as to time, place, personality, or amount. The difference need not be large. An accumulation of small differences is often the very essence of a sophisticated large fraud; i.e., the "salami-slicing" technique in computer fraud, in which a programmer instructs the computer to shave a dime or dollar from everyone's paycheck and add the total amount to his or her own paycheck.

The fraud auditor concentrates on small differences, whereas the financial auditing focuses on and detects large differences. We call those differences substantial, as though an exponential accumulation of small differences were insubstantial. Scientific insight has always depended on small exceptions and irregularities. In essence we might say that fraud auditing deals more with exceptions than general rules.

Here, then, are a few exceptions fraud auditors should look for:

1. Transactions that are odd as to:

    Time (of day, week, month, year, or season)

    Frequency (too many, too few)

    Places (too far, too near, and too "far out")

    Amount (too high, too low, too consistent, too alike, too different)

Parties or personalities (related parties, oddball personalities, strange and estranged relationships between parties, management performing clerical functions)

2. Internal controls that are unenforced or too often compromised by higher authorities

3. Employee motivation, morale, and job satisfaction levels that are chronically low

4. A corporate culture and reward system that supports unethical behavior toward employees, customers, competitors, lenders, and shareholders

Fraud abounds in environments in which there is low regard for truth, justice, and fair dealing, and high regard for monetary rewards and personal vanity.

TELLTALE SIGNS OF MANAGEMENT AND CORPORATE FRAUD

In every case of management and corporate fraud, telltale signs of the fraud exist for some period of time before a third party detects or discloses it. These signs may be:

1. Significant observed changes from the defrauder's past behavior pattern.

2. Knowledge that the defrauder was undergoing emotional trauma in his or her home life or work life.

3. Knowledge that the defrauder was betting heavily, drinking heavily, had a very expensive social life, or was sexually promiscuous.

4. Knowledge that the defrauder was heavily in debt.

5. Audit findings deemed to be errors and irregularities that were considered immaterial at the time.

6. Knowledge that the company was having financial difficulties such as frequent cash-flow shortages, declining sales and/or net profits, and loss of market share.

7. Knowledge that management was showing increasing signs of incompetence; i.e., poor planning, organization, communication, controls, motivation, and delegation; management indecision and confusion about corporate mission, goals, and strategies; and management ignorance of conditions in the industry and in the general economy.

8. Substantial growth beyond the industry norm in regulated industries.

These precipitating or predisposing conditions and events are called, in crisis-management parlance, *prodromal* or warning signs. (The word, derived from the Greek for "running before," means "running in a precrisis mode.")

For example, when a major midwestern bank came close to failure a few years ago, there were some prodromal conditions extant before the bank had to be bailed out by the Federal Deposit Insurance Corporation (FDIC). One such event was the discovery by the bank's internal auditors that a bank officer, who had purchased $800 million in oil and gas loans from the Penn Square Bank, had received $565,000 in loans from Penn Square Bank. Was that a red flag, a prodromal event? It is alleged that the bank's top management was not overly concerned about that kind of evidence of impropriety. It issued only a reprimand, a mild rebuke, because the officer had also brought in a portfolio of loans that could earn a gross return rate of 20 percent—if the loans performed. Unfortunately, most of the loans had to be written off a short time later.

As can be seen, not dealing with indications of management fraud when they first surface does not end it. And not dealing with it promptly when indications do fully surface may be costly in terms of the cash loss and loss of corporate image. Indications that first appear as oddities, for example, should be assessed as possible fraud. One may be able to ensure against the cash loss itself, but the damage to the image of the company and its products and services may be irreparable, particularly if the company is in the financial services business where faith, confidence, and trust in the industry and institution are the critical factors for success.

One further bit of advice: Prodromal events can become a way out for a company's fidelity insurance underwriter. The company auditor may be accused of acquiescing by ignoring an indicator of fraud and not reporting it within the time specified in the policy. If the insurance company's position holds up in court, an employer may not be able to recover on the cash loss. If so, the corporation's image may be damaged even further; the stockholders may decide to sue for managerial negligence.

Badges of Top-Management Fraud

A review of behaviors of corporate defrauders leads us to suggest that top-management defrauders:

- Tend to have highly material personal values. Success to them means financial success, not professional recognition.
- Tend to treat people as objects, not individuals, and often as objects for exploitation.
- Are highly self-centered.

- Are often eccentric in the way they display their wealth or spend their money. They tend to be conspicuous consumers and often boast of the things they have acquired, the friends they have in high office, and all the fine places they have visited.
- Speak about their cunning achievements and winnings more than their losses.
- Appear to be reckless or careless with facts and often enlarge on them.
- Appear to be hard working, almost compulsive, but most of their time at work is spent in scheming and designing short cuts to get ahead or beat the competition.
- May gamble or drink a great deal.
- Buy expensive gifts for their families, usually to compensate for spending so little time with them.
- Are hostile to people who oppose their views. They feel exempt from accountability and controls because of their station or position.
- Create a great deal of turnover among their subordinates and often set off one subordinate against another.
- Play favorites among their subordinates, but the relationship can cool very quickly because a subordinate often falls from grace after one mistake, even an insignificant one.
- Manage by crisis more often that by objectives. They tend to drift with the times and have no long-range plans.
- Tend to override internal controls with impunity and argue forcefully for less formality in controls.
- Demand absolute loyalty from subordinates, but they themselves are loyal only to their own self-interests.
- Have few real friends within their own industry or company. Their competitors and colleagues often dislike them.

Badges of Lower-Level Fraud

The behavior descriptors just listed are symptomatic of top-management fraud. What about lower-level profit-centered managers? Are there any patterns of behavior at those levels? Yes. First, recall that subordinates tend to mimic the behaviors of their superiors. The preceding list of fraud badges is useful here, too. But lower-level defrauders have symptoms of their own as well. Here are some of the conditions found in them or their environment:

- Their superiors exert great pressure to achieve high performance—higher sales, lower costs, more profits. Top management tolerates no justification or excuse for less than expected or demanded sales, cost, and profit targets.

- Bonuses are tied to short-term performance levels and do not take into consideration economic or competitive realities.
- Internal controls are absent or loosely enforced.
- Management controls consist mainly of pressures for performance: "Make your numbers come out right or we'll get somebody else."
- Business ethics are subordinated to economic self-interest.
- Vendors and suppliers are squeezed for the last ounce of profitability in their goods, wares, and services.
- There is a great deal of confusion about duties and responsibilities among subordinates.
- A high level of hostility exists among subordinates and between lower-level managers and their line and staff superiors.
- They believe the present level of responsibility exceeds the original job description.

EMBEZZLEMENT: WOULD YOU KNOW ONE IF YOU SAW ONE?

Detecting embezzlement is possible (1) through the traditional control concepts of separation of duties and audit trails, (2) through periodic financial and operational audits, (3) by gathering intelligence on the life-styles and personal habits of employees, (4) through allegations and complaints of fellow employees, (5) by logging exceptions to prescribed controls and procedures, (6) by reviewing variances in operating performance expectations (standards, goals, objectives, budgets, and plans), (7) through the intuition of the embezzler's superiors, and (8) through generalized suspicion (neurotic paranoia).

As can be seen in the above list of embezzlement-detection techniques, some are proactive approaches and others are reactive. Proactive approaches include (1) adequate internal controls, (2) financial and operational audits, (3) intelligence gathering, (4) logging of exceptions, and (5) review of variances. Reactive approaches include (1) allegations and complaints, (2) intuition, and (3) suspicion. All have a place in the general framework of embezzlement prevention, but ideally we should focus more on the proactive approaches than the reactive, although it would seem that at present the reactive approaches are more commonly used.

Are there any other audit and investigative caveats to embezzlement? Yes, there are several others. First, embezzlers usually do not make one grand hit for a million dollars and then run away. They are not hit-and-run criminals as confidence men and women are. Their peculations very often go on for years and very often get larger and larger over time. Sometimes this increase is necessary to maintain the scheme.

Second, each embezzler has a pattern of theft that is somewhat unique but discernable to an experienced fraud auditor, for example, an account category that gets an inordinate amount of padding to cover up the loss; a particular step in the audit-trail procedures that often gets bypassed or overridden; a favorite customer supplier or contractor whose account balance is manipulated; or an input document that often is fabricated, counterfeited, or forged. Most long-term embezzlement schemes, after discovery, are found to be very simple. This is a reflection of the embezzler's knowledge of the accounting system and those who interface with it. Fraudulent-pattern recognition is the unique skill of a trained and experienced fraud auditor.

IS CORPORATE FRAUD CYCLICAL?

Every aspect of economic life seems to have a season, a cycle, or a wave. These variations in movement over time facilitate business planning and government economic policy. Although the highs and lows of such economic trends cannot be predicted precisely on a short-term basis, they can be predicted from a long-term perspective. For example, the general economy of any country (and perhaps the world) goes from periods of prosperity to crisis to liquidation to expansion to upswing and finally back to prosperity.

Does the economic cycle have any impact on the incidence of corporate fraud? Logic would dictate that it does. Corporate fraud, being mainly a manifestation of economic greed and need, may well follow a similar cycle. But does fraudulent conduct by corporate executives peak during good economic times or during bad times? The answer is, during both good and bad times.

Fraudulent conduct by corporate managers peaks at the top of an economic cycle, when it is greed-based and at the bottom of the economic cycle, when it is need-based.

CAN MANAGEMENT CONTROLS BECOME TOO MUCH OF A GOOD THING?

Establishing effective and efficient management controls is a matter of balancing costs against benefits. Tipping the balance to either extreme—overcontrol or undercontrol—is inefficient and ineffective. But the cost of implementing controls is far easier to calculate than the intended benefits of such controls, because costs tend to be quantitative whereas benefits tend to be qualitative.

Deciding how much control should be exercised in any organization is not a simple matter. Furthermore, both economic and behavior considerations must be weighed. Economic considerations include direct and consequential costs (acquisition, implementation, and maintenance costs). Behavioral considerations have to do with the impact controls may have on personal productivity. Do controls add to workers' burdens, impose additional or distasteful tasks, make them less efficient, more suspicious of others, less trusting, or less trusted? Do control costs have an impact on human performance and job satisfaction? Worse yet, do controls take on the form of absolute rules, prohibitions, and mandatory actions and thus discourage judgment and discretion? Slavish compliance is required when controls are designed and enforced irrationally, without need, and without consideration for the sensitivities of the people affected by them. Then controls become more honored in the breach than in the observance. Covert and overt resistance can follow. In fact, in some organizational settings, overcontrol often results in petty acts of fraud and thievery—such as lying on expense accounts and fudging performance data—as methods of rebellion.

How can one overcome resistance to or negative reactions to controls?

- Make sure that goals, objectives, and control standards are realistic, not impossible or improbable to achieve. Standards, goals, and objectives should be challenging but attainable with ordinary, not extraordinary, effort.
- Involve in the control-setting process the employees who will be bound by the standards.
- Install controls only where they are necessary for prudent management, and evaluate their continued need and enhancement periodically. The real enemies to good and effective controls are undercontrol and overcontrol.
- Tight controls are fine as long as their administration and monitoring are placed as far down in the organization as possible. (Otherwise, the brass gets too bogged down in detail and control trivia, and lower-level managers become more and more like police officers.)
- Give output controls a slight edge over behavior controls as methodologies (i.e., monitor the quantity and quality of output against the present standard). Behavior controls (i.e., personal observations) are best used when performance requirements are clear and generally known; here, surveillance is perceived as less obtrusive. In fact, if coupled with positive reinforcements, such surveillance can promote efficiency and motivation. So both output and behavior controls play important roles in achieving organizational objectives.
- New and better controls do not of themselves solve problems. But together with enlightened management, good administration, and intelligent interpretation, controls lead to efficient and effective operations.
- Controls can be of two types: before the fact and after the fact. Before-the-fact controls are intended to prevent problems from occurring. They pinpoint violations of established policies and procedures and spot errors in

input accuracy and validity. After-the-fact controls are intended to detect problems that may quickly grow out of control, and require immediate remedies.

- Finally, people comply with rules when they are fair, rational, and needed for orderly procedure.

THE CLASSIC APPROACHES TO THE REDUCTION OF EMPLOYEE THEFT, FRAUD, AND EMBEZZLEMENT

1. The *Directive* approach: "Don't steal. If you do and we catch you, you'll be fired."
2. The *Prevention* approach: Screen out the probable thieves by (1) using background checks (employment verification, criminal record, credit and reference checks), (2) polygraph examination, and (3) psychological testing for honesty and integrity.
3. The *Detection* approach: Set up accounting controls and internal audit procedures to periodically verify the legitimacy of transactions and to confirm the existence of assets.
4. The *Observation* approach: Monitor employee conduct, the level of stocks of valuable and portable goods, and inspect outgoing parcels.
5. The *Investigation* approach: Follow-up all allegations of theft and variances in inventories of goods, tools, materials, and supplies to determine the nature and extent of the loss and the likely culprits.
6. The *Insurance* approach: Buy enough fidelity insurance to cover the firm against substantial loss. (While this does not reduce employee theft, it softens the blow when losses occur.)

But even by adopting all the so-called classic approaches, employee theft may continue on a large scale. That seems to be the experience of many firms today. What other options are available? What can we do to minimize the incidence rate and amount of loss from employee thievery?

If classic approaches are not working, it may be that the problem is no longer of a classic type.

What has changed in the work environment is that workers want, and often demand, the following:

- More participation in decisions that affect their job roles
- Fair and equitable treatment and opportunities for promotion
- Important and meaningful work—freedom from drudgery
- A safe and healthy work environment

- Inclusion in the work group
- Interpersonal trust
- Respect and recognition

The implications of the new approach to employee theft-prevention process are simply these:

1. Most prevention efforts focus on building more accounting and access controls or physical security controls.
2. We are approaching the limits of technology in those fields.
3. Our only hope for securing company assets is to shift the concentration of effort and cost to decreasing the probability of theft and fraud. The technique for executing that strategy is to improve the company's motivational and ethical climate.

PREVENTING FRAUD IN PARTICULAR ACCOUNT CATEGORIES

Cash skimming, receivables lapping, and using fictional employees and vendors generally are low-level-employee frauds; early booking of sales, expense deferral, and inventory overstatement are generally the handiwork of senior management. All are detected through auditing tests and techniques but only if an auditor elects to employ them. Attitude or mind-set makes the difference between finding a fraud by audit design or finding it by accident.

The fraud auditor's mind-set, or mentality, suggests that fraud can be found if it is pursued vigorously enough. While fraudsters try to bury their trails or conceal their crimes, an astute fraud auditor can follow the trail like a bloodhound.

In time, all frauds are revealed by auditing techniques such as counting, confirmation, inspection, observation, comparison, inquiries, ratio analysis, account analysis, and internal control testing.

Mautz and Sharaf summarized the qualities of a prudent auditor as follows:[2]

A prudent practitioner (auditor) is assumed to have a knowledge of the philosophy and practice of auditing, to have the degree of training, experience, and skill common to the average independent auditor, to have the ability to recognize indications of irregularities, and to keep abreast of developments in the perpetration and detection of irregularities. Due audit care requires the auditor to acquaint himself with the company under examination . . . to review the method of internal control operating in the company . . . obtain any knowledge readily available which is pertinent to the accounting and financial problems of the company . . . be responsive to unusual events and unfamiliar circumstances, to persist until he has eliminated from his own mind any reasonable doubts he may have about the existence of material irregularities, and to exercise caution in instructing his assistants and reviewing their work.

If frauds don't surface from these auditing techniques, they may surface from such other things as allegations and complaints from credible sources, from self-disclosure of defrauders, or from whistle blowers and paid informers.

CASES[3]

Management Fraud Case

Case History   In 1987 a senior bank official in a Middle Eastern country discovered a trunk that his predecessor had left in the bank's vault. A note on the trunk said: "Open only in the event of my death." His suspicions aroused, the official opened it immediately. Within, he found reams of documents that included deposit slips to banks in Switzerland for enormous sums of money. Although he didn't understand to what the documents referred, the official was certain that a fraud of some nature had taken place. The bank, which was owned by the government, knew of our reputation through international contacts. We were retained to investigate.

Approach   The first task was to sort through the documentation in the trunk. Although it was incomplete, there was sufficient information to reconstruct what turned out to be a startling tale. Between 1972 and 1985, several trusted employees at the bank had defrauded the government of approximately half a billion dollars. Their method was simple. A prominent government official, wanting to capitalize on the tremendous riches generated by the oil boom, persuaded the individuals to invest large sums of money on the government's behalf. They did so quite successfully and reported a most acceptable rate of return. But, unbeknownst to him, they were skimming off 2 percent of the interest for themselves. (When 2 percent of the interest translated to half a billion dollars, consider the value of the investments!)

The identity of those involved—apart from the bank official who had left the incriminating trunk—was determined by tracing the flight of the funds. The documentation led us to two banks in the United Kingdom, one in New York, and eight in Switzerland. A check of the banks revealed that the bank of England, in which large sums had been deposited, was owned by a family prominent in the Middle Eastern country. Further investigation revealed that the family had previously owned the bank where the documents had been found. (The government had purchased the bank after it had fallen into financial difficulty.) We also discovered that a firm of chartered accountants had prepared a net worth of the family in 1985. Among their findings were enormous unexplained management fees coming in from overseas. The final piece of incriminating evidence was that some of the diverted funds were traced to a man who was the personal secretary of the head of the family.

Results   On the basis of our report, a civil suit was launched against the family in England. At the time of writing, it appeared that at least £100 million will be recovered. Two members of the family were under house arrest in the Middle East, while a third was in self-exile.

A Graphic Conviction

Case History   Wealthy nursing home owner Helmuth Buxbaum of London, Ontario, was charged in 1984 with having contracted for the murder of his wife. Robert Barrett, a heroin junkie with a criminal record, told police that Buxbaum—who was mired in a world of drugs and prostitutes—had paid him approximately $35,000 in three installments to commit the crime. Buxbaum admitted to giving Barrett money for drugs but denied having paid him to kill. Because Barrett's credibility as a witness was open to challenge from the defense, the police believed that a conviction could not be obtained without financial evidence to corroborate his story. We were retained to provide that evidence.

Methodology   Buxbaum was a millionaire and paid cash for most of his illicit activities. We hypothesized that if Barrett's story was accurate—if he had received three large payments on three specific occasions—then supporting evidence would show up in Buxbaum's banking and other cash-source records. But if Buxbaum's explanation was truthful, his cash flow would be normal on those dates.

We examined Buxbaum's bank withdrawals, instant teller transactions (which are stored on computer tape), cash withdrawals on credit cards, and sale of gold for cash over the seven-month period in question. Sufficient documents were available to conclude that Buxbaum had spent between $1,000 and $4,000 in cash a week during that time. However, on the three occasions when Barrett said he received the large payments (approximately $15,000 in the third week of May 1984; $15,000 in the first week of July 1984, and $5,000 the week after), the cash withdrawals were significantly higher. On all three occasions, Buxbaum withdrew more than enough cash to cover the size of the payments described by Barrett.

Results   We prepared a simple graph that showed the three periods when large cash amounts were withdrawn, and how those periods corresponded to Barrett's testimony. The graph was presented to the jury as part of our expert testimony. Helmuth Buxbaum was convicted of first degree murder and sentenced to life imprisonment.

Nonprofit Dancing Dollars

Case History　In 1986, Cathy Towers was appointed executive director of Performance Partners, a nonprofit organization that represented various dance and theatrical groups within her province. Her employment letter of agreement stated she would be paid an annual salary of $30,000. Her position also gave her signing authority for the organization's annual $150,000 budget, which was funded by the Provincial Granting Agency (PGA).

Two years after her appointment, Towers and several other directors of Performance were replaced in what was described as a "palace revolt." The new board, on examining the books, found that there was an accumulated deficit of approximately $100,000. They retained our services to investigate what had taken place.

Methodology　An examination of Performance's bank account showed a large number of checks made out to Cathy Towers. The total far exceeded her annual salary. We also saw that bills from one year were actually paid from the budget of the following year. This was possible because Performance received its annual budget in quarterly advances. This had implications beyond its role in building up the $100,000 deficit, for under the agreement with PGA, Performance had to return any money not spent on *authorized* activities from each budget. Since the 1988 budget had been used to pay bills from 1987, and therefore, technically, the money had not been spent on authorized 1988 activities, theoretically, Performance could be asked to return $150,000 to PGA (although PGA had not indicated that this would happen). We also noted that no source deductions for employees (such as UIC or CPP) had been paid during Tower's tenure. If Revenue Canada performed an audit, Performance would be liable for whatever was owed.

When Towers was confronted with this information, she said that she had taken the money as payment for overtime and expenses. We calculated that she would have had to work 16 hours a day, 365 days a year, to account for the overtime being claimed.

In our report, we recommended that Performance Partners pursue remedies to recover its losses, and we presented a series of controls that could be implemented to prevent similar losses in the future.

Results　The matter was reported to the Canadian Royal Mounted Police, which declined to press charges because Tower's contract did not prohibit her from using the budget at her discretion, Performance Partners did not have the resources to proceed with civil litigation. However, PGA launched a civil action, which at the time of writing, was still in process.

REFERENCES

1. *SEC vs. AM International, Inc.,* Civil Action No. 83-1256, D.D.C. (May 2, 1983) Litigation Release No. 9980, February 27, 1984.
2. Mautz and Sharaf, *The Philosophy of Auditing,* American Accounting Association, 1961, p. 140.
3. Lindquist, Avey, Macdonald, Baskerville Inc., Toronto and Washington, D.C., (May 1994).

Chapter 6

Fraud Risk Assessment

The probability of fraud, theft, or embezzlement in any work environment is a product of the personality of the executive and employees, the working conditions, the controls, and the level of honesty therein.

Internal factors that enhance the probability of fraud, theft, and embezzlement include:

I. Inadequate rewards
   A. Pay, fringe benefits, recognition, job security, job responsibilities

II. Inadequate management controls
   A. Failure to articulate and communicate minimum standards of performance and personal conduct
   B. Ambiguity in job roles, duties, responsibilities, and areas of accountability

III. Lack of or inadequate reinforcement and performance feedback mechanisms
   A. Failure to counsel and take administrative action when performance levels or personal behavior falls below acceptable standards

IV. Inadequate support
   A. Lack of adequate resources to meet mandated standards

V. Inadequate operational reviews
   A. Lack of timely or periodic audits, inspections, and follow-through to ensure compliance with company goals, priorities, policies, procedures, and governmental regulations

VI. Lax enforcement of disciplinary rules
   A. Ambiguous corporate social values and ethical norms

VII. Fostering hostility
   A. Promoting or permitting destructive interpersonal or interdepartmental competitiveness

VIII. Other motivational issues
   A. Inadequate orientation and training on legal, ethical, and security issues

    B. Inadequate company policies with respect to sanctions for legal, ethical, and security breaches

    C. Failure to monitor and enforce policies on honesty, loyalty, and fairness

    D. General job-related stress or anxiety

Internal factors that reduce the probability of fraud, theft and embezzlement include:

I. Prevention measures
    A. Internal accounting controls
        1. Separation of duties
        2. Rotation of duties
        3. Periodic internal audits and surprise inspections
        4. Development and documentation of policies, procedures, systems, programs, and program modifications
    B. Computer access controls
        1. Identification defenses
        2. Authentication defenses
        3. Establishment of authorization by levels of security

II. Detection measures
    A. Logging of exceptions
        1. Out of sequence, out of priority, and aborted runs and entries
        2. Transactions that are too high, too low, too many, too few, too unusual (odd times, odd places, odd people)
        3. Attempted access beyond authorization level
        4. Repeated improper attempts to gain access (wrong identification, wrong password)
    B. Variance reporting
        1. Monitoring operational performance levels for
            a) variations from plans and standards
            b) deviations from accepted or mandated policies, procedures, and practices
            c) deviations from past quantitative relationships, for example, industry trends, past performance levels, normal profit and loss (P&L) and balance sheet ratios
    C. Intelligence gathering
        1. Monitoring employee attitudes, values, and job satisfaction levels
        2. Soliciting feedback from customers, vendors, and suppliers for evidence of employee dissatisfaction, inefficiency, inconsistency of policies, corruption, or dishonesty

HIGH-FRAUD AND LOW-FRAUD ENVIRONMENTS

Employee fraud, theft, and embezzlement are more prevalent in some organizations than in others. Conventional wisdom among members of the audit and security communities suggests that the organizations most vulnerable are those with the weakest management, accounting, and security controls; therefore, they propose the following solutions:

- Tight accounting and audit controls
- Thorough screening of applicants for employment
- Close supervision and monitoring of employee performance and behavior
- Explicit rules against theft, fraud, embezzlement, sabotage, and information piracy, and strict sanctions for their breach

Although we do not disagree with those solutions, we believe other considerations also have an impact on employee crime. Organizations that are most vulnerable to employee skullduggery can also be distinguished from those that are less vulnerable by the environmental and cultural contrasts shown in Exhibit 6.1.

Exhibit 6.1   The Corporate Fraud Environment Potential for Fraud

High Fraud Potential	Low Fraud Potential
Management style	**Management style**
Autocratic	Participative
Management orientation	**Management orientation**
Low trust	High trust
X Theory	Y Theory
Power driven	Achievement driven
Distribution of authority	**Distribution of authority**
Centralized, reserved by top management	Decentralized, delegated to all levels
Planning	**Planning**
Centralized	Decentralized
Short range	Long range
Performance	**Performance**
Measured quantitatively and on a short-term basis	Measured both qualitatively and quantitively and on a long-term basis
Profit focused	**Customer focused**

Exhibit 6.1 (*Continued*)

High Fraud Potential	Low Fraud Potential
Management by crisis	**Management by objectives**
Reporting by routine	**Reporting by exception**
Rigid rules strongly policed	**Reasonable rules fairly enforced**
Primary management concerns	**Primary management concerns**
Preservation of capital Profit maximization	Profit optimization Human, then capital and technological asset utilization
Reward system	**Reward system**
Punitive Penurious Politically administered	Reinforcing Generous Fairly administered
Feedback on performance	**Feedback on performance**
Critical Negative	Positive Supportive
Interaction mode	**Interaction mode**
Issues and personal differences are skirted or repressed	Issues and personal differences are confronted and addressed openly
Payoffs for good behavior	**Payoffs for good behavior**
Mainly monetary	Recognition, promotion, added responsibility, choice assignments, plus money
Business ethics	**Business ethics**
Ambivalent, rides the tides	Clearly defined and regularly followed
Internal relationships	**Internal relationships**
Highly competitive, hostile	**Friendly, competitive, supportive**
Values and beliefs	**Values and beliefs**
Economic, political Self-centered	Social, spiritual, group-centered
Success formula	**Success formula**
Works harder	Wroks smarter
Biggest human resource problem	**Biggest human resource problem**
High turnover Burnout Grievances Absenteeism	Not enough promotional opportunities for all the talent

Exhibit 6.1 *(Continued)*

High Fraud Potential	Low Fraud Potential
Company loyalty	**Company loyalty**
Low	High
Major financial concern	**Major financial concern**
Cash-flow shortage	Opportunities for new investments
Growth pattern	**Growth pattern**
Sporadic	Consistent
Relationship with competitors	**Relationship with competitors**
Hostile	Professional
CEO characteristics	**CEO characteristics**
Swinger, braggart, self-interested, driver, insensitive to people, feared, insecure, gambler, impulsive, tight-fisted, number- and things-oriented, profit seeker, vain, bombastic, highly emotional, partial, pretends to be more than he is	Professional, decisive, fast-paced, friendly, respected by peers, secure, risk-taker, thoughtful, generous with personal time and money, products- and markets-oriented, builder, helper, self-confident, composed, calm, deliberate, even disposition, fair, knows who he is, what he is, and where he is
Management structure, systems and controls	**Management structure, systems and controls**
Bureaucratic Regimented Inflexible Imposed controls	Collegial Systematic Open to change Self-controlled
Many-tiered structure, vertical	**Flat-structure, horizontal**
Everything documented, a rule for everything	**Documentation adequate** but not burdensome; some discretion afforded
Internal communication	**Internal communication**
Formal, written, stiff, pompous, ambiguous	Informal, oral, clear, friendly, open, candid
Peer relationships	**Peer relationships**
Hostile, aggressive, rivalrous	Cooperative, friendly

Source: Jack Bologna, *Forensic Accounting Review,* 1985.

RISK-MANAGEMENT CHECKLIST

This checklist shown in Exhibit 6.2 is designed to assist accountants in assessing and managing the risk of fraud in their organizations and those of their clients. Generally, all "No" answers require investigation and follow-up, the results of which should be documented. Where there is such additional documentation, the purpose of the "Ref" column is to cross-reference the checklist to the appropriate working paper (or to the notes on the reverse).

The checklist is intended for general use only. Using the checklist does not guarantee fraud prevention or detection, and it is not intended as a substitute for audit or similar procedures. If fraud prevention is an especially vital concern or if fraud is suspected, a specialist's advice should be sought.[1]

EMBEZZLEMENT RISK ASSESSMENT FOR THE BANKING INDUSTRY[2]

Cash is the inventory banks carry. So it should be no surprise that banks suffer extensively from embezzlement at the teller level. But most teller embezzlements create relatively small total losses as compared, for example, to the damage a bank's own money traders or its commercial lenders could cause. In this era of computerized banking, you might also think that electronic funds transfer clerks, who handle hundreds of millions of dollars a day, must be stealing like mad. We have seen little proof of that. There have been reports from banks in Los Angeles, Chicago, New York, London, and Zurich of attempts to fraudulently wire transfer bank funds, involving $10 million in one case, $20 million in another, and $60 million in still another. None of these attempts were successful.

But for the sake of experiential learning, compare the relative risks of bank funds transfer clerks committing acts of embezzlement vis-à-vis bank tellers, lenders, traders, purchasing department personnel, bookkeeper-accountants, operations supervisors, and so on, using the matrix form in Exhibit 6.3. When you complete the exercise, compare your assessment with a bank internal auditor's. How close were your responses to the expert's assessment? What factors did he or she rate more highly than you did? Why?

RISK FINANCING

An embezzlement risk assessment indicates whether the risk of fraud, theft, and embezzlement could be reduced with better controls, better personnel practices, better management, or all of these. But fraud, theft, and embezzlement

Exhibit 6.2   Risk-Management Checklist

	Yes	No	N/A	Ref
1. Does the organization have an adequate level of fraud awareness and are appropriate policies in place to minimize fraud risk, specifically:				
a. Generic Risk Factors				
• Has each employee been assigned a maximum "opportunity level" to commit fraud; for each employee, has management asked itself the question, "What is the maximum amount of which this employee could defraud the organization, and does this represent an acceptable risk?"	( )	( )	( )	____
• Has a "catastrophic" opportunity level been set; i.e., has management asked itself the question, "Have we ensured that no single employee—or group of employees in collusion—can commit a fraud that would place the organization in imminent risk of survival?"	( )	( )	( )	____
• Is it the organization's policy to immediately dismiss any employee who is found to have committed fraud?	( )	( )	( )	____
• Is it the organization's policy to report all frauds to the authorities and press charges?	( )	( )	( )	____
• For any and all frauds that the company has experienced in the past, have the reasons that led to the fraud been evaluated and corrective action taken?	( )	( )	( )	____
b. To manage individual risk factors; i.e., to promote moral behavior and minimize the motivation to commit fraud:				
• Does the organization have a corporate mission statement, which includes as an objective good corporate citizenship; i.e., maintaining good standing in the community?	( )	( )	( )	____
• Does the organization have a written code of ethics and business conduct?	( )	( )	( )	____
• Does the organization conduct ethical and security training for new employees with periodic updates for existing employees?	( )	( )	( )	____
• Does management set the right example; e.g., does it follow the corporate mission statement, code of ethics and business conduct, and other organization policies, and do the employees clearly see it doing so?	( )	( )	( )	____

Exhibit 6.2 (*Continued*)

	Yes	No	N/A	Ref
• Does the corporate culture avoid characteristics that promote unethical behavior; e.g., high or even hostile competitiveness within the organization, pushing employees to burnout, rigid and/or petty policies, or over-centralization of authority?	( )	( )	( )	_____
• When hiring, does the organization, to the extent possible, seek out individuals of high moral character and weed out those of low moral character?	( )	( )	( )	_____
• For especially sensitive positions, are screening and/or testing procedures used; e.g., psychological testing, drug testing, lie detector tests where legal?	( )	( )	( )	_____
• Does the organization provide and/or encourage counseling for employees with personal problems; e.g., alcohol and drug abuse?	( )	( )	( )	_____
• Does the organization have fair employee relations and compensation policies; e.g., salaries, fringe benefits, performance appraisal, promotions, severance pay? Do these policies compare favorably with competitors' and promote an environment that minimizes disenchantment and similar motivations to commit fraud?	( )	( )	( )	_____
• Are fair mechanisms in place for dealing with employee grievances?	( )	( )	( )	_____
• As a feedback mechanism on its policies with respect to employee relations, does the organization conduct exit interviews of departing employees?	( )	( )	( )	_____
c. Overall, does management exhibit an awareness of fraud and its possible manifestations; e.g., signs of employee problems such as drug addiction, and low-paid employees who suddenly appear with the trappings of wealth?	( )	( )	( )	_____
2. Does the organization have an adequate system of internal controls? Specifically:				
a. Has the need for fraud prevention been explicitly considered in the design and maintenance of the system of internal controls?	( )	( )	( )	_____
b. Control over physical and logical access:				
• Policy of locking doors, desks, and cabinets after hours and when unattended, especially for areas with valuable assets including files and records such as personnel and payroll, customer and vendor lists, corporate strategies, marketing plans, and research?	( )	( )	( )	_____

Exhibit 6.2   (*Continued*)

	Yes	No	N/A	Ref
• Use of IDs and passwords, such as those for computer files?	( )	( )	( )	___
• A stated and enforced policy that access is restricted to those requiring it to perform their job functions, including a strict policy against employees allowing access to unauthorized personnel by loaning keys, sharing passwords and so on?	( )	( )	( )	___
• For especially sensitive areas, computerized security and/or electronic surveillance systems?	( )	( )	( )	___
• To an impartial observer, does the workplace *appear* to have adequate access controls?	( )	( )	( )	___

c. Job descriptions:

	Yes	No	N/A	Ref
• Does the organization have written, specific job descriptions?	( )	( )	( )	___
• Are job descriptions adhered to?	( )	( )	( )	___
• Does the company have an organization chart that reflects and is consistent with the employee job descriptions?	( )	( )	( )	___
• Are incompatible duties segregated; i.e., handling of valuable assets, especially cash and related records?	( )	( )	( )	___
• Is the purchasing function properly segregated; for example, to ensure that one individual cannot requisition goods or services, approve and make the related payment, and access accounts payable records?	( )	( )	( )	___
• Are especially sensitive duties duplicated; i.e., the double-signing of checks over a specified amount?	( )	( )	( )	___
• Do job descriptions specify that annual vacations *must* be taken?	( )	( )	( )	___
• Overall, has the process of formulating job descriptions been an integrated one, giving adequate consideration to the importance of fraud prevention?	( )	( )	( )	___

d. Regular accounting reconciliations and analyses:

	Yes	No	N/A	Ref
• Bank reconciliations, for all accounts?	( )	( )	( )	___
• Accounts receivable reconciliations (month to month, general ledger to subledger)?	( )	( )	( )	___
• Accounts payable reconciliations (month to month, general ledger to subledger)?	( )	( )	( )	___

Exhibit 6.2 (*Continued*)

	Yes	No	N/A	Ref
• Variance analysis of general ledger accounts (budget to actual, current year versus prior year)?	( )	( )	( )	
• Vertical analysis of profit and loss accounts, i.e., as a percentage of sales, against historical and/or budget standards?	( )	( )	( )	
• Detailed sales and major expense analysis; i.e., by product line or geographic territory?	( )	( )	( )	____
e. Supervision:				
• Do supervisors and managers have adequate fraud awareness; i.e., are they alert to the possibility of fraud whenever an unusual or exceptional situation occurs, such as when supplier or customer complains about its account?	( )	( )	( )	____
• Do supervisors and managers diligently review the work of their subordinates; e.g., accounting reconciliations, and, where appropriate, even have the employee re-perform the work?	( )	( )	( )	____
• For smaller businesses or where division of duties is not possible, is close supervision in place so as to compensate for the lack of separation?	( )	( )	( )	____
• Is supervisory or management override (a manager or supervisor taking charge of, altering or otherwise interfering in the work of a subordinate) prohibited, and are others in the hierarchy alert to this situation as a fraud "red flag?"	( )	( )	( )	____
f. Audit:				
• Is there an internal audit function?	( )	( )	( )	____
• Does the internal audit function perform regular checks to ensure that fraud prevention mechanisms are in place and operating as intended?	( )	( )	( )	____
• Are external audits performed on a regular basis; i.e., quarterly for larger businesses?	( )	( )	( )	____
• Does management fully cooperate with external auditors with respect to its work in general and fraud matters in particular; i.e., through the audit committee?	( )	( )	( )	____
3. Has the organization addressed the following fraud prevention issues:				
a. Promoting an ethical environment?	( )	( )	( )	____
b. Risk financing	( )	( )	( )	____

Exhibit 6.3 Embezzlement Risk Assessment in the Banking Industry

Functional Roles	Probability of Occurrence*	Severity of Financial Loss*	Severity of Image Loss*	Weighted Average
Tellers				
Lenders				
Purchasers				
Traders				
Funds Transferors				
Bookkeepers/ Accountants				
Operations Supervisors				
Operations Clericals				
Data Input Clerks				
Computer Operators				
Programmer Analysts				
Systems Programmers				
Senior Management				

*Risk Level = 3 HIGH   Risk Level = 2 MEDIUM   Risk Level = 1 LOW

cannot be reduced to zero. Depending on the nature of the risk, its frequency and severity, there are some options for management. Management can elect to finance the risk in part or in whole, with insurance. If the risk is of catastrophic proportions, most management people would opt to transfer all or a large part of it to an insurance carrier.

External auditors do not view the risk of fraud, theft, and embezzlement from the same perspective as management people do. Their concern is a defensive one. External auditors see fraud from the perspective of professional liability; that is, if fraud is there and we miss it, will we be sued by the client, its shareholders, or even a third-party lender? External auditors are inclined to focus on transaction frauds; that is, expense voucher padding, and so on.

There is another element in this discourse on risk that we should cover as well. External auditors, according to SAS No. 53, "Should assess the risk that errors and irregularities may cause the financial statements to contain a material misstatement. Based on that assessment, the auditor should design the audit to provide reasonable assurance of detecting errors and irregularities that are material to the financial statements." (See Chapter 10 for full contents of SAS No. 53 and SAS No. 54, reprinted by permission of the AICPA.)

EVOLUTION OF AN ACCOUNTING SYSTEM FRAUD

1. Motivation
   a. Need, greed, revenge
2. Opportunity
   a. Access to assets and records
3. Control Weaknesses
   a. No audit trails or separation and rotation of duties, no internal audit function, no control policies, no ethics code
4. Formulation of Intent
   a. Rationalization of crime as borrowing, not stealing
5. Act of Theft, Fraud or Embezzlement
6. Concealment
   a. Alteration, forgery or destruction of records
7. Red Flags
   a. Variances detected, allegations made, behavior-pattern change noted
8. Audit Initiated
   a. Discrepancies detected

9. Investigation Initiated
    a. Evidence gathered, loss of assets confirmed and documented, inter-
        rogation of principals
10. Prosecution Recommended
    a. Civil recovery sought, insurance claim filed
11. Trial
    a. Presentation of facts and testimony

REFERENCES

1. Abstracted from *The Accountant's Handbook on Fraud and Commercial Crime,*
   G. J. Bologna, Robert J. Lindquist, and Joseph T. Wells, New York: Wiley, 1993.
2. Jack Bologna, Computer Protection Systems, Inc., 1994.

Chapter 7

Accounting Systems and Cycles

REVENUE CYCLE

The revenue cycle includes all systems that record the sale of goods and services, grant credit to customers, and receive and record customer remittances (Exhibit 7.1).

The details of a product sold for a price, or of professional services rendered for a fee, are set out in a document called a *sales invoice*. Details of the sales invoice are listed in the sales journal. When the customer pays, the company records the payment on a deposit slip that is ultimately listed in the cash receipts journal.

Business organizations also keep a list of those customers who owe money. This listing, produced by comparing the sales journal and the cash receipts journal, is called *accounts receivable*. It is usually prepared monthly and shows, for each customer listed, the age of the receivable—that is, if the customer has owed the money for 30, 60, 90, or more than 90 days.

Exhibit 7.1 Revenue Cycle

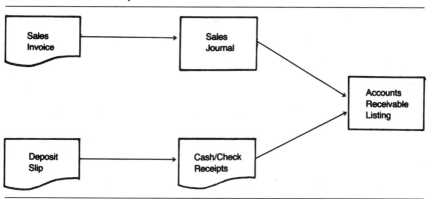

Thus the system of sales, receipts, and receivables constitutes the revenue cycle of any company. The primary documents are the sales invoice (evidence of the sale to the customer) and the deposit slip (evidence of the customer's payment to the company). The best evidence of payment is the customer's canceled check, which is returned directly to the customer's bank for processing.

PAYMENTS CYCLE

The payments cycle includes all systems that record the acquisition of goods and services for use in the business exchange for payment or promises to pay. Exhibit 7.2 charts this cycle.

In order to produce its product for sale, a company makes various types of expenditures. These may be for acquiring land, buildings, and equipment; purchasing materials and supplies; and paying company employees.

Purchases are made from many different suppliers. A supplier's invoice is evidence of a transaction. This invoice is sent to the company and sets out the details of the transaction. The company lists certain details of the supplier's invoice in the purchase journal.

If the company has the funds available, the supplier usually is paid within 30 days. This payment is evidenced by the company's canceled check. All checks are recorded in the company's check disbursements journal when they are issued. This journal is simply a list of the checks paid to the various suppliers and other creditors and individuals doing business with the company.

Most companies attempt to keep track of what they owe suppliers. This is usually done monthly. The company prepares an accounts payable listing by comparing what is recorded in the purchases journal with what is recorded as

Exhibit 7.2 Payments Cycle

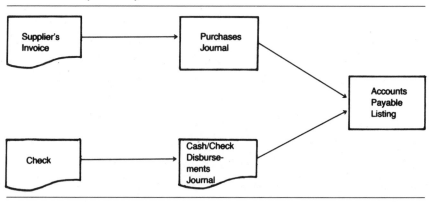

paid in the check disbursements journal. This list may detail how long they have owed various suppliers (for example, 30, 60, or 90 days).

BANK RECONCILIATION

The monies the company receives (as recorded in the cash receipts journal) and the monies the company pays out (as recorded in the check disbursements journal) are processed through the company's bank account. To ensure that the transactions recorded in these journals agree with those shown on the bank statement, a monthly bank reconciliation is prepared. Exhibit 7.3 charts this process.

GENERAL LEDGER

In the course of a year, many transactions are listed in each of the four journals. If these lists were totaled only annually, the room for error would be enormous, so businesses total the lists in each journal monthly and enter the totals in the general ledger.

The general ledger contains a separate ledger sheet for each account listed in the four journals. Someone looking at an individual sheet in the general ledger would expect to find up to one entry a month for each account. The monthly entry would be added to the accumulated total, so the total for the year-to-date activity is readily apparent.

Errors do occur within the books of account. To correct them, an entry is made in the general journal. This journal is kept for the specific purpose of adjusting the general ledger to make necessary changes, including the

Exhibit 7.3 Bank Reconciliation

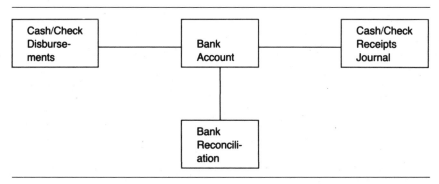

correction of errors. These entries should set out an explanation for the correction. A general journal entry has the effect of taking an amount from one account, say ABC, reducing the total in the ABC account and transferring that amount to the other account, XYZ, thereby increasing the total in XYZ. In this manner the general ledger balances are corrected. Once the correcting or adjusting entries are completed, the general ledger serves as the basis for preparing financial statements. Exhibits 7.4 and 7.5 illustrate the components and end product of the general ledger.

OTHER CORPORATE RECORDS

Other significant documents the company maintains are the corporate minute book and stockholder records. In many cases the corporate attorney holds these documents. The documents set out minutes of the meetings of both company shareholders and directors as well as details of the share certificates. The company ownership is set out as reflected on the certificates.

Exhibit 7.4   Documents in the Revenue Cycle

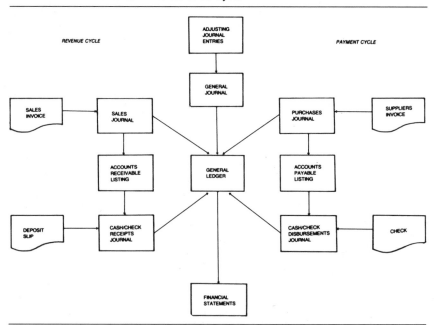

Exhibit 7.5 Documents in the Payment Cycle

Left side

Primary Document	Example	Information
SUPPLIER'S INVOICE:	Supplier's invoice	Date of preparation Name of supplier Description of product purchased Quantity of product purchased Cost per unit Total cost possibly with sales tax Address indicating where product delivered HOW FILED Alphabetically by supplier
	Purchase journal	
	Supplier's statement	
CANCELED CHECK:	Canceled check	Date of preparation Name of payee Amount of payment Name and account number of check Signing authority Endorsement Bank stamp indicating location and date negotiated by payee Preprinted number on check Description as to type of payment HOW FILED Numerical sequence by month with bank statement
	Check disbursement journal	

Center diagram

GENERAL LEDGER

— SALES JOURNAL
— PURCHASES JOURNAL
— CASH RECEIPTS JOURNAL
— CHECK DISBURSEMENTS JOURNAL

Right side

Primary Document	Information	Example
SALES INVOICE:	Date of preparation Name of customer Description of product sold Quantity of product sold price per unit Total price (sales value) possibly with sales tax Preprinted number on invoice HOW FILED Alphabetically by supplier Numerically by preprinted number	Sales invoice
SALES JOURNAL		Sales journal
DEPOSIT SLIP:	Date of preparation Whether cash or check Sometimes payor is named Bank stamp indicates date deposited Indicates if cash withdrawn at time of deposit HOW FILED Chronologically by date	Deposit slip
CASH RECEIPTS JOURNAL		Cash receipts journal
CUSTOMER CHECK:	Primary source document to prepare deposit slip, as the check is eventually returned to customer	

COMPUTERIZED ACCOUNTING SYSTEMS

Essentially, there are three major elements in a computerized accounting system: (1) key personnel, such as data input clerks, systems analysts, programmers, and librarians; (2) computer hardware—the physical equipment that includes the central processing unit and such "peripheral" devices as keyboards, printers, and video screens; and (3) computer software—the programs or instructions that enable the computer to manipulate the data input by the personnel.

These three elements are discussed below. It is important to note that these elements are over and above those in conventional (noncomputerized) accounting systems, and the normal procedures should still be in place. The major differences are that fewer personnel are directly connected with the actual manipulation of data, and instead of *people* producing reports, the *computer* produces the report.

Operation of a typical, centralized computer system such as a system using a mainframe or a minicomputer for corporatewide purposes is shown in a simplified flowchart in Exhibit 7.6.

Key Personnel

Most large organizations have a central information-processing department that services the entire organization. The employees in that department are computer specialists. They run the mainframe computer or minicomputer and maintain systems for the people in other departments—the systems users. This section briefly describes the jobs in the central computer department:

Systems Analyst   The systems analyst works with the various user departments to determine how their needs can best be met, what data must be entered, what processing must be carried out on the input data, what output must be produced, and with what frequency. The analyst also determines what equipment is necessary to meet the users' needs and how much memory and storage capacity are needed.

Programmer   The programmer carries on from the criteria the systems analyst develops. He or she writes, debugs, and installs new computer programs based on various specifications and the systems design the systems analyst prepares. Programmers are expected to document new programs in detail and to update the documentation when programs are changed. They are also on call in the event that software malfunctions.

Computer Operator   The computer operator directs the execution of various mechanical tasks by means of a console terminal. The operator schedules tasks for the computer to complete and is responsible for the proper use of

Exhibit 7.6 Typically Centralized Computer System: A Simplified Flowchart

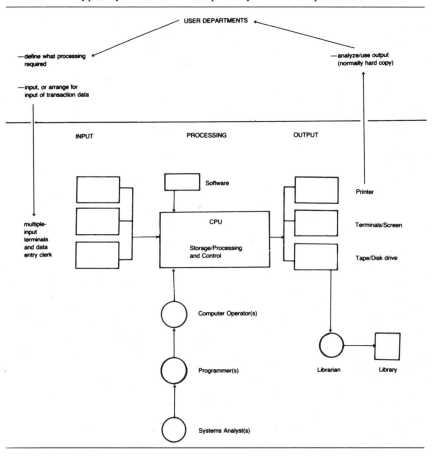

input and output devices. The operator usually maintains a computer-usage log recording whose programs were being run, and where and when the output was produced.

Data Entry Clerk   The data entry clerk enters all the data, which are then processed directly by the computer. The data can be accumulated and input in large batches or as transactions take place.

Librarian   The librarian stores and retrieves programs and data, usually at a location away from the computer site. Programs and data normally are stored on magnetic tape or disk and serve as a backup if the original software or transaction files are destroyed. The librarian also maintains, under normal circumstances, a log of borrowings from the library.

Decentralized Operators In addition to their central corporate computer, many organizations now have a network of terminals linked to it. The terminals may be linked via a local area network; the terminals and the mainframe are in the same building or a building nearby. This link between the terminals and the central computer may be achieved through ordinary telephone lines, or via satellite, microwave, or some other means if the terminals and the central computer are remote.

With a network in place, the need for a data-entry operator in the central department may disappear. Instead, operators using terminals or local area networks or at remote sites can enter data directly into the central computer. Clearly, this decentralized system of processing increases computer systems' vulnerability because more people have access to the computer under conditions that may be less easily controlled. Passwords and other methods of restricting access have to be relied on heavily, to prevent people from tampering with programs and files.

Computer Hardware

Computer equipment may be on-line or off-line. An on-line system permits the operator to access and manipulate information in the computer, changing the data base immediately and receiving information from the computer immediately. In contrast, off-line systems involve an intermediate step of some kind before processing takes place.

Generally, computer hardware includes (1) equipment for preparing data for processing, (2) input devices, (3) central processing unit, (4) auxiliary storage devices, and (5) output devices.

Data Preparation Equipment This equipment is used to convert the data into a machine-readable format. Depending on the method of inputting the information into the computer, numerous devices could be employed. These devices include magnetic tape, optical character readers, and paper-punch tape. Increasingly, preparatory stages are being bypassed altogether, and data is entered directly into the computer via on-line terminals.

Input Devices Input equipment includes such components as keyboards and video screens that show what is being entered, display instructions, and formats for inputting. Some screens respond to touch. Pointing devices (called "mice") can also be used with some microcomputers. Computers are available that will respond to a limited range of voice commands.

Central Processing Unit The CPU is the heart of the computer; it contains a series of operating programs and a translator that converts data into machine language (binary) on which the CPU itself operates. It stores programmed instructions and data; reads, writes, and moves data and instructions; interprets and performs programmed tasks; and synchronizes all of these activities.

Auxiliary Storage Devices In addition to its main memory, computers need auxiliary memory to store large volumes of data. The storage equipment holds either magnetic tape or magnetic disks. Stored data are extremely vulnerable to abuse, so methods of storing data are explained in more detail later.

Output Devices Output equipment includes printers, console typewriters, video display screens, and plotters. The technology of output as well as input devices is constantly being improved, because these devices constitute the interface between human beings and computers.

Computer Software

Software is the generic name for computer programs and their documentation. A program is a set of instructions that directs the computer to perform a task. Software is divided into two main classes: operating and application.

Operating software consists of the programs that keep the computer running as automatically as possible. They do not actually process anything (processing is the job of the application's software), but they monitor and perform operations that keep the computer system running.

Applications software consists of computer programs that apply the computer to the user's needs by carrying out a task the user wants performed (processing a payroll, for example). The normal sequence of instructions in an application program is as follows:

1. Read the information entered.
2. Process it (add, subtract).
3. Update existing files in the computer's memory with new information.
4. Output the new information by displaying, printing, or storing it (or all three).

PERSONAL COMPUTERS

Personal computers have all the components already described. They differ from large mainframe computers chiefly in size, performance, and price. Their performance limitations have been overcome rapidly, and their small size has many advantages—many are transportable (lap-sized models are truly portable), and they can fit comfortably on users' desks. They are also less expensive than mainframe computers, and in the past few years their use has skyrocketed.

The means used to store computer data are vulnerable to abuse and misuse. The earlier computers often used punchcards to input programs and data. Each punchcard represented a line of command and numbers, depending on where the punch occurred on the card. It was possible to alter information by taping over the punched holes or punching additional holes in strategic places. Because of the huge volume of punchcards, one card could easily be removed from or added to the deck without the user knowing that the data had been tampered with.

Paper Tape

At the same time, 8-channel paper tape was being used. This paper tape employed a series of round holes punched in six to eight lines or channels. The machine read their location. The paper tape permitted information to be stored and entered into the computer more easily than punched cards. Although information could not be readily changed on these paper tapes, the tapes themselves were quite fragile.

Magnetic Tape

Magnetic tape is still in use today, but disks, both floppy and hard, predominate. Information is stored on a disk in the same manner as on the magnetic tape. The disk resembles a magnetically coated record album. It has a series of concentric channels that encode the information. The major advantage of disks is that the computer can directly access information anywhere on the disk with great speed. In contrast, a magnetic tape must be read sequentially to find the relevant data or instructions.

The density of these disks determines the amount of information that can be stored on them.

Because they are small and light, floppy disks are easy to steal. When left lying about on desks they present a tempting target. Their surfaces are easily damaged and the magnetic dots can be obliterated by careless handling. Hard disks, on the other hand, are much less vulnerable, because they are protected by being housed within the computer's disk drive. Nevertheless, the data on both types of disks can be tampered with.

Paper and Microfilm

Data can be stored in hard-copy form, such as on paper or microfilm. Hard copies can show the result of data manipulation or processing by the computer, but not necessarily the transactions that occurred in arriving at the output. Paper is a familiar and stable medium but is bulky to store; as a result, more companies are using microfilm as the medium for storing records. Computerized records can be microfilmed directly from the disk or tape.

Other Media

As technology has advanced, so has the availability of other forms of storage—chief among them compact discs and optical storage media. These new media present their users with many advantages, particularly in the amount of information they can store and the ease and speed with which that information may be accessed, but of course they represent new opportunities for fraud and new challenges for hackers as well.

Chapter 8

Computer-Related Fraud

A computer-related crime, in very broad terms, means both a crime that has been committed or abetted through the use of a computer and a crime in which a computer itself is the victim. The usual crimes committed by computer include embezzlement, theft of property and proprietary information, fraud, forgery, and counterfeiting. Crimes committed against computers include sabotage, vandalism, and electronic wiretapping (gaining illegal access by impersonating an authorized user), and exceeding one's own authority (insider hacker).

Computer-related crime can be viewed as a phenomenon brought about by advances in information-processing technologies. Before we had computers, we had no computer crime, but we did have crime—both the white- and blue-collar varieties. We also had crimes of violence (crimes against people) and crimes against property. The computer did not usher in a new wave of crime; it merely changed the form of older crimes. Embezzlers can now steal by making electronic entries in books of account rather than by pen and ink or electromechanical entries.

Computer-related crime today is an occupational crime; that is, it is committed mainly by people with the requisite skills, knowledge, and access. Access can be gained more easily by organization insiders (employees) than by outsiders (intruders, hackers). Therefore, insiders represent a greater potential computer crime threat than outsiders, despite mass media commentators, who often suggest the opposite.

One might therefore conclude that computer-related crime is a phenomenon that involves knowledgeable people with questionable dispositions. But that also is too simple to be true. The idea that criminals are born crime prone has not won much favor from behavioral scientists. They suggest that cultural and environmental conditioning are more significant factors in understanding crime.

We therefore look at computer-related crime from a number of perspectives:

- The individual criminal, and his or her motivations
- The external environmental factors that exacerbate motivations to commit computer crime

- The internal organizational cultures that minimize or maximize the probability of such crimes

HISTORY AND EVOLUTION OF COMPUTER-RELATED CRIMES

Electronic computers were first introduced for commercial use in the United States in the mid-1950s. Before then the few computers that existed were used for governmental purposes (for tabulating the national census, for military applications, and for scientific research). Because we could have no computer-related crimes before we had computers, the history of the computer crime therefore begins in the mid-1950s.

Until 1958 no systematic tracking or tabulation of computer-related crime existed. In 1958 Stanford Research International (SRI) began tracking publicly reported incidents of computer abuse, some of which were criminal and others that involved the breach of civil laws such as the copyright and patent acts. SRI grouped these incidents into four categories:

1. Vandalism (against computers)
2. Information or property theft
3. Financial fraud or theft
4. Unauthorized use or sale of (computer) services

The first year in which 10 or more of these incidents were reported was 1968. There were a total of 13 incidents that year. Reported incidents rose until 1977, but in 1978 they dropped dramatically. Stanford Research discontinued tabulating such abuses after 1978 for several reasons. First, the publicly reported incidents bore no relationship to all incidents. Many, perhaps most, incidents of computer abuse were not publicly reported. So tabulating reported incidents by year could create the impression that computer abuse was growing or declining when, in fact, the reported incidents might not be fairly representative of all actual incidents of abuse. Also, with more and more computers being used, one could expect an increase in the number of incidents of abuse. Second, tabulating reported incidents of abuse would shed no light on the phenomenon itself or its causative factors. So SRI elected to look at each case individually for whatever insights it could glean on causations and other variables, such as the mental dispositions of the computer abusers and the employment conditions that made abuse more likely—demographic characteristics of abusers.

Now a word on what we do know about computer-related fraud versus what the mass public assumes to be true. The current computer-crime phenomenon is not significantly different from what businesses experienced 30 years ago. There is no conclusive evidence that the current rate of insider computer-related business crimes, such as employee theft, fraud, and embezzlement, is greater than it was in the past. But computing systems are more vulnerable to outsider attack by way of electronic eavesdropping and other illegal-access methods.

We can therefore sum up our theory of computer-related crime in a concept we call MOMM, an acronym for motivations, opportunities, means, and methods.

Motivations (Who and Why)

    Economic

    Ideological

    Egocentric

    Psychotic

Opportunities (What, When and Where)

    Inadequate systems controls

        Accounting controls

        Access controls

    Inadequacies in Management Controls

        Reward system

        Ethical climate

        Climate for trust

Means (How)

    Compromising controls

    Compromising personnel

    Compromising technology

Methods (How much, How often)

    Input scams

    Throughput scams

    Output scams

We can then depict computer-related theft as an iterative process. (Exhibit 8.1).

The personal motives that can lead to the commission of a computer crime are:

- Economic
- Egocentric
- Ideological
- Psychotic

Economic motives indicate that the perpetrator has as a main purpose, a need, or desire to secure a financial gain from the crime—money or things that can be disposed of for money.

Egocentric motives mean a need or desire for perpetrators to show off their talent in committing what the general public sees as a complex crime. Stealing money may be included in the criminal act, but it is not the primary purpose of the act. The stolen funds are a secondary consideration—the more the better, but only to demonstrate the prowess of the perpetrator. Youthful

Exhibit 8.1   The Computer Theft Iteration

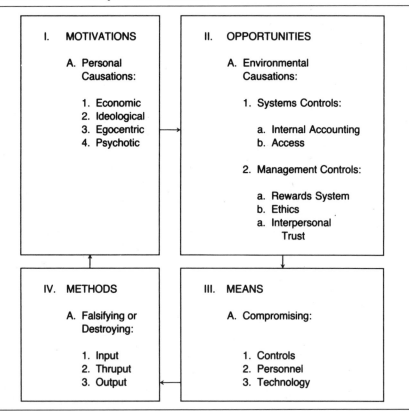

hackers usually fall into this category. Their intentions generally are not to steal money but to elicit information, to demonstrate how bright they are.

Ideological motives are demonstrated when perpetrators feel impelled to seek revenge against someone or something they believe is oppressing or exploiting them. Terrorist bombings of computer centers exemplify that mindset. Sabotage against computers by disgruntled employees is another example. Such criminals may think that computer technology threatens their economic and political survival or well-being.

Psychotic motives include a distorted sense of reality, delusions of grandeur or persecution, and exaggerated fears of computers, to a point where bizarre behavior is directed against computers to relieve anxieties. But there have been few reported incidents of computer abuse where psychotic motives were attributed to perpetrators.

Environmental conditions that have provided motives for computer-related crime and abuse include both the internal environment of the firm that operates a computer and the external environment (the world or marketplace in general). Internal influences that can add to the motive for computer-related crime and abuse include such things as:

- The work environment
- The reward system
- The level of interpersonal trust
- The level of ethics
- The level of stress (pressure for performance)
- The level of internal controls

Externally, motives for computer-related crime and abuse may be provided by the current mores and social values of society, competitive conditions in the industry, and economic conditions in the country or the world.

Computer-related crimes can be grouped into three categories that parallel the three stages of data processing: input tampering, throughput tampering, and output tampering. (We owe this classification to Robert Jacobson, a well-known computer security consultant in New York City.) Input crimes involve the entry of false or fraudulent data into a computer; i.e., data that have been altered, forged, or counterfeited—raised, lowered, destroyed, intentionally omitted, or fabricated. Input scams are probably the most common computer-related crimes, yet perhaps the easiest kind to prevent with effective supervision and controls (such as separation of duties and proper audit trails).

Throughput crimes require a knowledge of programming. Such colorful expressions as *salami slicing, trojan horses, trap doors, time bombs,* and *logic bombs* have been used to describe these computer abuses. The publicly reported cases of these abuses are far fewer than the input crimes mentioned earlier. If it is true that computer crimes, like most white-collar crimes, are economically motivated, it would seem reasonable to assume that the incident rate of throughput scams will be lower than input and output scams, because the chief culprits of these latter two types of computer crimes are data entry clerks and computer operators, who earn considerably less than programmers and analysts.

Output crimes, such as theft of computer-generated reports and information files (customer mailing lists, R & D results, long-range plans, employee lists, secret formulas, and so on) seem to be increasing in this era of intense competition, particularly among high technology manufacturers.

Among the publicly reported cases of computer crime, most have been the input and output and have involved lower-level data processing clerks—entry clerks and computer operators. However, because throughput crimes are more difficult to detect, we cannot say that their number is exceeded by the other two types. We simply do not know. Furthermore, throughput crimes may not be reported for other reasons as well; proving them is quite complex, and admitting that they even occurred is embarrassing to top management.

THE MOST COMMON COMPUTER-RELATED CRIMES

Whereas computer hacking (pranksters breaking into computers) has received most of the recent media attention, the most prevalent computer crime is the fraudulent disbursement of funds that is generally preceded by the submission of a spurious claim in the following forms:

- False vendor, supplier, or contractor invoice
- False governmental benefit claim
- False fringe benefit claim
- False refund or credit claim
- False payroll claim
- False expense claim

Fraudulent disbursement of funds usually requires a data entry clerk in accounts payable, payroll, or the benefits section, either acting alone or in collusion with an insider or outsider (depending on how tight the internal controls are). From an accountant's perspective, the claim is a false debit to an expense so that a corresponding credit can be posted to the cash account for the issuance of a check. Auditors assert such disbursement frauds represent more than half of all frauds by lower-level employees.

At higher management levels, the typical fraud involves overstating profits by the fabrication of such data as sales, which are increased arbitrarily (sales booked before the sales transaction is completed), and the understatement of expenses, which are arbitrarily reduced or disguised as deferrals to the next accounting period. There are numerous variations on these two main themes— overstatement of sales and understatement of expenses. One of the more common ploys to overstate profits is to arbitrarily increase the ending inventory of manufactured goods or merchandise held for sale. That ploy results in understating the cost of goods sold and thereby increasing the net profit.

The executive compensation system often provides the incentive to overstate profits. If bonus awards depend on profits, executives have an economic incentive to fudge the numbers. They may also be tempted to do so if they own a great deal of company stock whose value depends on investor perceptions of profitability. If profits are down, investors are unhappy and may rush to sell, thus causing a lowered stock's price and depressing the value of the executive's own stock.

Manipulations of this type often require line executives and personnel in accounting and data processing capacities to conspire together. We saw such an example in the Equity Funding case, and we have seen many others since then. Such conspiracies have become a recurring theme in business. The pressure on executives for high performance grows each year. We are therefore likely to see more of such frauds in the future.

THE NATURE OF COMPUTER-RELATED CRIME

Crimes like embezzlement and employee thefts of funds were not unheard of before computers came into being. Accountants attempted to discourage such crimes by requiring a separation of duties between people who handled cash or other assets and those who made entries in the books of account. Accessibility to assets and accountability for recording transactions concerning such assets were divided, on the theory that requiring two people to conspire to commit a theft of assets would reduce the probability of such a theft.

An added control measure accountants instituted is called the paper trail or audit trail. In essence that control measure requires that all business transactions be entered into journals and be supported by paper documents; (vendor invoices, purchase orders, receiving reports, canceled checks, disbursement vouchers, sales receipts, or customer invoices) before disbursements could be made.

But despite these control measures, employee thefts, frauds, and embezzlements were still possible. Accounting systems were not designed to be foolproof or fraud proof. A determined defrauder could still find ways to circumvent or override controls even in the era of manual accounting. Computers have not changed that human disposition. Fraud, thefts, and embezzlements are still possible in the computer era.

HACKERS AND PHONE PHREAKS

Coauthor Bologna's organization, Computer Protection Systems, Inc., has for the past several years published a monthly newsletter called "Computer Security Digest." That newsletter and the publication noted in each entry provide the selected information on computer crime that follows.[1]

> Do hackers mature and become more responsible with age? Kevin Poulsen, a former programmer for Sun Microsystems, Inc., was recently indicted by a San Francisco grand jury for allegedly stealing a secret Air Force military document that listed the names and locations of structures to be attacked in the event of war. Poulsen's network alias is "Dark Dante." He was charged with conspiring to break into government and Pacific Bell computers, stealing and trafficking telephone access codes, obtaining unpublished numbers for the Soviet Consulate in San Francisco, and wiretapping the conversations of Pacific Bell officials who were investigating him. Earlier, he was charged with illegally accessing computers at UCLA but was not prosecuted because he was a juvenile. (*Computerworld,* 12/14/92)

> *Forbes* magazine, 12/21/92, alleges that "serious computer crime is beginning to reach epidemic proportions." The new breed of hackers are not just youthful joy-riders, says the article, but cybercrooks. They steal information, software, and credit-card numbers.

> Bruce Sterling, a self-proclaimed cyberpunk novelist, in his recent book, *The Hackers Crackdown* (Bantam Books, 1992), says "Computer intrusion, as a nonprofit act of intellectual exploration and mastery, is in slow decline in the United States, but electronic fraud, especially telecommunications crime, is growing by leaps and bounds."

> Security officers use network analyzers to monitor outside hackers' keystroke activity. However, the federal wiretap law reveals that they may be breaking the law because they are intercepting messages. The legal eagles at the U.S. Department of Justice have come up with a 101-word warning message that federal agencies should use on their log-on screens to notify regular users and hackers that their keystrokes may be monitored. (*Computerworld,* 1/18/93)

> The FBI offers the following advice if you think your system is being hacked:

> • Promptly notify your network security officer and law-enforcement authorities.

> • Select one person in authority, such as the IS manager, who will be the main contact point and the person called to testify.

- Keep records, collect and secure evidence, and compile cost information.
- Plan what you will say and do if the intruder contacts you.
- Provide technical assistance to investigators.
- Do NOT "clean up the system" (which destroys evidence) or discuss the case over unsecured electronic mail. (*Computerworld,* 1/25/93)

The University of California's computer system was used as a springboard for 100 hackers who took a joy ride through Internet, where connections to CIA, DOD, and NASA computers were made. The hackers are under investigation by the FBI, but no arrests have been made. (*Info Week,* 2/1/93)

AT&T reports that it has thrown more than 1,000 alleged hackers off its 800 network and notified 1,000 customers per month of calling patterns that could be caused by toll fraud. (*Network World,* 2/8/93)

Toll call frauds conducted by jail inmates? Yes. A Boston jail inmate, masquerading as a New England Telephone and Telegraph Co. technician, accessed a phone company customer's system and made toll calls. Fortunately, the customer had a toll monitoring service provider who alerted her to the strange calling patterns. The calls were traced to the inmate. Around 150 calls were made before the inmate was nabbed. Toll frauds are said to cost the industry about $2 billion a year. (*Network World,* 3/1/93)

Telecommunications Advisors, Inc., a research and consulting firm in Portland, Oregon, that teaches companies about toll fraud, surveyed 624 users throughout the country on several aspects of telecommunications security. More than 70 percent of the 124 respondents were hit by hackers at least once during the past five years, with the average aggregate loss per victim, many of whom were struck more than once, at $125,000. (Computer Security Digest, May 1993)

According to news reports from China, Shi Biao, a computer hacker, was executed as a warning to others contemplating computer crime. In 1991 Biao defrauded the Agricultural Bank of China of around $200,000 through money transfers. (*Information Week,* May 17, 1993)

Info Security News (July–August 1993, p. 47) has an interesting piece on hacking, written by Marc Robins, called "Voice Processing System Security: How Hackers Do Their Dirty Work." Robins says: "One way hackers infiltrate systems is through a physical attack. The hacker, posing as an employee or service technician, enters the premises and locates the voice-processing system."

In a recent fax vote, *Information Week* probed readers' feelings about hiring hackers as the ultimate network security test.

Some results are eye-opening. For example, 15 percent of the respondents say hackers have approached them, although only 6 percent of the total say they have hired one. In the same survey, 10 percent of the respondents report that rival companies have broken into their systems to steal information. (*Information Week,* 8/16/93)

The technofreaks who gathered last week at the End of the Universe conference in the Netherlands had at least one thing in common with their sixties countercultural counterparts: They believed that rules are meant to be broken. In just 30 minutes, the hackers had already cracked the conference's network, reprogrammed the system, and rejected the password. (*Newsweek,* 8/16/93)

As users have chased hackers from DISA to voice mail, from voice mail to maintenance ports, and from maintenance ports to modem pools, there has been one constant: Hackers are relentless and will reattack the PBX from a different direction. To be effective in the long term, the antihacking system must stop and track attempts targeted at the entire communications environment. (*Network World,* 8/26/93)

New York Federal Court sentenced two computer hacker ring members, known as MOD or Masters of Disaster, to six months in prison, six months home detention, and 750 hours of community service. Both pled guilty in March to conspiracy in a scheme to break into corporate and university computer systems. (*Computerworld,* 8/2/93)

Public Access Network Corp., a commercial service known as Panix that sells customers access to the Internet, was penetrated by an unauthorized systems "cracker" who obtained high-level access to the system. Many other Internet-connected networks may have been affected too.

"We're seeing a tremendous increase in cracking," says Dain Gary, manager of the Computer Emergency Response Team (CERT), which helps network administrators cope with break-ins on the Internet. "The trend directly corresponds to the growth in the Internet." Mr. Gary says that his group logs three to four security breaches a day. This year he expects a 50 percent increase over last year's 773 reported security breaches. (*Wall Street Journal,* 11/1/93)

Recognizing fraud and abuse patterns is important in telecommunication fraud reduction. Because fraud and abuse often show up there, first review your monthly telecommunications bills. Check the following points when reviewing the billing detail:

- Billing amount for variance (last three months is advised).
- Call detail for calls made during off-business hours.
- Calls placed to international locations.
- Long-duration calls to unknown telephone numbers.

- Third party calls billed to your number.
- Collect calls billed to your number.

(ACFE-SEM Chapter newsletter, November 1993, in an article written by Joseph Mansfield, CFE.)

Estimates place the United States telecommunications fraud at around $4 billion annually, with fraud on cellular networks alone accounting for between $365 million and $600 million each year. (*Computerworld,* 11/1/93)

Michael Kabay, director of education for the National Computer Security Association, has an interesting piece on hackers in the 12/6/93 *Network World.* He concludes that: "Criminal hackers often claim that their depredations serve a useful social purpose by bringing security weaknesses to light. If they are sincere, they should negotiate with the owners of networks for mutually satisfactory testing arrangements. All of us should be reaching out to educate young people about network usage—in schools, in colleges and universities, even in youth clubs and scout troops. We must extend the rules of morality and civility—of respect and communications—into cyberspace. We support driver education classes; how about network education classes?"

Corporate data are less secure than they were a year ago, a Computer Security Institute survey says. The greatest threats are from hackers and disgruntled former employees. Sixty computer security managers also said that their security budgets are inadequate to meet the challenge of the next 12 months. (*Computerworld,* 12/13/93)

A former AT&T employee and his uncle were sentenced to 18 months in prison for conspiring to extort $1 million from the communications giant. Federal prosecutors in Newark, New Jersey, said the former AT&T project coordinator admitted to stealing computerized records from 4,000 customer accounts last April. His uncle then contacted AT&T and falsely warned the vendor that one of their employees was selling account information to AT&T competitors. He demanded $1 million from AT&T to plug the leak, prosecutors said. (*Computerworld,* 12/20/93)

An Internet security investigation team spotted what may be the largest computer security breach on the Internet and urged tens of thousands of users to change their passwords.

On January 1 a program that logs passwords was installed on computers at the University of California at Berkeley. The program collected more than 3,000 passwords between 7 a.m. and 9 p.m., forcing system administrators to notify users to change their passwords. Rob Robertson, a systems programmer, said he spent a week shoring up the system's security and assessing damage. There was none, he said.

Experts say the rush of commercial traffic onto the Internet has frustrated efforts to track and thwart breaches. Since mid-1990, the number of businesses connecting to the Internet has risen thirty-fold to 11,000, said Howard Funk, an Internet consultant. (*Wall Street Journal,* 2/7/94)

The Computer Emergency Response Team (CERT) at Carnegie-Mellon University advised users to batten down the hatches in the face of a rash of password thefts and other security breaches discovered in Unix-based computers on the Internet.

"In the past week, CERT has observed a dramatic increase in reports of intruders monitoring network traffic," the U.S. Department of Defense-sponsored group said in an advisory sent February 3 over the Internet. "Systems of some service providers have been compromised . . . [and] intruders have captured access to information for tens of thousands of systems across the Internet." (*Computerworld,* 2/7/94)

The *Washington Post* reported that Rice University in Houston and the University of California at Berkeley had been broken into and had well over 6,000 passwords stolen. (Computer Security Digest, March 1994)

A summary of Telecommunications Advisors, Inc.'s, "1994 Telecom Fraud Review," excluding massive but impossible to quantify indirect costs, can be:

- CPE Toll Fraud, $1.3 Billion
- "800" Calls by Hackers/Telecrooks, $115 Million
- Cellular Fraud, $400 Million
- Subscription Fraud, $475 Million
- Calling Card/Credit Card Fraud, $400 Million
- Prisoner Toll Fraud, $90 Million
- Pay Phone Fraud, $90 Million
- Call Forwarding Fraud, $65 Million
- Direct Hits to Switches/Networks, $190 Million
- 800/900 Number Fraud, $100 Million
- Social Engineering, $80 Million

Total for Telecom Fraud—$3,305 Billion
(Telecom & Network Security Business School, according to John L. Sullivan, Jr., a managing director in the Boston office of Korn/Ferry International, an executive recruiting firm.) (Computer Security Digest, April 1994)

William R. Cheswick and Steven M. Bellovin, two AT&T Bell Laboratories researchers who helped break the infamous "Berferd" hacker case, reveal their methods in *Firewalls and Internet Security: Repelling the Wily Hacker,* published in May 1994. The book shows readers how to evaluate the kinds of threats they face and put in place security measures that will thwart the most determined and sophisticated hackers. In particular, the authors provide step-by-step instructions for building a firewall gateway, a dedicated machine equipped with safeguards that act as a single, more easily defended Internet connection.

Computer crackers and information system security professionals face off in a special evening session called *Meet the Enemy—How You Will Be Attacked and What To Do About It* on June 14 at 7 p.m. during NetSec '94, the network security conference of the Computer Security Institute (CSI).

This unique session will allow NetSec '94 attendees to interact directly—via an anonymous audioconference—with members of the computer underground who are credentialed in the art of invading computerized infrastructures of corporations and government organizations.

"*Meet the Enemy* seeks to close the gap between security practitioners who protect computerized information assets and those who continue to successfully attack them," said Ray Kaplan of CyberSafe, who will lead the session. "In light of these ongoing system invasions, participants will discuss whether today's security professionals have the tools, techniques, and detailed understanding required to keep their data safe," Kaplan said. "Attendees are encouraged to bring specific questions about the computer underground and how it works," he added. (Computer Security Digest, May 1994)

Computer hackers posted illegal copies of new software from IBM, Microsoft, and other companies on the Internet, inviting hundreds and possibly thousands of users worldwide to download pirated versions of the programs. The unknown hackers broke into a computer system at Florida State University and deposited copies of IBM's new OS/2, a test version of Windows95, and about a dozen other programs. (*Wall Street Journal,* 10/31/94)

Computer hackers infiltrated General Electric computers connected to the Internet, according to a broadcast report by GE's local NBC television station in New York City.

The computer breach, which was confirmed by a GE spokesperson, gave the hackers access to research and proprietary information on GE computers in two cities, according to the report on WNBC-TV. The intruders, who managed to penetrate robust security barriers, known as firewalls, also looked at files pertaining to NBC, the report said. (*Wall Street Journal,* 11/28/94)

In February 1994, the Computer Emergency Response Team (CERT) at Carnegie Mellon University, which monitors Internet security, warned network administrators that a band of intruders had stolen tens of thousands of Internet passwords. In July, the Lawrence Livermore National Laboratory conceded that an employee had used its computers to distribute pornography. The number of Internet incidents reported by CERT reached 1,300 last year, up from 50 a few years earlier.

These episodes serve as a reality check. The Internet, which promises electronic intimacy with millions of potential customers, also may be fraught with bugs, snoops, and questionable characters. "The opportunities for creative fraud are vastly greater than they used to be," warns Peter G. Neumann, principal scientist at SRI International in Menlo Park, California. (*Business Week,* 11/14/94)

Hackers penetrated a number of General Electric Co. computers, which caused the company to sever all its links to the Internet for 72 hours.

Observers said GE's experience is part of a roaring wave of Internet-borne computer security breaches pushed by an explosion of new technology in the hands of poorly trained users. "We are seeing a lot more incidents—between eight and 14 new incidents a day," said Barbara Fraser, manager of product development at the Computer Emergency Response Team (CERT) at Carnegie Mellon University in Pittsburgh. "A single incident can involve thousands of computers," she said. (*Computerworld,* 12/5/94)

Critical Issues in Information Security

- Access controls
- Accuracy
- Auditing
- Authentication
- Availability
- Back-up and recovery
- Counterfeiting
- Cryptography
- Data interception
- Disaster planning
- Diversion of assets
- Destruction of records
- Electronic funds transfers
- Embezzlement
- Espionage
- Ethics
- False entries
- Fraudulent financial statements
- Hacking
- Impersonation
- Integrity
- Piracy
- Privacy
- Proprietary information theft
- Social engineering
- Terrorism
- Theft of data, time and supplies
- Timeliness of entries
- Toll fraud
- Viruses

THE VALUE OF STORED DATA

With the advent of computers, a new form of asset has been created: the data held in the computer. The data eventually may cause money to change hands as in EFT systems. Although the data are not a negotiable instrument (as is a bank check), it nonetheless has value. Further examples of these assets are bank-to-bank transfers, accounts receivable balances, inventory levels, funds-and-deposit balances, fixed assets listings, and accounts payable balances. Other more intangible assets include valued or confidential programs, scientific data files, programs a company can sell for a profit, confidential financial information, computer time, and so on.

COMPUTER COMMUNICATIONS

Computer communications may be defined as the ability to transfer messages between independent hardware devices. In order to communicate, the computer devices must, of course, be connected in some way. A network refers to the computer, the terminals, and any other peripheral devices that are interconnected. The enhancement of information technologies has increased the vulnerability of computer systems to such crimes as hacking and other telecom frauds. Client-server computing also allows for more risk exposure than in the traditional mainframe computer environment.

The idea of connecting computers is not new. For a number of years it has been possible to sit down at terminals that are in the same building as the mainframe computer to which the terminals are linked, or at remote terminals hundreds of miles from the mainframe computer, and send data back and forth between the terminals and the mainframe. Most computers of any size have one or more terminals attached to them (sometimes hundreds) and are part of a network. Terminals can communicate with the central or host computer via either telephone lines or dedicated data telecommunication lines.

The terminal may function simply as an input/output device enabling its user to run programs on the central computer. A terminal that cannot do any processing itself is called a *dumb* terminal. *Intelligent* or *smart* terminals, on the other hand, can process data downloaded from the central computer because they have their own software.

PC's today can communicate not only with an organization's own large computers, but with external computers containing data bases that the public can access for a fee, such as Compuserve. In addition to bibliographic information, public data bases offer users a wide variety of services, such as financial, stock market, and other statistical information; travel information; and access to electronic bulletin boards.

The network scene has become more complicated in recent years with the arrival of microcomputers in the workplace. Although most of the microcomputers now in use are *standalones* (they function completely independently), microcomputer users sooner or later are likely to communicate with each other and with the organization's central computer to share information and programs. The need to communicate has spurred the development of local area networks (LANs).

A LAN is a data communications system that links one or more independent services (microcomputers, printers, hard disks) and enables them to communicate. The LAN transmits data over short distances and usually is confined to a small area such as a department (one floor), a single building, or a warehouse. Cabling is used to link the equipment.

Microcomputers may be linked to other microcomputers in a LAN, or they may be linked to the central computer via a wide-area network, or both. They can then function as independent workstations, or can operate in conjunction with the other hardware devices that are on the LAN, or can function as terminals to the central computer.

CHARACTERISTICS OF THE COMPUTER ENVIRONMENT

Although computerized accounting systems are a natural progression from manual accounting systems, they do have special characteristics that make them more susceptible to criminal activity or abuse. To understand the potential impact and extent of computer-related crime, it is necessary to understand these characteristics.

Data Are Concentrated in One Place

Computer systems collect and combine data, usually from all departments within an organization. This information is processed and centrally stored. Centralization means that the data are in one location, and therefore all data in that location are vulnerable to abuse. By simply obtaining the appropriate password, a person could access any or all of a company's financial or other records.

The Storage Medium Is Vulnerable

Assets are widely recorded in magnetic form. This storage medium is volatile and easily abused, making the stored information vulnerable.

The Audit Trail May Be Obscure

The sheer volume of transactions, together with the on-line access and networks available on many systems, may result in confused or incomplete audit trails.

Visible Records May Be Nonexistent

Permanent records are often stored in machine-readable form. Any abuse of these records, whether data or actual programs, is therefore less likely to be detected by nonspecialists. In addition, a theft or other form of abuse may remain undetected for a long time, allowing perpetrators to cover their tracks or disappear.

Programs and Data Can Be Altered Leaving No Trace of the Alteration

Manual records may reveal tampering or alterations, whereas computer records stored on a magnetic medium may be altered by writing over a record, obliterating the previous record without leaving any trail of the source of the change.

Tampering Can Be Carried Out Almost Instantly

Computers cannot discriminate between legitimate and illegitimate users once a security system in place has been breached. The computer will change data instantly when commanded to do so. Its speed means that a computer criminal is at risk only briefly while actually committing the crime and is much less likely to be caught in the act.

Networks Increase the Risks

As mentioned earlier, networks increase the vulnerability of computer systems. Information can be stolen by copying it through a workstation or by tapping into transmission cables. There can be unauthorized entry through public telephone lines. Information may be downloaded from a highly secure central computer to a microcomputer whose operator then leaves the floppy disk containing the information unattended on a desktop. The more terminals there are, the more opportunities there are to gain unauthorized access to the central computer.

Computer Systems Are Not Widely Understood

In some ways computer systems become more and more complex as technology advances. One needs considerable expertise to understand what is happening in a computer environment, especially with regard to computer programs. Thus, abuses are not as likely to be detected as other types of crimes.

Security Features Are Not Always Built in

Much of the hardware and many of the operating systems in use today were designed without much thought being given to preventing computer abuse or crime.

Internal Control Features May Be Inadequate

Many computer analysts and programmers are not knowledgeable about accounting controls or the general principles of internal control. As a result, some systems are designed without adequate controls. In addition, many programs that have been operating for a long time have undergone extensive changes, but the changes may be poorly documented and the "patched" programs little understood. Anyone with sufficient knowledge of programming conceivably could manipulate or change the programs to his or her benefit without a change being discovered.

Trusted Personnel May Circumvent Controls

By the very nature of their jobs, programmers and data entry clerks are in a position to manipulate records. A high degree of trust must be reposed in them, and a corresponding degree of risk for the organization exists.

Technical personnel may be able to get around built-in controls, or may deliberately exploit a flaw they discover in the course of their work. Disgruntled employees, or employees who enjoy seeing the computer "tripped up," may also abuse computer systems. Finally, managers may override normal controls that were built into the system.

COMPUTER SYSTEM THREATS

There are three main categories of threats to computer systems:

1. Theft, including theft of assets, data, and programs
2. Manipulation, including the additions or deletions of information in data files or programs
3. Theft of computer time

Some examples of fraudulent activities that may be employed are:

- Adding, deleting, or changing input data, or entering fraudulent data
- Misposting or partially posting transactions

- Producing counterfeit output, or suppressing, destroying, or stealing output
- Tampering with programs; e.g., to take money from many accounts in small amounts
- Altering or deleting master files, or holding them for ransom
- Overriding internal controls to gain access to confidential information
- Exploiting intersystem deficiencies
- Committing sabotage
- Stealing computer time
- Conducting electronic surveillance of data as it is transmitted
- Browsing or insider hacking, i.e., probing into the data base

Besides these and other threats, computerized accounting systems are vulnerable to all the dangers inherent in any accounting system, whether computerized or manual.

REFERENCES

1. Jack Bologna, *Computer Security Digest,* 1993–1995 issues.

Chapter 9

The Auditor as an Expert Witness

Lay witnesses in civil and criminal cases are generally restricted from giving legal testimony consisting of opinions, conclusions, and characterizations, although they may estimate the speed of a moving vehicle, approximate temperature and distances, identify common smells, and testify in matters of physical description such as age, height, and weight.

However, qualified experts may give their professional opinions. Consider the following Michigan Supreme Court Rules of Evidence on this point:[1]

Rule 702 Testimony by Experts

If the court determines that recognized scientific, technical, or other specialized knowledge will assist the trier of fact to understand the evidence or to determine a fact in issue, a witness qualified as an expert by knowledge, skill, experience, training, or education, may testify thereto in the form of an opinion or otherwise.

Rule 703 Bases of Opinion Testimony by Experts

The facts or data in the particular case upon which an expert bases an opinion or inference may be those perceived by or made known to him at or before the hearing. The court may require that underlying facts or data essential to an opinion or inference be in evidence.

Rule 704 Opinion on Ultimate Issue

Testimony in the form of an opinion or inference otherwise admissible is not objectionable because it embraces an ultimate issue to be decided by the trier of fact.

Rule 705 Disclosure of Facts or Data Underlying Expert Opinion

The expert may testify in terms of opinion or inference and give his reasons therefor without prior disclosure of the underlying facts or data, unless the court requires otherwise. The expert may in any event be required to disclose the underlying facts or data on cross-examination.

Rule 706 Court-Appointed Experts

(a)*Appointment.* The court may on its own motion or on the motion of any party enter an order to show cause why expert witnesses should be appointed, and may request the parties to submit nominations. The court may appoint any expert witnesses agreed upon by the parties, and may appoint expert witnesses of its own selection. An expert witness shall not be appointed by the court unless he consents to act. A witness so appointed shall be informed of his duties by the court in writing, a copy of which shall be filed with the clerk, or at a conference in which the parties shall have opportunity to participate. A witness so appointed shall advise the parties of his findings, if any, his deposition may be taken by any party, and he may be called to testify by the court or any party. He shall be subject to cross-examination by each party, including a party calling him as a witness.

(b)*Compensation.* Expert witnesses so appointed are entitled to reasonable compensation in whatever sum the court may allow. The compensation thus fixed is payable from funds which may be provided by law in criminal cases and civil actions and proceedings involving just compensation under the Fifth Amendment. In other civil actions and proceedings the compensation shall be paid by the parties in such proportion and at such time as the court directs, and thereafter charged in like manner as other costs.

(c)*Disclosure of appointment.* In the exercise of its discretion, the court may authorize disclosure to the jury of the fact that the court appointed the expert witness.

(d)*Parties' experts of own selection.* Nothing in this rule limits the parties in calling expert witnesses of their own selection.

Rule 707 Use of Learned Treatises for Impeachment

To the extent called to the attention of an expert witness upon cross-examination or relied upon by him in direct examination, statements contained in published treatises, periodicals, or pamphlets on a subject of history, medicine, or other science or art, established as a reliable authority by the testimony or admission of the witness or by other expert testimony or by judicial notice, are admissible for impeachment purposes only.

Expert witnesses may be cross-examined as any other witness and especially as to qualifications, bases of opinions, and compensation for testifying.

Expert witnesses may express opinions in response to hypothetical questions, if the hypothesized facts in the questions are supported by the evidence of the case.

Accountants and auditors are often called upon to provide testimony in litigation support matters and criminal prosecutions in which their services are utilized to support investigations of such crimes as financial frauds, embezzlement, misapplication of funds, arson for profit, bankruptcy fraud, and tax evasion. Accountants and auditors may also be utilized as defense witnesses or as support to the defendant's counsel on matters that involve accounting or audit issues.

QUALIFICATION AND ADMISSIBILITY OF ACCOUNTING SCHEDULES

To qualify accountants and auditors as technical experts generally is not a difficult task. Questions are posed to them concerning their professional credentials—education, work experience, licensing or certification, technical-training courses taken, technical books and journal articles written, offices held in professional associations, and awards and commendations received.

Defense lawyers generally are not prone to challenge the expertise of accountants and auditors, assuming they meet at least minimum standards of professional competence. To do so might give these experts an opportunity to fully highlight their professional credentials and perhaps make a greater impression on the jury or judge, thus adding more weight to their testimony. So defense attorneys often pass on the opportunity to challenge these expert witnesses.

When accountants and auditors are called by the prosecution they generally testify about their investigative findings; when they are called by the defense, they may testify about the quality of the findings or the opinions expressed by the prosecution's accounting expert, in order to create doubt in the minds of members of the jury about the credibility or weight to give to the prosecution's expert.

To be a credible expert witness, accountants and auditors should be knowledgeable in their own fields by education and experience and members in good standing of the profession or of some specialized aspect of practice that would be pertinent to the case at hand. But there are other considerations as well to make an expert witness credible. Experts will appear credible when they follow these suggestions:

- Speak clearly and audibly.
- Refrain from using professional jargon.
- Use simple rather than complex terms to describe findings and opinions.
- Address the specific questions asked; do not go off on tangents or volunteer more than a question asks.
- Do not verbally fence with the defense attorney or prosecutor.
- Look directly at the question poser (prosecutor or defense counsel).
- Maintain a professional demeanor; do not smile gratuitously at the judge, the jury, the lawyer who hired you, or the opponent's counsel.

- Be calm and deliberate in responding to questions; speak neither too slowly nor too rapidly.
- Dress conservatively.
- Have hair neatly combed and shoes newly shined.
- Use graphs, charts, and other visual aids if they help to clarify a point.
- Do not read from notes if you can avoid it. (The opposition lawyer will probably demand to see such notes if you do, and you will then appear to have rehearsed your testimony.)
- If you have documents to introduce, have them organized so that you can quickly retrieve them when asked to do so by the counsel for whose side you are testifying.
- Do not hem and haw or stammer. Retain your composure when a tough or complex question is posed.
- Ask for repetition or clarification if you do not fully understand the question.
- If you do not know the answer, say so—don't guess.
- In cross-examination do not respond too quickly. Counsel for your side may wish to interpose an objection to the question.
- If the judge elects to ask a question, respond to it by looking at him or her.
- Do not stare off into space, or at the floor or ceiling.
- Be friendly to all sides.
- Do not raise your voice in anger if the opponent's lawyer tries to bait you.
- Be honest. Don't invent. Don't inflate. Don't evade.

The goal of forensic accountants is to make their findings understandable to counsel, judges, and juries, and to avoid resorting to jargon and academic polemics about accounting rules and standards. The facts, stated simply and briefly, are all the audience needs or cares to hear. Anything beyond that only makes accounting and auditing more obscure.

Qualifying as an Expert Witness

The extract reproduced from the proceedings in *Regina v. Scheel* shows how the accountant's qualifications as an expert witness can be established and how accounting exhibits might be introduced.

Robert John Lindquist: Sworn
Examination-in-Chief by Mr. Hunt (Crown):

Q. Mr. Lindquist, where do you reside, sir?
A. I live in Toronto, Ontario.

Q.   And what is your occupation?

A.   I am a chartered accountant.

Q.   And do you practice on your own or with someone else?

A.   I practice in partnership with other chartered accountants under the firm name of Lindquist, Holmes, and Company.

Q.   And how long have you been operating the partnership as a chartered accountant?

A.   Close to six years now.

Q.   And prior to that were you associated with any other firm?

A.   Yes, prior to that I worked for a period of six years with a national accounting firm where I studied after my graduation from University.

Q.   And in what year did you qualify as a chartered accountant?

A.   In 1972.

Q.   And since that date have you had occasion to testify in court with respect to accounting matters?

A.   I have.

Q.   And on approximately how many occasions would that have occurred?

A.   An estimate of some 50 occasions.

Q.   Your Honor, I tender Mr. Lindquist as a witness who should be classified as an expert witness on the basis of his qualifications that I have elicited.

Mr. Hermiston:

I am content with the qualifications, Your Honor.

His Honor:

Thank you.

Mr. Hunt:

Mr. Lindquist, I understand that you have prepared a number of documents relating to various transactions dealing with Metro Pallet Repair?

A.   Yes, I have.

Q.   Could I see Exhibit A? I am presenting to you a document, a rather large document, marked Exhibit A on the Voir Dire. I would ask you to look at that document and tell me if you recognize that?

A.   Yes, I do.

Q.   And did you prepare that document yourself?

A.   Yes, I did.

Q.   And I wonder if, so the jury can see it, you would hold it in such a way that the jury will be able to see the structure of the document. It appears to consist of a number of columns, vertical columns; am I correct?

A.   That's correct.

Q.   And the document is headed what?

A.   It's headed, "Analysis of Sales for the Period August 1, 1973, to October 3, 1973."[2]

Admissibility of Accounting Evidence

Documentary accounting evidence may be presented in a court of law in two forms: (1) primary, including original, individual accounting documents obtained from the parties concerned or other sources, and (2) secondary, including summaries and schedules based on the original documents. These are produced by an accountant based on an examination of the primary evidence.

> The admissibility of such evidence is well established in the United States. In *Hoyer v. United States,* 8 Cir., 223 F.2d 134 (1955), the Court held that in a prosecution for attempting to evade income taxes, summaries prepared from documentary and oral evidence were admissible to show the defendant's correct net income. Gardner, Chief Judge, delivering the judgment of the Court said:[3] ". . . these exhibits so compiled and prepared purported to show the correct net income of the defendant for the years covered by the indictment. They were prepared by experts from documentary evidence introduced and from oral testimony. As the documentary evidence had already been introduced, counsel for the defendant had ample opportunity to examine it and to cross-examine the expert as to the basic testimony and his calculations based thereon. The evidence was clearly admissible.
>
> The documentary evidence presented a complicated situation and required elaborate compilations which could not have been made by the jury. It is also to be noted in this connection that the Court advised the jury that the testimony of the experts was advisory and need not be accepted by them as a verity."

In *Daniel v. United States,* 5 Cir., 343 F.2d 785 (1965), Hunter, District Judge, delivering the judgment of the Court, said:[4]

> . . . The rule is that a summary of books and records is admissible, provided cross-examination is allowed and the original records are available. Here the records of which the exhibits are summaries were in evidence, and the man who prepared them was available for cross-examination.
>
> It is perfectly proper that litigants be permitted the use of illustrative charts to summarize varying computations and to thus make the primary proof upon which such charts must be based more enlightening to the jury. The district judge did not abuse his discretion by permitting the use of these summaries.
>
> I would also observe that in the present case the summaries were helpful to the appellant, with respect to some of the counts.

The introduction of the summaries did not offend against the rule that requires the production of original documents, since the documents which were the primary source of the summaries were in evidence. It is accordingly unnecessary in this case to invoke the exception to the rule referred to by Wigmore in the following passage:

Where a fact could be ascertained only by the inspection of a large number of documents made up of very *numerous detailed shipments* . . . as the net balance resulting from a year's vouchers of a treasurer or a year's accounts in a bank ledger—it is obvious that it would often be practically out of the question to apply the present principle by requiring the production of the entire mass of documents and entries to be perused by the jury or read aloud to them. The convenience of trials demands that other evidence be allowed to be offered, in the shape of the testimony of a competent witness who has perused the entire mass and will state summarily the net result. Such a practice is well established to be proper.

Most courts require, as a condition, that the mass thus summarily testified to shall, if the occasion seems to require it, be placed at hand in court, or at least be made accessible to the opposing party, in order that the correctness of the evidence may be tested by inspection if desired, or that the material for cross-examination may be made available. . . ."

Accordingly, we were of the view that the learned trial judge did not err in admitting the summaries previously described.

PROFILE OF THE EXPERT WITNESS

Expert accounting witnesses must have a thorough knowledge not only of generally accepted accounting principles but also of the current promulgations of their institute. Often, the expert's expertise may involve special knowledge of a specific industry, such as construction accounting or accounting in a stock market environment. In this case, the expert should be aware of recent developments and any important accounting issues within that area.

Experts must also be analytical and possess the ability to work with incomplete data; however, they may not always be able to recognize when data is incomplete. As a result, the experts may make various assumptions that would then be open to interpretation or attack. If all data have *not* been made available, then it is quite possible that the opposing counsel may be able to offer alternate scenarios that are more plausible under the circumstances, thus discrediting the expert.

Experts must have the ability to simplify complex issues. It is helpful if they can communicate very directly and simply, keeping in mind that they are talking to nonaccountants and that the expert's role is to clarify complex issues so that everyone can understand them. In view of this, some background or experience in teaching often is helpful.

The question of whether or not being a chartered accountant is sufficient to qualify oneself as an expert often arises. Generally, persons *may* be experts in their particular field of expertise if they have sufficient experience and are members of their institute. This does not mean that chartered accountants are automatically experts; however, it passes the first hurdle. It is helpful to have prior experience with litigation or criminal matters, to be considered an expert. This is primarily as a result of the awareness that is instilled during the testifying experience. Further, it is often helpful to have been accepted as an expert in other matters, thereby easing current acceptance. A danger exists, however, of appearing to be an expert at being an expert witness.

Often, the counsel introducing the witness will read the expert's qualifications or ask specific questions of the witness to establish his or her credentials. On occasion, the qualifications of the expert witness are read directly into the court record. Although the expert's qualifications are not often contested, it is a distinct possibility. Over and above being accepted by both parties, it is most important that the expert witness be accepted by the court.

THE EXPERT'S ROLE IN THE LITIGATION TEAM

Generally, experts play an ongoing part in the litigation team. In particular, their involvement may be at various stages throughout the development of the case, most notably:

1. Case assessment.
2. Identification of documentation required to support the case, both additional and currently available.
3. Evaluation of the scope of work.
4. Preparation of initial financial assessment and analysis.
5. Consultation with counsel on legal issues and approach.
6. Preparation of report and accounting schedules and, if necessary, a document brief.
7. Negotiations between parties.
8. Assistance to counsel in court.
9. Expert evidence in court.

The accountant may also be called on to give a different opinion than that reached by an equally credible expert accountant on the other side. This may arise because of different interpretations of the facts of the case or various alternative accounting techniques that might be available under the circumstances. In some cases, given equally plausible alternatives, the case often is decided on whichever side has the most credible expert witness.

PRETESTIMONY ACTIVITIES

Pretestimony activities generally encompass preparing the report of the expert witness to a final stage. Without stating that the list is all inclusive or appropriate in all circumstances, reports should include a discussion of the following financial aspects:

- Issues
- Reliance on data to achieve conclusion
- Assumptions made in arriving at conclusion
- Restriction on assumptions
- Date of information cut-off
- Opinion and conclusion based on the available documentation
- Limitations of opinion and sensitivity to assumptions
- Detailed schedules and documents supporting the opinion and conclusion

One important problem in preparing reports and accounting summaries arises from the delegation of tasks to junior accountants. If the person giving evidence has not had direct knowledge or has not examined the specific documents or prepared the accounting summaries, it may be possible that the expert will be trapped under the hearsay rule. If tasks are delegated, it is important that the review process entail review of all work to original documentation on a 100 percent basis.

It is also important to know the effect of other assumptions on the conclusion or opinion reached in the report. It is often possible to trap an expert into giving alternate opinions, based on other assumptions that had not been considered. Generally, working papers supporting the report and accounting schedules should not show contradictory conclusions to the report, as they are producible in court. This does not advocate that working papers should be deleted or amended subsequent to preparation; rather, it is a caution that these papers should be prepared with the precept that they could ultimately be submitted to the court and, as such, should take the appropriate form when they are prepared.

Another aspect of pretrial preparation relates to the availability of all notes that the witness intends to use or rely on. These notes may be requested in evidence for the court or may be producible during examination.

Further activities could consist of determining whether sufficient material is present to support the report. It may be necessary to derive information from other witnesses to support the expert's conclusions. This normally is done by reference to discoveries or earlier will-says. Unfortunately, the witness cannot refer to these unless he or she has direct knowledge of their contents. If the accountant has relied on opinions or information presented by other witnesses then he or she must either hear that evidence in court or have the transcript or agreed statement of facts available. Otherwise, that information and any opinions drawn from it would not be allowable.

It often is useful to have a list of all other witnesses including the witnesses for the other side. This is important so that the expert is not surprised by the existence of other experts or reports. One can then determine if it is necessary that the expert be present for the testimony of those witnesses and obtain the related court approval. If another expert will be present, then it is incumbent on the expert witness to examine the alternate reports and assess whether reasonable points are brought by the other side that may affect the credibility of the expert's report.

Other pretestimony activities encompass ensuring that any required graphic displays are ready and available, that all important discussions with the lawyer have been held as part of the pretestimony meetings, and that the expert completely understands the report and all other relevant issues in the trial *whether accounting-related or not.* Most important, experts must ensure that they agree with counsel as to the sequence of the experts' evidence and the strategy for presenting it. It is often useful to have a dry run at the direct testimony, with all the questions being posed by the counsel to the expert witness in order to avoid surprises during trial.

At pretestimony meetings, it is often appropriate to discuss the witness's qualifications again to assure that they are current, to discuss the strengths and weaknesses of the case, and to discuss and agree on which parts of the expert's reports, if not all, are to be entered into court as exhibits.

ON THE STAND: DEMEANOR AND APPEARANCE

Judges and juries often base their assessments of expert witnesses at least in part on how the witnesses look. Therefore, it is important that witnesses be well-groomed and neatly dressed. In the case of an accountant, a dark business suit is the expected image. This appearance may enhance the image to psychological advantage. In the witness box, the witness should maintain a poised, alert appearance, stand still, and be ready to take the oath. It is important to control the hands, avoid fidgeting, and to maintain eye contact with the questioner. As the judge will be taking notes, the witness should speak slowly enough to ensure that the judge does not fall behind. The voice should be strong and directed to the questioner. The witness should enunciate clearly.

Several things should be avoided in giving evidence. These range from drinking five cups of coffee immediately before testifying or chewing bubble gum while giving evidence, to small physical mannerisms that may affect your appearance. These physical mannerisms, which might be as simple as rubbing your hands together continually, looking down at your hands, continually moving in the stand, or jingling coins in a pocket, could quickly become irritating to the judge.

DIRECT EXAMINATION

The purpose of direct examination is to enable counsel for the side you represent to draw out the financial evidence to prove the case. Most likely, this will be only a reiteration of what has been discussed previously with your counsel outside of the courtroom. It is still very important, however, to refresh your memory by reference to anything you may have read, written, or given in evidence on the case beforehand.

Direct examination is the most organized aspect of the trial; it is the stage in which the expert's credibility must be established with the judge or jury. According to the concept of the primary memory feature, people remember best what they hear first and last. This is often a useful idea to employ in giving or structuring evidence. A further noteworthy point is that the jury will often have a limited attention span in a long trial; thus, it is often useful to use a "grab/give/conclude" method of presenting evidence.

For a witness, the interpretation of questions and the ability to listen are crucial skills. Even though the witness already may have gone through a mock direct examination, it is critical that each question be evaluated carefully again; the witness should reflect on the questions asked and not anticipate them (they may have been changed since the time of rehearsal). Throughout, it is useful to remember that this aspect of testimony was rehearsed in advance and so is the easiest aspect of examination.

It is necessary to be honest in answering questions. Less obvious, however, is the need to avoid bias and prejudice when answering. The answers to all questions should be clear and concise, and when complex terms are used they should be clarified. Use of notes should be limited as much as possible in order to maintain eye contact with both the judge and the rest of the court.

Accounting schedules should be described accurately and succinctly in layperson's terms. Schedules are by their nature concise documents and should be described in that manner. If opinions are given, they should be given with conviction once the appropriate groundwork has been laid.

CROSS-EXAMINATION

Cross-examination is truly the highlight of the adversarial court system; it is geared to allow counsel to either clarify or make points at the witness's expense. As such, it is generally the most difficult part of the trial process for any witness. Anything unexpected can turn up that might refute or embarrass the witness, whose credibility is constantly called into question.

The goals of the opposing counsel during cross-examination are threefold. The first is to diminish the importance of the expert testimony just presented. The second might be to have the expert testify in support of the opposing position by providing a series of assumptions. The third is to attack the opinion itself or to show the inadequacies of the expert's work in arriving at his or her opinion, thereby discrediting the opinion, the report, and the witness in the eyes of the court.

The opposing counsel can attack or question anything that was said or entered into court. This includes notes, working papers, affidavits, will-says, reports, and preliminary trial or discovery transcripts. Often, cross-examination is conducted in an atmosphere of confrontation and contradiction. At all times, remember that the financial expert witness, however crucial to the case, is merely a piece of the puzzle.

Most important, witnesses must not take attacks or attempts to discredit them personally. There are many ways to discredit an expert witness. Throughout the process it is important for the witness to maintain pride and professional integrity. An adage to remember is that "even mud can be worn well."

In general, proper attitude and demeanor during direct examination are also applicable to cross-examination, except that opposing counsel wants to reduce or limit the impact of the witness's evidence. It is natural to feel a certain amount of apprehension at this stage, and this does a great deal to keep the witness alert.

The jury often watches the judge, and therefore the expert often can take a clue as to the tempo and reaction of the jury and the judge to the evidence being presented. Slight changes in style and presentation can be made accordingly.

The opposing counsel usually has a plan of cross-examination in mind, and an expert witness should be able to establish this direction to prevent falling into a trap or erring. A danger of this, of course, is that the witness will spend as much time planning ahead as answering the questions and may not be giving appropriate weight to the immediate questions. Further, in attempting to anticipate questions, the witness may misunderstand the one being asked.

When asked questions, the expert should evaluate them carefully and take time to consider the answers. The witness should be calm and pause before answering, and tread very carefully towards the answer, knowing exactly how it relates to both the question and the issues before the court.

When answering it is important to be honest and to avoid the appearance of bias and prejudice. It is equally important not to exaggerate, ramble, allow oneself to be baited, or attempt to be humorous. One of the most devastating blows to a litigation or defendant is having an expert witness make a transparent attempt to hide errors or lose his or her temper.

Generally, it is a rule of thumb for expert witnesses not to give away or volunteer information. Further, during the answer, it may often be extremely difficult to avoid being trapped in various assumptions, "what if" scenarios, and generalities presented by counsel during cross-examination. If this occurs, retrench by asking for the question to be rephrased in smaller components.

It is critical never, *never* to underestimate the accounting expertise of the opposing counsel. Often, opposing counsel will be underplaying their understanding of the issues in order to lull the expert into a sense of security. Obviously, this can lead the expert into a difficult situation.

In general terms, opposing counsel's golden rule is to cross-examine only if the cross-examination would benefit a case. In questioning the witness, opposing counsel will generally ask either simply worded short questions or leading questions. Usually counsel know the answers to their questions in order to eliminate any surprises and to allow them to lead the witness along. Several techniques are also available to destroy witnesses without touching their evidence.

The opposing counsel generally will evaluate answers and then take a specific approach that furthers their arguments. Generally, witnesses will not be allowed to explain or elaborate on answers at that time as that would allow a witness to alter the thrust of the carefully orchestrated cross-examination. Opposing counsel is also continually questioning or evaluating how its last question and answer could be used against the witness. If the question has raised new ground, can it be developed and used to enhance the opposing counsel's position?

Opposing counsel will often prepare by reading all the witness's earlier testimony and publications. The opposing counsel might also speak to other lawyers about the witness's earlier performance in court. This may indicate specific weaknesses a witness may have. If any are discovered, the questioning of the witness will probably be directed to that area.

Opposing counsel may also attempt to take psychological control of a witness by:

- Using his or her physical presence to intimidate
- Maintaining nonstop eye contact
- Challenging the space of the witness
- Posing fast-pace questions to confuse the witness
- Not allowing the expert to explain or deviate from the exact question

Opposing counsel often uses physical domination. Opposing counsel will quickly discover the expert's response pattern, and might take an aggressive stance to lead the expert to the point where he or she is unsure, with devastating results.

Strategies Employed in Cross-Examination

The following strategic methods could be employed by opposing counsel to discredit witnesses or to diminish the importance of their testimony. These methods could be used singly or in conjunction with one another, and are not an all-encompassing list. A good counsel in cross-examination will quickly discover the witness's weak areas and employ any possible techniques to achieve his or her goal. Thus, it is often useful to have an overall understanding of some of the more common methods employed.

Myopic Vision   Myopic vision entails getting the expert to admit to excessive time being spent in the investigation of a matter, then highlighting an area of which the expert is unsure or in which he or she has not done much work. This area may not be central to the issues in the case but must be relevant to conclusions reached. Then, the opposing counsel will make a large issue of it and prove that the expert's vision is myopic in that the work was limited in extent or scope and, as such, substandard. At the same time, the question of fees could be drawn in to show that large sums were expended to have this "obviously incomplete" work done.

Safety/Good Guy   Often, the opposing counsel will begin a cross examination gently, not attacking the expert and so lulling him or her into a feeling of false security. Then, opposing counsel might find a small hole that could be enlarged quickly. Often the opposing counsel appears friendly and conciliatory, so that the jury becomes sympathetic to his or her cause. Opposing counsel may also attempt to achieve a rapport with the witness that will make the witness want to help the opposition to bring out information in the matter. Doing so might result in the witness giving information that otherwise would not have been given. With this additional information, it might be possible to find a chink or hole in the evidence and develop it further.

Contradiction   Opposing counsel might use leading questions to force the witness into a hard or contradictory position. Alternately, counsel can establish the credibility in court of a potentially contradicting document or quote from other articles written by other experts in the field. If these documents or articles contradict the expert, then the expert might admit to that contradiction. If the contradiction exists, the expert might be drawn into an argument as to who is the most appropriate or experienced expert in the circumstances. Instances also have occurred when witnesses have contradicted themselves or their own articles written several years earlier merely because they have forgotten or have become confused by the attack.

New Information   Opposing counsel may introduce new information of which the expert might not be aware, or refer to a specific relevance in the conclusions the expert witness reaches. This is normally done to confuse witness so that the witness might contradict himself or herself or develop a series of alternate scenarios, given the new information that shows that his or her report and opinions are no longer of value.

Support Opposing Sides Theory   This approach establishes and recognizes an expert's qualifications and evidence. The same information the expert uses is then used and interpreted by opposing counsel in a different way to support an alternate theory. By getting the expert to agree to the alternate interpretation of the facts and theory, the opposing counsel has in effect made the expert a witness for the other side. This technique is useful to obtain concessions from witnesses that would damage their conclusions and, ultimately, their credibility.

Bias   This method draws the expert's counsel and the expert together to show possible collusion in the evidence being presented in testimony, and hence show bias. This can be shown if the opposing counsel determines that the expert's counsel had instructed the witness about what to say, or by limiting the expert's scope and hence conclusions. This approach can also focus on the question of whether or not the expert was told by the client what to do and look for. With this approach, opposing counsel can attempt to show that the expert overlooked important documentation in an effort to assist his or her client.

Confrontation   This very simple method is the continued use of a confrontation of wills to put witnesses into a situation in which they might lose control and become angry. Once a witness has exploded, credibility disappears.

Sounding Board   This method uses the witness as a sounding board to reacquaint the jury with the favorable aspects (to opposing counsel) of the case. This technique often uses the "Is it not true" and "Would you agree with me" approach. Constant nonstop agreement is useful to browbeat the expert. To the judge and jury, agreement with various questions the opposing counsel raises may also be interpreted as a general concurrence with the opposing counsel's position. This is often a valuable psychological tool.

Fees   This method attacks the witness for taking an inordinate amount of time to achieve the result. Further, the attack may indicate incomplete work and may be correlated to the fees charged. This method is often related to "bias" and "myopic vision." Because of high fees or reoccurring engagements with a client, it may be suggested that the witness and his or her opinion are biased for the client. This technique often builds to a conclusion in which the opposing counsel shows that the work was superficial and unprofessional, but the expert received a great deal of money for this and other areas of service to the client; the direct implication is that the testimony was purchased or that the expert was paid to overlook facts contradictory to his or her conclusions.

Terms of Engagement   This technique normally starts by opposing counsel obtaining the original engagement letter and examining the terms of engagement, then showing that the expert intended to examine only items in support of his or her client and glossed over any alternative theories, generally to the detriment of the opposition. Therefore, the witness could be portrayed as partial.

Discrediting the Witness   Discrediting the witness is the concept of proving that the expert is unworthy to be a credible witness. This often is accomplished by showing that the expert currently is, or has previously been, grossly biased, prejudiced, corrupt, convicted of criminal activities, shown to engage in immoral activities, made inconsistent statements, acquired a reputation for a lack of veracity, and/or exaggerated his or her qualifications.

Discrediting might also look at the quality of the experts' educational background to reveal any other unusual activities that might bias them or exclude them from the court as experts.

SURVIVAL TECHNIQUES

Here are ten points for the expert witness to remember both in preparing for and in giving evidence at trial. Remember to:

1. Prepare your material completely.
2. Know your material thoroughly.
3. Plan your testimony in advance.
4. Be alert.
5. Listen carefully.
6. Carefully consider each answer, and pause before answering.
7. Be honest and avoid bias.
8. Clarify—use simple words.

9. Keep your cool.

10. Maintain professional pride and integrity throughout.

REFERENCES

1. Michigan Supreme Court Rules of Evidence, Rules 702, 703, 704, 705, 706, 707.
2. Ontario Court of Appeals, Regina v. Scheel, May 12, 1978.
3. *Hoyer v. U.S.,* 8 Cir., 223 F.2d 134, 1955, p. 138.
4. *Daniel v. U.S.* 5 Cir., 343 F.2d 785, 1965, Hunter District Judge, p. 789.

Chapter 10

General Criteria and Standards for Evaluating an Expert's Qualifications*

Determining that a given person is sufficiently knowledgeable and capable of serving as an expert depends on two factors. First, does the candidate possess the objective qualifications for the job? Does he or she have the appropriate credentials, relevant prior experience, and critical information that bears on successful resolution of the case?

Second, does the expert, though sufficiently qualified, have the personal characteristics to effectively function as part of the investigative team? Is the individual a team player? Does his or her professional reputation and the quality of previous work recommend using him or her in the case at hand? Can the expert explain technical complexities in such a way that both the criminal justice practitioners—investigators, prosecutors, and judges—and the jury can clearly understand their meaning and importance? Does the expert project a professional manner? Can he or she build and keep rapport with others? The following sections address in detail both the requisite formal credentials and the essential personal characteristics that effective consultants and expert witnesses must display.

CREDENTIALS

Credentials and standards vary for assessing the knowledgeability of out-of-court experts, depending on the area of expertise. Even with regard to laying the foundation at trial for the court to accept a witness as an expert, the criteria, though generally standardized between fields of expertise in the eyes of

*Excerpted from the *Computer Crime Expert Witness Manuel,* 1980, Koba Associates, Inc. Reprinted with permission of the Bureau of Justice Statistics, U.S. Department of Justice.

207

the law, are not inflexible and are subject to some variation. With these caveats in mind, there are several broad areas in which experts are expected to have credentials and qualifications that distinguish them from laypeople. These include the following:

- Professional licensure, certification, or registration by a recognized professional body in the field of expertise in question
- Undergraduate, graduate, and postgraduate academic degrees that are either in the field of expertise or serve as a suitable background to it
- Specialized training and/or continuing professional education beyond academic degrees that indicate up-to-date familiarity with the latest technical developments in the subject area
- Writings and publications that display technical opinions and are available as part of the general body of knowledge in the subject area
- Relevant teaching, lecturing and/or other consultancies that indicate that he or she is held in high professional esteem in the subject area
- Affiliation with professional associations
- Directly relevant prior experience gained through similar assignments, whether as technical advisor or expert witness, in the subject area
- Special status, or access to privileged information, peculiar to the case at hand, which renders the individual an expert

Professional Licensure, Certification, or Registration

Most professional organizations to some degree, regulate their members and feature mechanisms for reviewing a practitioner's qualifications—often at periodic intervals. Endorsements about competence—a license to practice the profession, a certification in a specialty area, or registration at a central professional regulatory authority in the jurisdiction—are all common practices. A professional license, certification, or registration is an important factor in assessing the level of basic competence for technical advisors in most areas of expertise useful in financial and computer-related crime investigations. Establishing that an individual has a license or certification in his or her profession, and/or is registered in the jurisdiction as a practitioner of that profession, is a standard step in laying the foundation at trial for the court to accept the testimony of such a person as an expert.

Determining what standards are used to qualify a practitioner in a given profession can easily be determined by inquiring of the professional licensing or certifying body in question. In addition, many jurisdictions require practitioners in a wide variety of professions, who may have acquired their credentials elsewhere, to register with a central government authority if they want to practice their profession locally. The central registering authority can be a useful source of information on professional licensing standards locally and perhaps a source of expert referrals.

Many of the more traditional professional organizations supply experts in crime cases. Those include lawyers, engineers, and forensic chemists. Most states have laws that dictate the criteria for professional licensing in these broader professions.

Academic Degrees

Traditionally, the academic degrees they hold has been key to determining whether professionals will qualify as expert witnesses.[1] Even when experts are used only behind the scenes in the investigation of computer-related crimes, their backgrounds can be investigated by the defense and their credentials will be considered. This is particularly true because as technical advisors they become potential expert witnesses.

Despite the strategic importance of appropriate academic credential for experts whose credibility the defense may challenge, it is important not to rely too heavily on academic qualifications alone. Many universities do not have well developed courses about computer-related crime, especially on the postgraduate level, and because the field is changing so rapidly the courses they do have may not be current. Therefore, knowledgeable sources agree that when an expert witness's academic credentials are considered, how recently the degrees were awarded and whether he or she has continued to take courses in the field should be considered as well.

Training and Continuing Education Experience

Developments in computer programming, electronics, telecommunications engineering, EDP auditing, computer security, and other specializations are increasing rapidly. Training and continuing education in these areas, and such fields as combating white-collar crime, economic crime, and computer crime, are being offered widely. Professional associations and regulatory bodies frequently offer certificates of completion and other objective indicators of ungraded skills for attending such courses.

How many current, relevant training courses and continuing education courses has the prospective technical expert attended? How up to date is he or she on the state of the art in this technical field? A showing of such currency is generally a corollary to the presentation of academic credentials to the court when an expert witness's qualifications are reviewed. The absence of such current educational updates would not only have a strong affect on the quality of the expert advice given to the government, but it can lead to the government's expert witness being impeached on cross-examination and the technical accuracy of aspects of the government's case being challenged.

Writings and Publications

Whether prospective expert witnesses have published in the field of their purported expertise is traditionally an important factor to review when laying the foundation at trial for the technical advisor to take the stand as an expert witness. Prior publications may be less relevant when experts are used as technical advisors to the investigative or prosecutive team during the case preparation stages. However, this is not necessarily the case. The prior publications of computer-related crime scholars/researchers retained to assist in profiling the computer felon(s) and determining the modus operandi in complex computer fraud cases will be directly relevant. Their availability could greatly assist the team by providing them with an orientation, and such published views could be challenged if the technical advisor's identity is discoverable during pretrial.

What books or articles has the technical advisor written on the subject in question? Were they published, and if so, how recently? How were the expert's works received by his or her professional peers? Are the expert's works considered authoritative? Do other published works in the same field challenge or contradict the expert's published views? Are the experts' published views consistent in all of their writings? Are their published views, while consistent among themselves, congruent with the expert's current views on the case at hand? These are all critical questions to be addressed when selecting an expert. Especially if there is to be an established or prolonged professional relationship with the expert, the consultant's published works must be analyzed and monitored during pretrial preparation to avoid significant discrepancies that may arise between the expert's present planned testimony and past, possibly contradictory, positions he or she has taken.

Teaching and Other Consultancies

Activities that show a consultant's prior acceptance as an expert advisor or instructor go to the issue of his or her reliability and credibility as part of the government's team. Such activities as teaching or consulting in a given field traditionally are considered at the time an expert's credentials are presented to the court before he or she takes the stand as an expert witness. Because of the newness and rapid evolution of computer-related technology, such credentials may hold more weight in a computer-related crime case than academic degrees or publications. A careful check with past users of the prospective experts' service—trainees or clients for whom they have consulted—can be an excellent way to assess their reliability and stature, plus the currency and nature of their views before retaining them in a given case.

Government experts' extensive prior teaching and/or consultancies, if they have been retained for a fee, can sometimes work to the detriment of the prosecution. For example, experts who for a fee have done extensive training of investigators and prosecutors of computer crime, and/or who have for a fee testified frequently for the prosecution in such cases, but not for the defense, could be impeached for bias and/or financial interest if the government calls them as expert witnesses.[2] Especially when a substantial part of an expert's income derives from such services to law enforcement, his or her comparative usefulness as an expert witness may be compromised.

Even if such experts are not potential expert witnesses, their identity and involvement in preparing the case may prove discoverable by the defense and lead to allegations of bias in the technical advice rendered at the investigatory stage. These considerations aside, retention of an expert who has extensively trained and consulted for *only one side* in such cases can lessen the fundamental value of having an outside expert on the investigative team to begin with.

Professional Associations

As in the case of professional licensure, prospective experts' certification or membership in professional associations adds to a presumption of competence and is routinely included in the proffering of an expert's credentials to the court before presenting expert testimony. As with the matters of licensure, academic degrees, continuing education, and prior consultancies, membership in professional associations is subject to verification checks and to the gathering of references from the expert's professional peers. This is an important and useful quality-control check.

Previous Similar Experience

Because the various computer technology fields are new and new developments in computer technology occur so quickly, formal credentials are less important in computer-related crime cases than direct prior experience with the victim company's computer operations, the brands of hardware or software the victim used, and the software applications involved. In addition, prior experience in investigating computer-related crimes, providing computer security, or computer-related crime research can be the critical element that renders a particular party an expert advisor. Identifying trustworthy and objective advisors who have such direct prior experience can be the most important factor in selecting an expert. Despite traditional criteria, such as formal credentials, by which a proffered expert's qualifications to testify as an expert witness are normally assessed, the trial judge has broad discretion to base a decision that an individual is an expert qualified to testify on a given subject primarily—or even solely—on that person's prior relevant experience.

There are pitfalls in over reliance on technical advisors with extensive prior experience in a subject area. Maintaining control over the overall management and direction of the case can be one difficulty. Susceptibility to defense charges of partisanship and bias against experts with extensive prior experience disproportionately on the government's side only is another hazard. Regardless, past experience remains the single most important qualification of experts in computer-related crime.

Sole Access to Privileged Information or Facts

Employees of the victimized agency or of the manufacturer, vendor, or service organization whose computer products the victims used can be among the most useful technical advisors when investigating a computer-related crime case or preparing one for trial. The background, education, and other credentials of such people can vary tremendously; this group can include top management at the victim organization, in-house computer technologists, data providers, equipment operators, and others who handle relevant data or are in sole possession of facts about the victim's operations. As a result, these people's qualifications in their own fields, while important, will prove secondary to their familiarity with aspects of the victim's operations and equipment. For the narrow purpose of laying out what such operational practices routinely were or what equipment capabilities and vulnerabilities are, courts can be expected to admit expert testimony from such people, if the prosecution is able to demonstrate their familiarity with such factors and their general competence.

The greatest pitfalls in using such individuals as pretrial technical advisors or as expert witnesses at trial are: (1) distinguishing the true area of competence and (2) bias. Employees or service personnel may be qualified to speak authoritatively on only very narrow points and be completely unqualified on other related points. In addition, loyalty to the employer, job security considerations, or, on the other hand, a grudge against the employer or another employee may taint the individual's objectivity and hence his or her utility. And, of course, the investigative team must be especially circumspect about bringing such persons in as technical advisors, unless and until their possible complicity in the crime is completely ruled out.

Personal Qualities of the Expert

The other standards in deciding whether to use a particular person as a technical advisor or expert witness are the personal qualities of the prospective expert. Because this area is primarily subjective, as distinguished from the relative objectiveness of credentials, it is difficult to say what the key factors are and how they should be assessed. However, eight considerations hold true for the use of technical advisors or expert witnesses in any major case, whether or not they are computer related. The following sections present these considerations.

1. Ability to Work as Part of a Team Regardless of the area of their professional competence, many individuals are not temperamentally or attitudinally geared to working as part of a team. Doubtless this problem is more prevalent with certain professions than with others because of the nature of the work and other factors. Assessing whether a prospective expert will be a team player is a critical decision that must be made very early in the relationship, before the expert is retained. Reference checks and personal interviews help in making this determination. Effective management of the expert in the case, the security of sensitive investigative data, and the effectiveness of the expert as a witness on the stand are only a few of the overriding considerations that dictate using only team players in expert roles.

2. Trustworthiness and Integrity Despite the advisability of limiting a technical advisor's access to casework on a "need-to-know" basis, the expert invariably will be exposed to sensitive information during the course of the case. At the very least, this will extend to a knowledge of his or her own role in the case, of those aspects of the investigation where he or she has been providing input, and the identities of others on the investigative team. The trustworthiness and discretion of the expert must be assured and maintained.

As with the problem of ensuring that the expert is a team player, detailed reference checks and personal interviews must be used to check the expert's trustworthiness and integrity.

3. Professional Reputation and Recognition As important as academic degrees and publications is an expert's stature and reputation among his or her peers. While this will be partly a product of the authoritativeness of his or her views and credentials and experience in the field, it will also be reflective of his or her qualities. Many of the qualities will be directly relevant to whether the expert will be able to establish a harmonious working relationship with others on the case.

Experts' reputations can cut both ways with regard to their credibility as expert witnesses on the stand: If their views are controversial or even contested, the greater the experts' fame, the more likely the defense will be able to identify counterexperts familiar with the views and at odds with them. On the other hand, increased fame can go to the issue of stature and authoritativeness, by which opposing expert opinion can be overshadowed.

Reference checks and a review of the literature in the field to accurately gauge experts' professional stature and reputation are important steps to take before retaining them. Even if they are not retained as potential expert witnesses, the nature of their role in the case or the nature of the retainer agreement can make experts' identities discoverable by the defense at the pretrial stage, and thus their reputations are open to attack.

4. Quality and Timeliness of Previous Work It is critically important to assess the quality of experts' work *before* retaining them. Most directly, the quality of their prior consultancies and service as expert witnesses must be checked out in great detail. The professional community's perception of the quality of the experts' work, publication, teaching, or lectures should be determined. If the government's expert is a potential expert witness, assume that the defense will make a thorough assessment in this area, and will attempt to impeach the witness. The investigative and prosecutive team cannot afford surprises on cross-examination in this regard. Employers, prior clients, professional references, and professional and regulatory agencies, among others, should be contacted for an assessment of the quality and timeliness of the prospective experts' work.

5. Professional Bearing and Demeanor Perhaps subtle, but always significant, is the professional bearing and demeanor of the technical advisor. The ability to speak authoritatively, to sustain composure under vigorous cross-examination, to avoid argumentativeness with opposing counsel, and to simplify for the judge and jury without condescension are essential characteristics. The absence of any of these should exclude the admitted expert from consideration as an expert witness. Moreover, the behind-the-scenes technical advisor must also possess these qualities, because he or she must work closely with the other members of the investigative team, often under pressure.

Determining professional bearing and demeanor can be complicated. Initial impressions during interviews and preliminary discussions about the case are important, as are assessments by references and other outsiders. However, all of these observations are of limited utility. Engaging in role-play early in the process with other investigators or prosecutors simulating an interrogation or cross-examination will provide useful information about the experts' reactions under pressure and in response to challenges to their expertise. Playing devil's advocate in a discussion with experts about their views or opinions on technical issues, or asking them to discuss the weaknesses in their own positions, or probing them on subjects beyond their area of expertise to assess the degree to which they are opinionated by nature are also useful techniques. In short, stress-interviews for experts, whether or not they are viewed as potential expert witnesses, are an essential tool to gauge bearing and demeanor.

6. "Presence" Before a Group The ability to present ideas effectively to a group is a learned skill. However, many individuals in all areas of endeavor lack this skill. An expert whose knowledge of a technical area is sound and who can effectively advise investigators behind the scenes may or may not possess an effective presence before a group.

This is a critical skill in any expert witness; for potential expert witnesses, advance screening for the presence of this skill, and practice sessions to enhance it for trial, are a must. However, the ability to make effective presentations to groups may also be a necessary attribute of the behind-the-scenes technical advisor; this should be considered when retaining *any* expert.

Advisors at the investigative or pretrial stages of complex cases may be called upon to give orientation sessions on technical aspects of the case to a large group of investigators and other technical advisors. This requires experts to be effective at group presentation. In addition, should the identity of the technical advisors become known to the defense at the pretrial stage, depending on the nature of their relationship with the government and their role in the case, they may be subpoenaed to testify. This would require them to have the same ability to effectively command the attention of a group as if they had been designated by the government as potential expert witnesses.

7. Ability to Explain Technical Issues in Lay Terms A thorough grounding in their field of expertise and the ability to make an effective group presentation are undercut if technical advisors are unable to simplify complex technical matters so that intelligent laypeople can understand them. Indeed, this is the most fundamental skill technical advisors or expert witnesses must possess. The ability to make technical points understandable to the members of the investigative or prosecutorial team is critical to their ability to erect a sound theory of the case and to implement an effective strategy to break the case and/or obtain a conviction. Similarly, the ability to bring important technical points home to the judge and jury, without confusion or condescension, will have a direct impact on the likelihood of a favorable verdict.

If the experts have performed other consultancies in the past or served previously as expert witnesses, determining whether they have this skill should prove easy by performing a thorough reference check. However, in the absence of these prior experiences, an effective technique would be to have prospective experts explain to a group of lay office staff the meaning of a few technical terms or concepts the interviewer selects. If the office staff cannot grasp the expert's explanation, chances are that other laypeople on the investigative team or the jury will not readily understand either. The presence or absence of strong interpersonal communications skills in experts is universally acknowledged as a key factor in the advisability of retaining them.

8. Mannerisms and Idiosyncrasies Distinctions distract. Peculiar mannerisms, unusual modes of dress, and other aspects of experts' personalities tend to deflect attention from their message. The use of vulgarity or excessive humor at inappropriate times and derogatory remarks about professional rivals alienates listeners and turns them against the speaker and thus against the message. Such distractions must be eliminated at all costs in the case of potential expert witnesses, by either modifying their behavior or replacing them. Again, because behind-the-scenes technical advisors can under certain circumstances be subpoenaed to testify, these caveats are not limited solely to designated expert witnesses.

SOURCES FOR LOCATING EXPERT WITNESSES

Technical advisors for use in crime cases can be selected or drawn from a number of sources. These include the following:

1. In-house sources.
2. Other law enforcement agencies.
3. Other agencies of state or local government.
4. State and local licensing, certifying, and registering bodies.
5. Law enforcement professional associations.
6. Professional associations in the subject area of expert knowledge sought.
7. The victimized organization.
8. The manufacturers/vendors and serving organizations who supply equipment or interface services to the victim.
9. Other organizations in the victim's field of activity or industry.
10. Area universities and research centers.
11. Private consulting firms specializing in the subject area. Determining which source(s) to use for a particular sort of expert will be dictated by a mix of factors (Exhibit 10.1).
12. Prior experience at obtaining experts.
13. Preexisting relationships with other agencies and referral sources.
14. The facts and circumstances of each case.

DISTINGUISHING THE ACTUAL AREA OF COMPETENCE

A concluding consideration when selecting an expert is offered as a caveat: Be certain of precisely for which area(s) of expertise the investigative team needs other advisors, and carefully distinguish between these various areas of technical expertise when selecting a given consultant. For example, the decision to retain an EDP programmer, an EDP auditor, and a computer-security specialist as a core team of outside technical advisors when undertaking a complex computer-related crime case will be a common decision. However, selecting a programmer who is proficient in the programming language of the victimized company will be equally essential. Selecting a programmer and an EDP auditor who are familiar with business applications of computer technology within the victim's field or industry will be necessary. When selecting a computer-security consultant, you must decide whether you need a physical-security specialist, a data-security specialist, or both. (Most computer-security consultants are not expert in both.) These examples could be expanded almost infinitely.

Exhibit 10.1   Likely Sources of Technical Advisors in Computer-Related Crime Cases, by Type of Experience

TYPES OF EXPERTS REQUIRED	IN-HOUSE RESOURCES	OTHER AGENCIES OF GOVERNMENT	LICENSING BODIES	PROFESSIONAL ASSN'S IN SUBJECT AREA	LAW ENFORCEMENT PROFESSIONAL ASSN'S	VICTIM COMPANY OR ORGANIZATION	HW/SW MANUFACTURER VENDOR/SERVICERS	OTHER ORGANIZATIONS IN VICTIM'S INDUSTRY	AREA UNIVERSITIES, RESEARCH CENTERS	PRIVATE CONSULTING FIRMS	OTHER LAW ENFORCEMENT AGENCIES
COMPUTER SCIENTISTS		X	X	X		X	X	X	X	X	
ELECTRONIC ENGINEERS		X	X	X		X	X	X	X	X	
TELECOMMUNICATIONS ENGINEERS		X	X	X		X	X	X	X	X	
COMPUTER CRIME SCHOLARS			X	X	X				X	X	X
SUBJECT MATTER EXPERTS FROM VICTIM'S INDUSTRY				X		X	X	X			
COMPUTER USERS						X	X	X			
DATA PROVIDERS						X	X	X			
COMPUTER OPERATORS						X	X	X			
NON COMPUTER PERSONNEL WHO INTERFACE IN VICTIM'S OPERATION						X	X	X			
EDP PROGRAMMERS	X	X	X	X	X	X	X	X	X	X	X
SYSTEMS ANALYSTS	X	X	X	X	X	X	X	X	X	X	X
DATABASE MANAGERS				X		X	X	X			
EDP AUDITORS	X	X	X	X	X	X	X	X	X	X	X
COMPUTER-SECURITY SPECIALISTS	X	X	X	X	X	X	X	X	X	X	X
EXPERIENCED COMPUTER-RELATED CRIME INVESTIGATORS	X	X	X	X	X		X		X		
FORENSIC SCIENTISTS	X	X	X	X	X		X		X		X

Distinguishing the area(s) of specialized expertise needed must be coupled with distinguishing the true area(s) of a given consultant's expert competence from other areas in which he or she is not truly expert. This process is made more difficult because experts in one area are often unaware, or unwilling to admit, the limitations of their expertise. In such situations, representatives of the victimized organization or the manufacturers or vendors of the computer hardware or software equipment involved in the crime may be the best sources of guidance as to precisely what outside expertise is needed and what types of people would be likely to have the requisite capabilities. Consultation with experienced computer crime investigators or prosecutors, whether they are local or from other jurisdictions, can provide helpful information about the legal ramifications of securing outside technical advice.

REFERENCES

1. J. D. Kogan, "On Being a Good Expert Witness in a Criminal Case," *Journal of Forensic Science,* (January, 1978), p. 195.
2. Michael H. Graham, "Impeaching the Professional Expert Witness by a Showing of Financial Interest," 53 Ind. L.J. 35, 44–47 (Winter 1977), p. 198.

Chapter 11

Gathering Evidence

RULES OF EVIDENCE

A court trial is intended to deduce the truth of a given proposition. In a criminal case, the proposition is the guilt or innocence of an accused person. The evidence introduced to and received by the court to prove the charge must be beyond a reasonable doubt—not necessarily to a moral certainty—and the quantity and quality of evidence must convince an honest and reasonable layperson that the defendant is guilty after it is all considered and weighed impartially.

But what is evidence and how can it be weighed and introduced? In a broad sense, evidence is anything perceptible by the five senses and any species of proof such as testimony of witnesses, records, documents, facts, data, or concrete objects, legally presented at a trial to prove a contention and induce a belief in the minds of the court or jury. In weighing evidence, the court or jury may consider such things as the demeanor of witnesses, their bias for or against an accused, and any relationship to the accused. Thus, evidence can be testimonial, circumstantial, demonstrative, inferential, and even theoretical when given by a qualified expert. Evidence is simply anything that proves and disproves any matter in question.

To be *legally* acceptable as evidence, however, testimony, documents, objects, or facts must be competent, relevant, and material to the issues being litigated, and be gathered lawfully. Otherwise, on motion by the opposite side, the evidence may be excluded. Now perhaps we should elaborate on relevancy, materiality, and competency: Relevancy of evidence does not depend on the conclusiveness of the testimony offered, but on its legitimate tendency to establish a controverted fact.[1]

Some of the evidentiary matters considered relevant and therefore admissible are:

- The motive for the crime
- The defendant's ability to commit the crime
- The defendant's opportunity to commit the crime

- Threats or expressions of ill will by the accused
- The means of committing the offense (possession of a weapon, tool, or skills used in committing the crime)
- Physical evidence at the scene linking the accused to the crime
- The suspect's conduct and comments at the time of arrest
- The attempt to conceal identity
- The attempt to destroy evidence
- Valid confessions

The materiality rule requires that evidence must have an important value to a case or prove a point at issue. Unimportant details only extend the period of time for trial. Accordingly, a trial court judge may rule against the introduction of evidence that is repetitive or additive (that merely proves the same point in another way), or evidence that tends to be remote even though it is relevant. Materiality, then, is the degree of relevancy. The court cannot become preoccupied with trifles or unnecessary details. For example, the physical presence of a suspect in the computer room or tape library or near a terminal on a day when a spurious transaction was generated may be relevant and material. One's presence in a non-computer-related area of the building may be relevant, but immaterial.

Competency of evidence means that which is adequately sufficient, reliable, and relevant to the case and presented by a qualified and capable (and sane) witness; the presence of those characteristics or the absence of those disabilities that render a witness legally fit and qualified to give testimony in a court applies in the same sense to documents or other forms of written evidence. But competency differs from credibility. Competency is a question that arises before a witness's testimony can be considered; credibility is that witness's veracity. Competency is for the judge to determine; credibility is for the jury to decide.

The competency rule also dictates that conclusions or opinions of a nonexpert witness on matters that require technical expertise be excluded. For example, testimony by an investigating officer on the cause of death may not be appropriate or competent in a trial for murder or wrongful death, because the officer is not qualified by education, study, or experience to make such an assessment. The officer testifying that there were "no visible signs of life" when the body was found may be acceptable, however.

When an expert witness is called on to testify, a foundation must be laid before testimony is accepted or allowed. Laying a foundation means that the witness's expertise must be established before a professional opinion is rendered. Qualifying a witness as an expert means demonstrating to the judge's satisfaction that by formal education, advanced study, and experience, the witness is knowledgeable about the topic on which his or her testimony will bear. The testimony of experts is an exception to the hearsay rule.

The hearsay rule is based on the theory that testimony that merely repeats what some other person said should not be admitted because of the possibility of distortion or misunderstanding. Furthermore, the person who made the actual statement is unavailable for cross-examination and has not been sworn in as a witness. Generally speaking, witnesses can testify only to those things of which they have personal and direct knowledge, and not give conclusions or opinions.

But there are occasions—exceptions—when hearsay evidence is admissible. Some examples are:

- Dying declarations, either verbal or written
- Valid confessions
- Tacit admissions
- Public records that do not require an opinion but speak for themselves
- *Res gestae* statements—spontaneous explanations, if spoken as part of the criminal act or immediately following the commission of such criminal act
- Earlier testimony given under oath
- Business entries made in the normal course of business

Photocopies of original business documents and other writings and printed matter are often made to preserve evidence. Investigators use these so that the original records needed to run a business are not removed and to ensure that in the event of an inadvertent destruction of such originals a certified true copy of the document is still available as proof. Investigators may also use the certified copy to document their case reports. At the trial, however, the original document—if still available—is the best evidence and must be presented. The best evidence in this context means primary evidence, not secondary; original as distinguished from substitutionary; the highest evidence of which the nature of the case is susceptible: "A written instrument is itself always regarded as the primary or best possible evidence of its existence and contents; a copy, or the recollection of a witness, would be secondary evidence.[2] Further, "Contents of a document must be proved by producing the document itself."[3]

HEARSAY EXCEPTIONS

In an idealistic sense, a court trial is a quest to determine the truth. However, the means of acquiring evidence vary. Some means are legal, others are illegal; for example, they may violate constitutional guarantees against unreasonable search and seizure, forced confessions, or failure to be represented by counsel. Realistically, therefore, a court trial can result only in a measure of truth and not in absolute truth in the philosophical sense.

Yet, in the Anglo-American tradition, witnesses other than experts, cannot generally testify as to probabilities, opinions, assumptions, impressions, generalizations, or conclusions, but only as to things, people, and events they have seen, felt, tasted, smelled, or heard firsthand. And even those things must be legally and logically relevant. Logical relevancy means that the evidence being offered must tend to prove or disprove a fact of consequence. Even if it is logically relevant, a court may exclude evidence if it is likely to inflame or confuse a jury or consume too much time. And testimony as to the statistical probability of guilt is considered too prejudicial and unreliable to be accepted.

Testimony as to the character and reputation of an accused may be admissible under certain conditions, even though it would seem to violate the hearsay rule. Such testimony may be admitted when character is an element of the action; that is, when the mental condition or legal competency of the accused is in question.

Evidence of other crimes an accused committed is not generally admissible to prove character. It may be admitted for other purposes, however, such as proof of motive, opportunity, or intent to commit an act.

A witness's credibility may also be attacked by a showing that he or she was convicted of a serious crime (punishable by death or imprisonment for more than a year) or for such crimes as theft, dishonesty, or false statement. Such conviction should have occurred in recent years—usually within the last 10 years.

Evidence can be direct or circumstantial. Direct evidence proves a fact directly; if the evidence is believed, the fact is established. Circumstantial evidence proves the desired fact indirectly and depends on the strength of the inferences the evidence raises. For example, a letter properly addressed, stamped, and mailed is assumed (inferred) to have been received by the addressee. Testimony that a letter was so addressed, stamped, and mailed raises an inference that it was received. The inference may be rebutted by testimony that is was not in fact received.

The best evidence rule deals with written documents proffered as evidence. The rule requires that the original, if available, and not a copy thereof, be presented at a trial. If the original was destroyed or is in the hands of an opposite party and not subject to legal process by search warrant or subpoena, an authenticated copy may be substituted. Business records and documents kept in the ordinary course of business may be presented as evidence, too, even if the person who made the entries or prepared the documents is unavailable.

OTHER RULES OF EVIDENCE

Chain of Custody

When evidence in the form of document or object (means or instrument) is seized at a crime scene, or as a result of subpoena *duces tecum* (for documents), or discovered in the course of audit and investigation, it should be marked, identified, inventoried, and preserved to maintain it in its original condition and to establish a clear chain of custody until it is introduced at the trial. If gaps in possession or custody occur, the evidence may be challenged at the trial on the theory that the writing or object introduced may not be the original or is not in its original condition and therefore is of doubtful authenticity.

For a seized document to be admissible as evidence, it is necessary to prove that it is the same document that was seized and that it is in the same condition as it was when it was seized. Because several people may handle it in the interval between seizure and trial, it should be adequately marked at the time of seizure for later identification, and its custody must be shown from that time until it is introduced in court.

Investigators or auditors who seize or secure documents should quickly identify them by some marking, so they can later testify that they are the documents seized and that they are in the same condition as they were when seized. Investigators might, for instance, write their initials and the date of seizure on the margin, in a corner, or at some other inconspicuous place on the front or back of each document. If circumstances suggest that such marking might render the document subject to attack on the grounds that it has been defaced or it is not in the same condition as when seized, the investigators or auditors can, after making a copy for comparison or for use as an exhibit to the report, put the document into an envelope, write a description and any other identifying information on the front of the envelope, and seal it.

These techniques should be applied any time investigators or auditors come into possession of original documents that might be used as evidence in a trial. If auditors make copies of documentary evidence, they should take steps to preserve their authenticity in case they are needed as secondary evidence if the original documents are not available for the trial.

Secondary Evidence

To introduce secondary evidence, one must explain satisfactorily to the court the absence of the original document. Secondary evidence is not restricted to photocopies of the document; it may be the testimony of witnesses or transcripts of the document's contents. Whereas the federal courts give no preference to the type of secondary evidence, most other jurisdictions do. Under the majority rule, testimony (*parol evidence*) will not be allowed to prove the contents of a document if there is secondary documentary evidence available to prove its contents. However, before secondary evidence of the original document may be introduced, the party offering the contents of the substitute must have used all reasonable and diligent means to obtain the original. Again, this is a matter for the court to determine.

When the original document has been destroyed by the party attempting to prove its contents, secondary evidence will be admitted if the destruction was in the ordinary course of business, or by mistake, or even intentional, provided it was not done for any fraudulent purpose.

Privileged Communications

The rule supporting privileged communications is based on the belief that it is necessary to maintain the confidentiality of certain communications. It covers only those communications that are a unique product of the protected relationship. The basic reason behind these protected communications is the belief that the protection of certain relationships is more important to society than the possible harm resulting from the loss of such evidence. Legal jurisdictions vary as to what communications are protected. Some of the more prevalent privileged relationships are:

- Attorney–client
- Husband–wife
- Physician–patient
- Clergy–congregant
- Law enforcement officer–informant

When dealing with privileged communications, consider the following basic principles:

1. Only the holder of a privilege, or someone authorized by the holder, can assert the privilege.
2. If the holder fails to assert it after having notice and an opportunity to assert it, the privilege is waived.
3. The privilege may also be waived if the holder discloses a significant part of the communication to a party not within the protected relationship.
4. The communication, to be within the privilege, must be sufficiently related to the relationship protected (for example, communications between an attorney and client must be related to legal consultation).

Under common law a person cannot testify against his or her spouse in a criminal trial. While they are married, neither may waive this testimonial incompetency.

Conversations in the known presence of third parties are not protected. Protected communications are those that are in fact confidential or induced by the marriage or other relationship. Ordinary conversations relating to matters not deemed to be confidential are not within the purview of the privilege.

The laws of different states vary widely in the application of the principles of privileged communications. Depending on what protected relationship is involved, different rules may apply regarding what communications are protected, the methods of waiver, and the duration of the privilege.

Whenever an auditor/investigator is confronted with the need to use evidence that consists of communications between parties in one of these relationships, he or she should consult with an attorney, especially if the evidence is crucial to the case.

ADMISSIONS AND CONFESSIONS

Criminal phenomena occur as a result of four factors:

1. The criminal's motivations.
2. Opportunities to commit crimes, presented by weaknesses in people, internal controls, safeguards, or protection measures.
3. Means to commit crimes—resources (knowledge of weaknesses), skill in exploiting them, and a mental disposition to do so (confederates and tools).
4. Methods—the plans to execute crimes while minimizing the risk of capture.

Crime is a risk for both victim and victimizer. The victim's risk is the loss of something valuable—life, limb, or property. The victimizer's risk is the loss of freedom, social status, and possibly of life, limb, and property, too. But criminals intend to gain something as a result of a crime, something to which they are not legally entitled. So criminals, rational ones, at least, must concern themselves with weighing the risk of discovery, apprehension, and conviction against the intended gain.

If the risk of discovery and the amount of the possible gain are great, then more time and thought must be spent on planning, disguising, surprise, escape, and possibly covering up the crime. Fortunately for police authorities, criminals tend to act in haste. Their plans often go awry. They do not anticipate everything that can happen. They usually add to their arsenal of defenses rationalizations for their misconduct, or alibis. "It wasn't me; I was elsewhere." "The devil made me do it." "I am poor and misunderstood, a victim of oppression." "He [the victim] had it coming." "I must have been crazy for doing what I did."

These rationalizations are what police interrogations are intended to sort through. Here again, intuition may play an important role. Criminals usually offer an excuse or justification for what they do. Sometimes they feign ignorance or illness. Sometimes they even feign amnesia. Interrogation cuts through these defenses, excuses, and rationalizations.

During an interrogation it is important to remain sensitive not only to what the suspect is saying but to the manner in which it is being said, and to observe facial expressions, body and eye movements, word choices, and posture. Verbal fencing with the suspect like Perry Mason conducting a cross-examination, does not help. Challenging the suspect's comments on the basis of pure logic and rationality does not persuade most criminals to confess. Suspects can stay with a lame excuse forever and almost come to believe it after a while. The reason they persist in lying is that their crimes were not committed out of a sense of logic, but mainly for emotional reasons such as lust, greed, anger, or envy. So in interrogating suspects, one must be prepared to deal with their emotions. "Why did you do it?" is not a very good question early on. It calls for intellectualizing by the suspect, or rationalizing, a much more common response to that type of question.

A better choice are questions that do not get to the *gravamen* (main issue) of the crime at all—questions about a suspect's feelings and emotions:

How are you feeling?
Can I get anything for you?
Do you feel like talking?
Can I call anyone for you?

The purpose of these innocuous questions is to build rapport, first at the emotional level and later at a rational level. Not all criminal suspects feel compelled to talk about their crimes, but most do, if an interrogator can establish rapport with them. And rapport can be established even after they are advised of their right to remain silent.

An apprehended suspect, or one merely being informally interviewed before arrest, is under great emotional strain. Fears of conviction and incarceration are exacerbated. These fears must be overcome before intelligent conversation can be achieved. The tone and demeanor of the interrogator/interviewer must be reassuring, if not friendly. Intuition enters this process only if the investigator remains calm, dispassionate, and sensitive to the emotional needs and concerns of the suspect or witness. Intuition does not work when his or her mind is cluttered with isolated facts or a list of questions about the details of a crime.

Once investigators have learned something about the suspect's history, family, friends, and feelings, they can discern the most appropriate interrogation technique. If the suspect remains cold, aloof, and noncommunicative while innocuous questions are posed, he or she will be the same when the questions get more serious. The investigator needs a command of all the known facts of the crime to gain a confession in that case.

If the suspect responds openly to the investigator's offers of kindness and civility, the latter can lead by general questioning. The investigator will let the suspect describe the crime and not get in the way by verbal bantering, accusation, or sparring. The suspect should be allowed to tell the story in his or her own way, even if the investigator knows some of the facts are being distorted. The investigator can always come back and ask for clarification, and then compare the conflicts with the testimony of witnesses or confederates.

The importance of confessions and admissions in resolving crime should not be understated. Without such confessions and admissions, many crimes would never be solved. In some fraud cases, accounting books and records do not provide enough evidence to convict a suspect. So a confession from a thief, defrauder, or embezzler makes fraud prosecutions easier. A freely given confession often details the scheme, the accounts manipulated, and the uses to which the purloined funds were applied. The evidence gathered after a confession may corroborate the crime. A confession alone will not support a criminal conviction, however, so the auditor will have to retrieve from the data available within the accounting system and from third-party sources enough corroborating evidence to support the confession.

REFERENCES

1. *ICC v. Baird,* 24 S. C.T. 563, 194, U.S. 25, 48 L. Ed. 860.
2. *Manhattan Malting Co. v. Swetland,* 14 Mont. 269, 36, p. 84.
3. *Nunan v. Timberlake,* 85 F. 2d 407, 66 App. D.C. 150.

Chapter 12

Case Studies

The case-study method of instruction originated in the law schools of the United Kingdom, the United States, and Canada. The case method requires that students digest the salient facts, determine the legal issues involved, and critique the legal opinion of the court on the basis of past legal precedents and legal reasoning.

Accountants get a taste of the case method in the practice sets they use to master principles of accounting and auditing. We have therefore included a selection of case studies on fraud incidents that readers can use for their own self-study.

The following cases will provide a measure of experiential learning for auditors who are new to the field of fraud auditing and forensic accounting. Obviously a few short and simple cases won't make anyone an expert, but it is a good first step in the process of mastering the subject.

The cases (with name changes) were taken from the forensic practice of Lindquist Avey Macdonald and Baskerville, Inc., of Toronto, Ontario and Washington D.C.[1]

DAVE FLAG CASE

Dave Flag, the purchasing manager for a state government, had authority to approve supplier invoices under $5,000. Flag's subordinates often complained of his autocratic style, which became worse after Flag was passed over for promotion. State officials became suspicious after a clerk experienced repeated difficulty in contacting representatives of the ABC Paper Company, which had purportedly delivered paper supplies to the state. An investigation revealed that Flag had approved numerous invoices to ABC, a company that Flag had owned for several years and from which no goods had been received.

> *Question 1:* What are the weaknesses in internal controls that allowed this fraud to occur?
>
> *Question 2:* How could this fraud have been discovered earlier?

MAXI LUMBER CASE

First State Bank loaned approximately $6.8 million to Maxi Lumber. The loans were secured by accounts receivable from Maxi's list of reputable customers. When Maxi went bankrupt, the bank discovered that only $2 million in receivables were genuine; the other $4.8 million were for projects that had not been started or were entirely fictitious. The bank sued Maxi's auditors for negligence.

The auditors had sent confirmation requests to Maxi's customers. It was common practice in this industry for companies to ignore requests from auditors to confirm balances owing. During the last two years of the auditors' work, however, the number of confirmations customers returned was astonishingly high, and all agreed with Maxi's records. Investigative accountants discovered that the confirmations purportedly returned by customers were not the same documents as those that were sent by the auditors, and had been completed by management of Maxi. In addition, the auditors failed to identify Maxi's practice of prebilling invoices for contracts that had not yet been started.

Question 1: What weaknesses do you see in the audit procedures?

Question 2: How could the external auditors have discovered this fraud earlier?

ROY'S RETAIL CASE

In 1993, Roy's Retail reported an inventory shrink of 7 percent of sales, or $30 million, well above the industry average of 3 percent of sales. (Shrink is the difference between inventory reported on the books and the actual amount on hand.) Management suspected widespread theft and fraud. Forensic accountants retained by management attributed the shrink to poor internal controls.

Forensic accountants found that the head office staff were able to alter the store's inventory records unbeknownst to store management and were approving supplier invoices without ensuring that the warehouse had received the merchandise and that the vendor was an approved supplier. The warehouse had installed a new shipment-tracking system that had not been properly tested and was recording duplicate shipments of merchandise from numerous fly-by-night suppliers. Many poor purchasing decisions were made that resulted in selling the merchandise at well below cost. Although these factors made it possible for fraud to occur, none was discovered, and the shrink was attributed to the poor controls and resulting accounting errors.

Question 1: What weaknesses do you see in internal controls?

Question 2: How could the external auditors have found this fraud earlier?

PLASTICS, LTD., CASE

Plastics, Ltd., manufactured plastic wraps and bags for industrial use. At year end, the company's auditors were unable to determine why inventory on the books was $5 million higher than inventory on hand. Management suspected widescale fraud. Forensic accountants found that the wraps and bags were being manufactured with slightly more material than called for in the engineering specs. The accounting system, however, was relieving inventory based on the lesser production quantity and was the main cause of the overstatement.

Question 1: What weaknesses do you see in internal controls?

Question 2: How could external auditors have found this fraud earlier?

U.S. JEWELRY CONSORTIUM

The U.S. Jewelry Consortium is an organization begun and maintained by jewelry retailers to obtain supplier price discounts through volume purchasing. Blain was hired as general manager and he was responsible for a wide range of duties, including preparing accounting records and handling the banking function. Blain altered some accounting records of the U.S. Jewelry Consortium to conceal business losses resulting from a catalog/flyer sales promotion program. Accounts receivable and sales balances were inflated. Misappropriations of funds for Blain's personal benefit were concealed by further account alterations. The audited financial statements reflected amounts including these alternations. Blain made his actions known to the board of directors, who appointed a new auditor.

Question 1: What weaknesses do you see in internal controls?

Question 2: How could the external auditors have found this fraud earlier?

MONEY, MONEY, MONEY CASE

Part 1

Brian Money, a 29-year-old assistant branch manager and lending officer of a large downtown Toronto bank, defrauded the bank of some $10.2 million over a 20-month period. He fabricated loans to real and fictitious customers and gambled away the proceeds at an Atlantic City casino. Money was such a valued customer that the casino flew its corporate jet to Toronto to pick him up for weekend jaunts.

The defalcation came to light when Canadian law enforcement authorities arrested Money for a traffic violation on his return from a trip to Atlantic City. A search of his person disclosed that he was carrying about $29,000 in currency. That information was passed on to the bank, which then conducted an audit and found the fictional loans and transfers of funds to the casino. The bank is suing the casino to recover at least part of its loss.

Money used a *lapping scheme* to keep auditors off his trail—that is, he paid off earlier loans with subsequent loans so that no delinquencies would show. However, the fictional loan balances grew and grew. Money's superior at the branch had approved the larger loans because "he had no reason to mistrust him." The branch manager was subsequently suspended along with the assistant branch manager for administration, a credit officer, and an auditor.

Question 1: What are the weaknesses in internal controls that allowed this fraud to occur?

Question 2: How could this fraud have been discovered earlier?

Part 2

- Mr. Money was authorized to grant loans up to $25,000. He was also responsible for servicing all loans in his portfolio under the supervision of Mr. Boss.
- Mr. Boss had the authority to approve loans up to $100,000. Loans exceeding $100,000 required approval from the head office.
- Mr. Money's personnel file indicates that he was well regarded by both employees and customers of the financial institution. He had worked for two years under the supervision of Mr. Boss, who considered him to be highly competent and trustworthy. The personnel file also indicated that Mr. Money worked long hours and had not taken his vacation entitlement for the previous year. Mr. Boss had observed that the employee received numerous personal messages during working hours.
- Mr. Money had a personal checking account with the financial institution in which his salary was deposited. He also operated an investment club account for a group of horse racing enthusiasts.

Internal Audit Findings:

- The branch's loan portfolio included approximately 5,000 loan accounts, with a total loan value of $75 million. This volume represented an increase of $25 million since the previous audit.
- Five individual loans accounted for $20 million of the total loan portfolio. These loan accounts were with established customers, all with histories of large loans with the financial institution.

- The auditor's inquiries concerning the significant increase in the total loan value revealed that a substantial portion of the increase was attributable to the use by major customers of unused portions of approved lines of credit.
- The audit identified one new major customer, Mr. Spender, who had loans with the bank that exceeded $100,000 from time to time. The loan balance at the time of the audit was $20,000. The purpose of the loan account was described as an investment loan for the purchase and sale of government bonds.

Highlights of analysis of the major loans, including Mr. Spender's account:

1. The major accounts had the required approvals from the head office for the lines of credit.

2. All the major loans were current, with interest regularly being paid. A few large advances between $700,000 and $1 million were repaid within a short period of the advances.

3. Although the increases in the loans of the major customers were within the approved lines of credit, three of the loans were in U.S. dollars, whereas all previous loans for these customers were in Canadian dollars. These customers had current operating accounts in Canadian and U.S. dollars. Interest payments on the U.S. dollar loans were made from additional loan advances.

4. No confirmation with major customers of the loans outstanding at the time of the audit was undertaken for the following reasons:
   - The lines of credit had the appropriate head office approvals on file.
   - The lines of credit were confirmed with the customer during the last audit.
   - The loans were current with interest regularly being paid.
   - No losses had been incurred with these customers.

5. The files contained several pre-signed (by the customer) demand notes that had been presigned by the customer. The explanation was that Mr. Money held these pre-signed notes to allow for the customers' immediate cash requirements, thus allowing them to avoid waiting for their notes to reach the bank.

6. The auditor analyzed the account of the new major customer, Mr. Spender, found the following characteristics:
   - The loan was to be used to make investments in the purchase and sale of governmental bonds.
   - The loan was approved by Mr. Money and Mr. Boss.
   - The loan balance fluctuated between $20,000 and $150,000 with $20,000 owing at the time of the audit.

- No current operating account for the customer existed. Loans were repaid by the sale of government bonds. The loans advanced were used to purchase bank drafts payable to a securities firm. However, the paid drafts were not examined by auditors.
- Several advances were made with dummy demand notes. The explanation Mr. Money gave was that Mr. Spender had been traveling a lot but had agreed to come into the bank to sign the notes "all at once."
- The auditor wished to confirm details of the loan directly with Mr. Spender. Mr. Money indicated that Mr. Spender required absolute discretion. Therefore, the financial institution held all correspondence regarding the loan for pickup, and Mr. Money did not want a confirmation letter sent.
- The auditor discussed the account with Mr. Money's supervisor, Mr. Boss, who indicated that Mr. Spender was a wealthy acquaintance of Mr. Money's. Mr. Boss agreed with Mr. Money to hold all mail and suggested that the auditor confirm the loan by alternative means. Mr. Boss assured the auditor that he had complete faith in Mr. Money and watched the loan closely to ensure that the account was secure.
- The auditor requested that head-office approval be obtained, because the loan at times exceeded $100,000. Mr. Boss agreed. The auditor also noted the account for follow-up in the next audit, but because there was no evidence of any current problems with the account he decided not to confirm the account directly with the customer.

Question: For each of the areas noted below, identify those factors or characteristics you consider red-flag warnings for possible fraud:

Employee lifestyle information

Loan-portfolio growth

Mr. Spender's account

TRADING MANIA

Bank A provides a large array of financial services to its customers, including foreign exchange trading. Mr. Arnold is the senior foreign exchange trader, and he heads the department as well. Arnold's prowess as a trader was undisputed by top management—until now. He was generally left alone to do as he deemed appropriate, particularly since no one else at the bank understood foreign currency exchange trading. The bank, however, did not permit trading in foreign currency options—it allowed only forward contracts. Despite that policy, Arnold traded on futures, on the bank's account and on his own. His record in such trades proved disastrous. The bank lost millions. He concealed his losses by rolling them over and manipulating accounting records with the help of personnel in his department.

Question 1: What internal control weaknesses do you see in this case?
Question 2: How could this fraud have been detected earlier?

SHARP RENTALS CASE

Rumors of management corruption at its main plant in Dallas, Texas, reached the Canadian head office of Sharp Rentals, Inc., in May, 1989, through an anonymous letter. Sharp, which rented large and expensive tools to oil and drilling companies, had annual revenues of $40 million. The news was shocking to senior management in Canada because they had placed great trust in Andy Buell, who ran the Dallas operation. According to the allegations, Buell and his second-in-command, Ronald Bates, were stealing contracts from Sharp and renting their own tools to Sharp's customers. Forensic accountants were retained to assist management in determining whether the charges were true and, if so, how to get rid of the two employees.

We accompanied the president and three vice presidents from the head office on a visit to Dallas. Buell responded to our presence with considerable hostility. During our two days on site we examined the books and records and interviewed company personnel. On our departure, Buell said that if his name wasn't cleared within a few days, he would resign.

Because no obvious signs of wrongdoing had been found, the consensus among management in Canada was to drop any further investigation. Buell was considered a valuable employee who would be difficult to replace. However, in a private meeting with the president we suggested there were indeed grounds to continue the investigation. We presented a list of 50 opportunities for fraud, based on the limited information to which we had access during our visit. Two items were particularly noteworthy. One was a piece of paper found in Buell's files that referred to a company called SRI, which, we noted, are the initials of Sharp Rentals, Inc. A check of state records uncovered no company registered under that name. The other item was the information that Buell personally retrieved and opened the company's mail each day, an action that seemed suspicious for the head of an operation of this size. Sharp's president agreed to let us return to Dallas without anyone else knowing our plans.

Through interviews and surveillance work conducted late at night, we confirmed that Buell and Bates were operating a phony company called SRI, and that SRI had its own tools, which it rented to Sharp's customers. From other interviews, we learned that the SRI tools were removed from Sharp's property just prior to visits by the comptroller from Canada. We also discovered that all bank deposits were made by Buell, Bates, or their sons, who also worked in the Dallas plant. No other employees were allowed to make banking transactions. On our return from Dallas, we had sufficient evidence to dismiss Buell and Bates.

A few days later, we returned to Dallas with the president and several other executives and entered the office in the early morning before anyone else arrived. This allowed us time to review all the files. Among our findings were Sharp invoices that included the company name SRI. Also, we found checks that customers had made out jointly to Sharp and SRI. These checks had been endorsed by Buell, who had no such authority, and subsequently they had been cashed. We later discovered that Buell had been cashing checks from many customers in this manner. Later that day, Buell and Bates were served with a letter informing them of their dismissal.

Question: What internal control weaknesses do you see in this case?

DOUBLE-PAID VACATIONS CASE

The president of The Flagstaff Corp. received an anonymous letter at company headquarters in Toronto, Ontario, in March 1989, which said that senior executives at a Quebec plant were misappropriating funds for lavish expenses and for constructing fishing and hunting camps for their own use. At the same time, the company learned that a secret slush fund had been set up at the same plant. The money from that fund was apparently being used to take clients on promotional trips, including hunting and fishing excursions. Although the anonymous letter was written in English, the grammar and syntax indicated that the author was francophone. Toronto executives surmised that the letter writer was probably referring to the slush fund, but inexact language made it seem as if actual camps were being built.

Flagstaff retained our services to look into the matter of the slush fund. However, it restricted the scope of our investigation. The plant in question was its most profitable, and the executives under suspicion were its top performers. We were instructed not to talk to any third parties, such as suppliers or customers, nor to any employees except the three who were accused of involvement with the fund.

During interviews with the suspected employees—the comptroller, the vice president of marketing, and the vice president of operations—we were told the following story.

In 1987, their supervisor had been let go and was not replaced. Instead, a new line-reporting procedure was introduced that left them without anyone at the plant to report to. The vice president of operations, in collusion with the other two, seized the opportunity to negotiate a new deal with two agents who sold a Flagstaff byproduct to farmers as cattle feed. He stopped paying them commission, but instead created a joint marketing program and paid them an incentive that he could absorb through existing budgets. The new deal, which was negotiated verbally, was not reported to the head office. Commission continued to be recorded in the books, but the money was put into a secret slush fund and used to entertain customers—among other ways, by taking them on fishing and hunting trips. At the time of our investigation, approximately $35,000 had been used in this manner. Full exposure, the amount of commission money available to them, was only $70,000.

We prepared our report for the head office, stating that some records existed to verify their suspicions, but those records were far from complete. We also reported that an ownership search of fishing and hunting camps did not turn up the names of any of the three executives, nor, from a brief lifestyle review, did they appear to be living in excess of their means. Since the only personal benefit seemed to be that at least one of them went on a holiday excursion each year, Flagstaff decided not to take any action beyond issuing a mild reprimand.

However, as we were filing our report, the head office received two more anonymous letters saying that the allegations in the original letter were accurate, and that while our investigation had scared the trio, still we had not dug deeply enough. Then a supervisor from the plant telephoned the head office offering to talk.

The supervisor provided a file of photocopies of suppliers' invoices that he considered suspicious. We used those as the starting point of this second phase of our investigation. This time we had the mandate to conduct a full-scale review, which began with a meticulous examination of all documentation as we searched for anything that looked out of the ordinary. We interviewed a supplier to try to verify one of the suspicious invoices. This supplier revealed that he had sent patio furniture to the home of one of the three men, and then, at the executive's insistence, billed Flagstaff with a false invoice for electronic equipment. When we compared the codes on a cash register receipt from a lumber supplier with the actual products, we found that the men had bought materials that could be used to build a fishing lodge. Further investigation proved that the executives were indeed building a lodge in northern Quebec.

Our investigation found that customers had never gone on any of the trips paid for by the slush fund. Instead, we discovered that three types of fraud involving travel expenses had taken place: (1) the executives, their wives, and their friends went on trips to the lodges; (2) the executives, their wives, and their friends went on trips to Florida and other southern resorts; and (3) expenses were filed for trips that never took place at all. We also realized that the amount of money that had been misappropriated far exceeded the value of the slush fund.

In the course of the investigation, auditors noticed two checks worth $8,000 that had been put through check requisitions to a nonregistered outfitter. They had been cashed at the same bank branch in which the vice president of marketing had a personal account. That led to the discovery that the trio had invested in a second camp—a lodge located in northern Ontario. We estimated the loss to the company to be a minimum of $300,000.

Question: How could this fraud have been prevented?

THE MONEY-LAUNDERING LAWYER CASE

Mike Brewer, an Ontario lawyer, found it considerably more profitable to launder drug money than to practice his profession. During a six-month period in the early 1980s, Brewer laundered millions of dollars from drug sales, mostly in Toronto and Buffalo. An undercover investigation discovered his criminal activity. We were retained by the Royal Canadian Mounted Police, a regional police force, and the attorney general of Ontario to quantify the amount of laundered money and determine how the laundering had taken place. In the course of the investigation, it became evident that Brewer was also involved in another illegal scheme connected to the money laundering.

Brewer incorporated a company called Brewer Currency Exchange to try to legitimize the large sums of cash he regularly took to the bank. Although he maintained no books or records for the company, almost $12 million in cash was processed through the account in a six-month period. Brewer's commission was apparently a modest 3 percent. It was learned from interviews with his office staff that Brewer had purchased an expensive Pitney Bowes money counter. When certain clients came to the office, Brewer closed his door and the machine was heard whirring away. Brewer then took the money to his bank and exchanged it for a bank draft or had it sent in a Brinks truck to the United States where he purchased U.S. bearer bonds. By tracing bank and Brinks records, the pattern and quantity of cash transactions were determined.

During our investigation, we saw that Brewer was also involved in a real estate scheme that had evolved from his money-laundering activities. As one way of providing his drug clients with a means of legitimizing their large amounts of cash, Brewer established the following ruse: He set up an offshore company called ABC; a client gave him money—for example $300,000—which he deposited to his trust account; the funds were transferred to ABC; the client purchased a property for $300,000 and ABC advanced $300,000 for the purchase, secured by a mortgage. The net result was that the client was both mortgagee (the lender) and mortgagor (the borrower). If the client were ever asked where he got the money to buy the property, he could produce a registered mortgage. The difficulty in determining who was behind the offshore company or getting access to a lawyer's trust account made the laundering activities unlikely to be detected.

The success of this scam encouraged Brewer to expand his real estate activities. He approached a major bank and explained that he wanted to borrow money at one rate (12 percent, for example) to establish a mortgage company that would, in turn, lend to customers at a higher rate (14 percent or 15 percent, for example). The normal security for this type of transaction is the mortgage itself. However, Brewer somehow convinced the bank to accept the pledge of the proceeds of the mortgage instead. That meant that Brewer owned the mortgage and the bank's security was the receivable due to Brewer. If the mortgagor couldn't make his payments, Brewer could assume ownership of the property; the bank could be left with nothing.

To ensure that would happen, Brewer loaned large sums of money to a group of investors who were already in financial difficulty. The group subsequently invested too deeply in the real estate market through Brewer's mortgage company, and soon went bankrupt, leaving Brewer with property worth approximately $1 million and the bank with an unsecured debt.

Question: Could this fraud have been detected earlier? How?

LIVING HIGH ON YOUR PARTNER'S MONEY

Montreal's Guy Montpetit had a background in psychology. In the 1960s, he worked in Geneva with the eminent psychologist Dr. Jean Piaget in the field of genetic epistemology. In 1968, he was invited to the Massachusetts Institute of Technology to help develop its artificial intelligence program. During the 1970s, Montpetit established several computer firms, including Logo Computer Systems, Inc., which developed and sold a personal computer program language for schools.

It was Montpetit's dream to create a semiconductor (silicon chip) industry in Quebec. Between 1983 and 1987, he formed several companies in the province with that objective in mind. Although he received considerable government financial assistance along the way, by 1987 he was in dire need of funds to keep going. In 1986, he met Takayuki Tsuru, a Japanese businessman who was involved with developing a Logo program in Japan. Tsuru wanted to purchase control of Logo Canada (with which Montpetit was no longer associated) to help advance that project. In May 1987, Tsuru agreed to loan one of Montpetit's companies, Gigamos Holdings, Inc., $9 million to be used primarily to acquire control of Logo Canada and to purchase the assets of Lisp Machines, Inc., a U.S. company in the field of artificial intelligence. At the time, Lisp was under Chapter 11 of the U.S. Bankruptcy Act.

By August, Gigamos Holdings had spent the money. Control of Logo Canada had indeed been acquired by Holdings for $1.4 million. However,

Holdings had loaned approximately $3 million to a company that was 100 percent owned by Montpetit. The company, in turn, had purchased Lisp's assets. Thus, contrary to the agreement with Tsuru, Montpetit (rather than Holdings) owned Lisp's assets. With most of the remaining money, Montpetit put a down payment on a 12-story building in Vaudreuil, Quebec, valued at approximately $15 million, which he wanted to use as headquarters for his semiconductor business.

In the next few months, Montpetit desperately tried to find additional funding to pay off the remainder of the building. The federal and Quebec governments were considering up to $45 million in loans, grants, or both, but only on condition that Montpetit find investors willing to contribute $13 million in shares. In October 1987, Tsuru agreed to lend Gigamos Real Estate, Inc., another of Montpetit's companies, $30 million, which was delivered in a series of payments before the end of the year. The money was to enable Montpetit to complete purchase of the building and still have $13 million he needed to meet the requirements of the two governments. It was understood that Montpetit would continue to seek $30 million in funding from other sources in order to repay Tsuru as quickly as possible.

By October 1988, Tsuru began to have doubts about what had happened to his money. Repeated attempts to get answers from Montpetit produced no results. He therefore petitioned the Quebec Superior Court under the Canada Business Corporations Act (CBCA) to help him find out what had occurred. One of our partners was appointed inspector by the court, and given the fullest powers of search, seizure, and questioning.

Montpetit was the sole owner or a partner in 15 companies located in Quebec, Manitoba, Saskatchewan, the United States and Bermuda. Through a myriad of transactions, he moved the $39 million loaned by Tsuru in, out and around those companies—some of which existed in name only. In October 1988, when the inspector was appointed, the bank accounts of the companies and of Guy Montpetit showed a total balance of approximately $600,000. The essence of this complicated case was to determine what had been done with the rest of the $39 million, and if it had been used in accordance with the agreements the parties had reached, both verbally and in writing. Our charge was to assist the court in deciding whether the transactions of Holdings and Real Estate should be reversed and the monies returned to the accounts in which they were originally deposited, as Tsuru had requested. The question of possible criminal or civil charges was not an issue under these procedures.

From the copious documentation, most of which was found on the 12th floor of the building in Vaudreuil, we were able to trace the movement of the funds. Among the transactions were the purchase of the building in Vaudreuil; advances totaling $6.5 million to Gigamos Systems, Inc., a U.S. company owned 100 percent by Guy Montpetit; the purchase of a $3-million private jet (by a company called Gigamos Air Services, Inc., which Montpetit also owned 100 percent; the purchase of a $1.5 million house; extensive renovations to the house and the construction of a tennis court; and the repayment of a $1 million personal loan that Montpetit owed. In all, we concluded there were apparent personal benefits to Montpetit in the order of $10 to $12 million.

Question: Could this alleged fraud have been detected any earlier?

THE 28-HOUR-DAY CASE

The vast majority of lawyer Ezra Turnbull's clients were funded by a provincial Legal Aid Plan (LAP). Under the plan, lawyers submitted invoices for services rendered. Payment was governed by a fee schedule based on time spent and the procedure performed. Some procedures were assessed a flat fee no matter how many hours were involved. However, if a lawyer felt that he or she had performed an exceptional amount of work for a procedure, a discretionary increase request could be filed.

Ezra Turnbull was one of LAP's highest billers. He was also a frequent petitioner for discretionary increases. This was cause for concern to LAP, which prompted an investigation by the governing body into Turnbull's billing practices. Legal counsel for the governing body engaged our services to examine Turnbull's invoices for the years 1982, 1983, and 1984.

We analyzed Turnbull's 423 invoices, which had been submitted in a disorderly manner, for the three years in question. Some invoices included charges for a large number of procedures, but the information was not always presented in chronological order. Bills for time spent on the telephone were not detailed by the date of the calls but by a wide range of dates. This haphazard method made it difficult to determine what specific services had been performed on a particular date. To make sense of the information, we developed a computer model that enabled us to analyze the details, and to summarize the time Turnbull charged for each year.

Turnbull's billings to LAP for 1982 were 1894 hours; for 1983, 3596 hours; and for 1984, 2719 hours. The total for the three years we assessed was 8209 hours. A study of the legal profession, conducted in 1986, found that the average lawyer in Canada bills clients for 1100 hours per annum. Turnbull's average was almost three times greater than the norm.

Included in Turnbull's billings were charges for 21,267 telephone calls over the three-year period, totaling 2895 hours. Based on those figures, we estimated Turnbull would have had to make an average of two hours and forty minutes of phone calls a day for 365 days for each of the three years. Naturally, for every day that he made no calls (for example, when he was in court, at meetings, or took the day off) he would have needed to make almost six hours of calls the next day to maintain the average.

Although Turnbull's billings far exceeded the norm, we tried to see whether it was possible to have worked the number of hours that he claimed. While it was physically possible, as long as he worked almost around the clock, we found 75 days for which he submitted conflicting bills. For example, one invoice included charges for eight hours in court on a certain day. Another included charges for six hours of meetings and preparation work that, according to his invoices, took place on that same day, when he was supposed to have been in court. In analyzing his invoices further, we found a number of days when he billed for more than 24 hours of work. He also submitted invoices that included charges for court attendance on Saturdays and Sundays, when court does not sit, and charges for court attendance on behalf of non-legal-aid clients.

Question: What control procedures would you recommend to the provincial legal aid plan?

SECRET COMMISSIONS CASE

Following a directors' meeting of a major department store chain in Florida in the late 1970s, a primary supplier of toys and confections to the company's Canadian operations complained that he was not being allowed to show his products to the Canadian head office. "If you have a good product and sell at a competitive price, then you shouldn't have a problem," he was told. "Well, I'm being frozen out," he said, and then named Albert Grace, the company's vice president of purchasing, as the person imposing the freeze. Disturbed by the allegations, the company hired a private investigator who uncovered sufficient grounds for concern to call in the police. The police retained our services to help determine what documents should be identified in a search warrant, and to examine the documents once they were seized to see what they revealed.

Albert Grace's uncle had been president of the company, but Grace had been passed over for that position for a number of years. However, by all accounts, he was an excellent executive, responsible for purchasing approximately $100 million of product annually.

Our investigation revealed that Grace was in collusion with a supplier named Jim Corson. In the toy industry, one of the biggest problems is inventory. Goods imported from the Far East might end up sitting in inventory for considerable periods of time, with attendant costs for financing, storage, and the like. For example, if a supplier sold a product to a department store for a dollar, the supplier's cost might be 60 cents plus another 10 cents for inventory costs, leaving a profit of 30 cents. That level of gross profit would leave little money for payment of general selling and administrative expenses.

Grace arranged to exclude other suppliers and to deal only with Corson. He told Corson exactly what he wanted to purchase and when, eliminating the need for Corson to stock inventory and saving him the inventory carrying costs. Corson passed some of that saving on to the department store, which made Grace look good to his superiors, and they shared the overall profit. On millions of dollars' worth of purchases, made over many years, that secret commission (as it is called by lawyers) amounted to a considerable sum of money.

An analysis of the documentation showed that the revenue from the secret commission flowed through a series of companies: Some had Grace's and Corson's wives as principal shareholders; others had the shares held in trust by various lawyers. Unraveling the complex structure of the numerous companies was a difficult and protracted task. It was accomplished by diligently piecing together the parts of the puzzle as each fragment of evidence emerged.

Grace and Corson were charged under the Criminal Code with secret commissions. They pled not guilty, arguing that the department store chain suffered no actual loss. They also contended that because all income from their own companies was declared to Revenue Canada, no attempt had been made to cover up any wrongdoing. The reason for using so many different companies, lawyers, and accountants, they said, was for tax planning.

None of their arguments mitigated the fact that Grace, as an agent of the department store chain, received a benefit through a secret commission to which he would not have been entitled had the department store known of his actions. It was a clear contradiction of the conflict of interest guidelines he had signed as an employee.

Question: How could this fraud have been prevented?

THE RAINBOW SYNDROME CASE

The Sportswear Shop, which purchased raw materials in the Far East for assembly in Ontario, was a division of a large and successful company in the retail garment industry. In 1984, Sportswear was losing money, which prompted it to recruit new members to the management team. One addition was Patrick Lane, who was lured away from a competitor by a lucrative three-year guaranteed contract for $250,000 per annum, plus a percentage of profits, to head up the division. The contract specified that the only possible grounds for terminating the contract would be if Lane committed fraud.

The number-two person in the division was Harry Blake, who had held the same position under Lane's predecessor. Blake was primarily responsible for finding and purchasing raw materials—over the years, he had developed many contacts in the Far East. Lane's principal mandate was to increase the division's profits and deal with management in Ontario. After Lane's first year, the division experienced little success. The second was even worse, prompting Lane to become more involved with the overseas activities. That included joining Blake on one of the purchasing expeditions.

At home, employees were grumbling that Lane was not easy to work for, perhaps exemplified by the fact that both of his two secretaries had resigned.

At management meetings during his first two years at Sportswear, Lane presented highly favorable reports and projections that made it seem as if his division were doing much better than it was. By the third year, though, the financial results simply didn't back up what was on paper. Syd Greenberg, the division's CEO, confronted Lane. In his defense, Lane accused Blake of monumental mismanagement, particularly in respect to his dealings in the Far East. According to Lane, Blake was overpaying for raw materials that he purchased from friends overseas. Lane said that he witnessed this when he accompanied Blake on one of his trips. For those reasons, Lane said, he was firing Blake.

Blake, who believed himself to have been a loyal employee for many years, responded by launching a lawsuit for wrongful dismissal. When that happened, Syd Greenberg didn't know whom to believe. We were retained by Greenberg's lawyer to find out the truth. Our investigation, though, had to be conducted in a way that didn't disrupt the company or put Lane in a position where he would be forced to resign because of innuendo. If there were innuendo, and it proved false, Lane would be able to sue for constructive dismissal.

When there are contrasting versions of the facts, we place considerable weight on personal interviews with the parties involved. We talked first with Lane and other senior people to try to reconstruct the events that led up to his dismissal of Blake. This interview was broad in scope, covering financial and personal information from the time of Lane's appointment to the present. We came away feeling his story was rife with inconsistencies and omissions.

The next move was to talk with Blake. We asked Greenberg to call him, saying that in our experience we found that when people have nothing to hide they consent to be interviewed. Blake agreed to meet at his home. We went over the same material that we covered with Lane. His story seemed thorough and consistent. His emotions were believable. (He had kept notes from the trip they took together to the Far East.)

In a second interview with Lane, we asked directly about the major areas of disagreement between him and Blake. This session convinced us that Lane was not telling the truth. The key issue was the trip to China and Korea where, according to Lane, improprieties had taken place. Blake had produced invoices from suppliers verifying his contention that no overpayments or kickbacks were made. Lane was unable to offer any evidence to the contrary.

Our final report concluded that Lane was an incompetent manager who had risen beyond his capacity. A study of his records unearthed documents—which he had withheld from senior management—that showed the true picture of his division's performance. Lane was suffering from the "rainbow syndrome"—the hope that things will eventually turn around for the better.

Question 1: How could this fraud have been detected earlier?

Question 2: How could this fraud have been prevented?

REFERENCES

1. Lindquist Avey Macdonald and Baskerville, Inc., May 9, 1994, Toronto, Ontario, and Washington, D.C.

Index

A

Accountants, auditors:
  qualifying for, 193
  as technical experts, 192
Accounting evidence:
  admissibility of, 5
Accounting records:
  manipulation of, 4
Accounting system fraud:
  evolution of, 157
American Jurisprudence,
  64–65
Applications software, 167
Arson for profit, 4, 120
  evidence of, 121
Assets:
  current, 169
  fixed, 170
  noncurrent, 169–170
Auditing:
  financial, 5, 32
  fraud, 5, 26, 27, 31
Auditor, mind-set of, 141
AuditorPlus, 58

B

Balance sheet, 169
Banc-Audit, 53
Bank reconciliation, 161
BreachComber, 58
Bribery, 8

C

CA-Examine, 59
CA-PanAudit Plus, 59
Case studies:
  Dave Flag, 228
  Double-Paid Vacations, 235–237
  Graphic Conviction, 143–144
  Living High, 238–240
  Management Fraud, 142–143
  Maxi Lumber, 229
  Money, Money, Money,
    230–232
  Money-Laundering Lawyer
    Case, 237
  Non-profit Dancing Dollars, 144
  Plastics, Ltd., 230
  Rainbow Syndrome, 242–244
  Regina *v.* Barter, 98–99
  Regina *v.* Campbell and Mitchell,
    126–128
  Regina *v.* Down & Out, 99
  Regina *v.* Harvey, 109–110
  Regina *v.* Kotowski, 105–106
  Regina *v.* Lipsome, 97–98
  Regina *v.* Rosen, 112
  Regina *v.* Serplus, 116–121
  Roy's Retail, 229
  Secret Commission, 241–242
  Sharp Rentals, 234
  Trading Mania, 233
  28-Hour Day, 240
  U.S. Jewelry Consortium, 230

Check kiting, 8
Clayton Act, 28
Clinton Financial Services, 55–56
Codes of ethics, 123
Commercial billing:
  red flags, 126
Commercial bribery, 4
Company assets, 92
  stealing, embezzling of, 92
Computer communication:
  definition of, 185
Computer crime:
  commission of, 173–174
  common, 176
  economic motives, 174
  egocentric motives, 174
  environmental conditions, 175
  external motives, 175
  ideological motives, 175
  internal influences, 175
  psychotic, 175
Computer environment, 186
  characteristics of, 187–188
Computer hardware:
  auxiliary storage devices, 167
  Central Processing Unit (CPU),
    166–167
  data preparation equipment,
    166
  input devices, 166
  off-line, 166
  on-line, 166
  output devices, 167
Computerized accounting systems:
  elements of, 164–166
Computer operator, 164–165
Computer-related crime, 171
  evolution of, 172
  nature of, 177
Computer-related crime categories,
  175
Computer-related theft, 172
"Computer Security Digest," 178

Computer software:
  applications software, 167
Computer system, 188
  threats of, 188–189
Corporate defrauders:
  behavior of, 135–136
Corporate fraud, 9
Corporate minute book, 162
Corporate tax evasion, 4
Corruption, 4
Crime, white collar, 92
Criminal phenomena:
  result of, 225
Current liabilities, 170

D

Data-entry clerk, 165
Decentralized operators, 166
Detecting fraud, 133

E

EEO, 21
Embezzlement, 4
  detecting of, 137–138
  probability of, 146
Employee Retirement Income
    Security Act (ERISA), 28
Employee theft:
  reduction of, 140–141
Environmental law:
  violation of, 4
Equity Funding, 10, 106–109
E.S.M. Government Securities, 71
Expert witnesses:
  credentials of, 207–215
  cross examination of, 200–202
  cross examination strategies, 203
  demeanor, appearance, 199–200
  direct examination of, 200
  general criteria, 207
  location, sources of, 216

profile of, 196
qualifying, 193, 195
role in litigation team, 197
survival techniques, 205
External auditors, 157
External frauds, 4
Evidence, rules of, 219–221

F

False advertising, 4
False expense reports, 93
False information:
examples of, 95
False sales invoice, 94–95
False suppliers' invoices, 94
Federal regulatory agencies:
creation of, 50
Federal Trade Commission, 28
Financial auditors:
focus on large differences, 133
Financial Executive Institute, 1
Financial statements:
preparation of, 169
FINDER, 56–57
Forensic:
definition of, 42
Forensic accountant, 43
be able to do, 44–45
Forensic accounting:
corporate investigations,
43–44
in criminal matters, 43
government, 44
insurance claims, 44
reflections on, 46–49
Forensic expert:
role of, 42
Fraud-auditing course, 50
learning outcomes of, 50–52
software tools, 53
Fraud auditors, 5, 26–29
attributes of, 6

concerns of, 33
detecting fraud responsibility,
64
differences of, 133
look for, 133
mind-set of, 39–40, 141
standard care of, 64
"thinker types," 36
Fraud detection, 53–55
Frauds, 134
accounting-type of, 35
civil, 3
against the company, 4
for the company, 17, 21
conditions of, 33
corporate, 4, 17
as a crime, 9
criminal, 4
definition of, 33
front-end, 8, 20, 95–96
internal, 4
layperson's definition of, 10
lower-level, 136, 137
management, 4
on-the-job, 7
for the organization, 17
probability of, 146
prodromal signs of, 135
receivable receipts, 95
signs of, 134
statement, 6
as a tort, 9
transaction, 6
varieties of, 15
Fraudulent conduct:
by corporate managers, 138
Fraudulent disbursement, 176–177
Fraudulent insurance claims, 4

G

General journal, 161
General ledger, 161–162

Generally Accepted Accounting
    Standards (GAAS), 65

H

Hackers, 178–184
Hearsay exceptions, 221–222
High-fraud, low-fraud environments,
    148–150

I

Information security:
    critical issues of, 184
Information Technology Co., 53
In Our Opinion, 66
Input tampering, 175
Insider fraud:
    against the company, 20
INSIGHT Consulting Inc., 56
Institute of Internal Auditors, 1
    tool kit, 59
Internal Revenue Act, 28
International Association of
    Certified Fraud Examiners, 1
Investigative accountants, 124
    issues to resolve, 124
Investigative accounting, 5
    in murder, arson, commercial
        bribery, 114–115
Investigative concerns, 45
Investigative data bases research:
    bibliography, 62–63
    names, locations of, 60–62
    resources needed, 59
    varieties of, 59–60
Investigative mentality, 45
Inventory manipulations, 20
"Invitations to fraud," 129

J

Jung, Carl, 36

K

Kiting, 8

L

Labor-Management Reporting and
    Disclosure Act, 28
LAN, 186
Lapping, 8, 95, 97
Larceny, 4
Lay witnesses, 190
Left-brain thinker, 42
Librarian, 165
Litigation support, 5, 43
Logic bombs, 175
Long-term liabilities, 170

M

Macdonald Commission, 72, 78–79,
    80–81
Magnetic tape, 168
Management controls, 138–139
Management fraud, 10
Michigan Supreme Court Rules of
    Evidence, 190–192
MOMM, 173

N

National Association of Management
    Accountants, 1
NETMAP, 57

O

Office of Price Administration
    (OPA), 28
Organizational fraud, 5
OSHA, 21
Output tampering, 175–176
Outsider fraud, against company, 21

P

Paper, microfilm, 167
Paper tape, 168
Payables scam, 7
Payments cycle, 160
Payment systems, 7
Payroll manipulations, 20
Personal computers, 167
Phone phreaks, 178–184
Planned bankruptcy, 4, 11, 112, 114,
    120
Price fixing, 4, 21
Privileged communications, 224
Programmer, 164
Purchases, payables, payments, fraud
    in, 93

R

Receipt systems, 7
Receivable scam, 7
Red flags:
    internal environment, 130–132
Revenue cycle, 159
Right-brain thinker, 42
Risk management checklist, 151–153

S

Salami slicing, 175
SAS No. 16, 66–70
SAS No. 53, 157
SAS No. 54, 157
Secondary evidence, 223–224
Secret commissions, 123, 124–125
Securities and Exchange
    Commission Act (SEC), 28
SEC *v.* AM International Inc., 130
SEC *v.* McCormick & Co., 130

SEC *v.* U.S. Surgical Corp., 130–131
Shad, John, 71
Shareholders' equity, 170
Short counts and weights, 4
Skimming, 8
Smoothing profits, 21
Software AG, 58
Stanford Research Int'l. (SRI), 172
Statement of income, 170
Stockholder records, 162
Systems analyst, 164

T

Time bombs, 175
Toledo Personnel Management
    Association, 24
Trap doors, 175
Trojan horses, 175

U

United States *v.* Arthur Young &
    Co., 65–66
United States *v.* Goldblum, Levin,
    Lewis, et al., 11

V

Valuation analysis, 5

W

Wage and Hour Law, 28
Welfare Pension Fund Act, 28
White-collar crime, 13, 21, 23
White-collar criminals, 15
    in accounting systems, 92
    problems of, 23

FRAUD AUDITING AND FORENSIC ACCOUNTING

New Tools and Techniques

Second Edition

Fraud, in the words of the authors, is no simple vice.

Recent years have seen it grow both in size and complexity, to the point where some estimates place losses due to fraud at well over $100 billion a year. And, with the increasing complexity of financial structures and the intensity of business competition, fraud has become harder to detect and more tempting to commit.

Since much of the responsibility for detecting fraud has been assumed by the accounting profession, accountants need to learn how to recognize its signs and investigate it. *Fraud Auditing and Forensic Accounting, Second Edition* focuses on the investigation, detection, documentation, and prevention of accounting frauds, stock frauds, and employee theft and embezzlement. Written by recognized experts in the field of white-collar crime, this comprehensive book provides an incisive, in-depth analysis of how fraud occurs within an organization and explains the latest techniques for fighting it. The authors have brought together up-to-date material to show practicing professionals how to:

- Recognize the characteristics of organizations in which fraud is likely to occur

- Detect and deter accounting fraud, using the most recently developed techniques

- Conduct an efficient, systematic fraud investigation

- Use the latest methods for documenting fraud and preparing evidence— and much more